"This book is funny. Really funny. It's an unsentimental look at imperfect people. We may not want to BE them, but they sure are wild tour-guides for this crazed ride through our deeply flawed culture."

Writer/Director Billy Ray, *Captain Phillips*,
The Comey Rule, *Shattered Glass*.

"A period of recent American history, often ignored by most scribes, gets a wild and brilliant revision in *Bootleg Heroes* via the insightful and retro imagination of author Peter Cook. As a kindred spirit, I highly endorse this rollicking tale of 1980 Americana."

Dwayne Epstein, NY Times bestselling author of *Lee Marvin: Point Blank* and *Killin' Generals: The Making of The Dirty Dozen, The Most Iconic WWII Movie of All Time.*

"Peter Cook's rollicking tilt-a-whirl ride of a novel catalogues an era when American Empire bestrode the world like a hard-partying colossus. Combining the blunt-force satirical wit of Norman Mailer's *Naked and the Dead* with the nostalgia of Robert Towne's *The Last Detail*, *Bootleg Heroes* is a postcard from hell pasted with a postage stamp of the American flag."

Producer/ Screenwriter William Wheeler, *Ray Donovan*,
The Prime Gig, *The Hoax*, *The Queen of Katwe*.

"If you like your aguardiente con Devil's Breath, check this out - *Bootleg Heroes* is an American GI jungle saga that makes *Fast and Furious* look dull and torpid, set in Ecuador circa 1980, where romance is elusive and man's inhumanity and harsh realities rule. Filled to the brim with Hollywood love and lore, this book is a real pow to the kisser."

Patrick McGilligan, author of *Funny Man: Mel Brooks*,
Alfred Hitchcock: A Life in Darkness and Light.

"*Bootleg Heroes* shocked me out of my serenity with its super-realistic dialogue and vivid, colorful characters. It's a sensorial assault that catapults you into a book that reads like an action movie. Peter Cook's story-telling is compelling. His writing is super-charged. A story of innocence lost and experience gained during a tour of duty, as told by a former Marine. A glorious, unrelenting, unforgettable ride. Hold on!"

Actor Harry E. Northup, *Taxi Driver, Mean Streets, The Silence of the Lambs.*

"If you enjoyed *The Year of Living Dangerously* with a bit of *Catch-22* thrown in for fun, *Bootleg Heroes* is your next must-read! Cook's flair for capturing real life heroes, warts and all, dominates throughout. This is vivid storytelling at its finest for a new generation of readers. Bravo!"

Dr. Carl Cohn, *Professor Emeritus and Senior Research Fellow – Claremont Graduate University.*

"*Bootleg Heroes* is an intelligently crafted, riveting story that takes the reader along for a narrative of growth and exploration. It's a coming-of-age adventure that doesn't stoop to giving answers. Instead, it poses questions about the contradictions that we all face on this journey of life."

Director Jon Kean, *Swimming in Auschwitz.*

"Reading as a former Army M.P., *Bootleg Heroes* exceeded all expectations. Cook presents a hilariously funny, true to life examination of a military culture that reverberates with absolute authenticity. As I read the hierarchy that I'd lived, I found myself racing home to grab the book, return to '80's and laugh away the woes of my day."

Dr. Alan-Michael Graves, *Director of Teaching and Capacity Building, The Good Plus Foundation.*

"*Bootleg Heroes* is both poignant and brimming with belly laughs. In his facile and engaging style, Cook provides a truly engrossing coming of age novel."

Producer Alex Barnow, *The Goldbergs*.

"Gloriously authentic. *Bootleg Heroes* is quick witted, with great characters and fabulous one-liners. I was totally engrossed in this crazy world. *Bootleg Heroes* rocks the comic vibe of *M*A*S*H* and *Catch-22*."

Director Alfredo Ramos *Road Dogz, Kill Kapone, Welcome to Our World*.

"This is a richly drawn escape into the picaresque adventures of a young Marine, circa 1980, told with rare authenticity and heart and with such vivid detail, you can almost smell the coffee and the bedsheets. A hilarious coming of age tale, *Bootleg Heroes* reads as if Holden Caulfield had joined the Marines."

CEO Dani Klein, of *Laughter on Call* and Author of *Take My Spouse, Please...*

"From the bumpy ride in, to the emotional ride out, this is one Mister Toad's Wild Ride! Cook gives us a coming-of-age story at the U.S. Embassy in Quito, Ecuador during Carter/Reagan hostage time in America. The smattering of side trips and life lessons learned leaves one with a feeling of hope, if just enough people would read this and hear the call. When they make the movie, I want in!"

Actor Peter Jason, *The Long Riders, 48 Hours, Hail Caesar!*

"In *Bootleg Heroes*, there are two stories; one - of a young U.S. Marine doing his job in a foreign country - where the rules are different and danger is not far away - and a second story of this same young man's memories that tear at him, haunt him and ultimately lift him up. In this funny and powerful narrative, we may even discover ourselves. A worthy and surprising book."

Author / Screenwriter Gerald DiPego, *Cheevy, With a Vengeance, Phenomenon, Message in a Bottle, Sharky's Machine*.

"*Bootleg Heroes* captures the authentic, tribal behaviors of a handful of U.S. Marines stationed in South America circa 1980. It's a fast-paced, well-executed novel written by an insider. *Bootleg Heroes* made me laugh - and wince!"

> Dr. Peter Kuznick, *Director, Nuclear Studies Institute at American University, NY Times Bestselling Co-author (w/ Oliver Stone) of The Untold History of the United States.*

"*Bootleg Heroes* tells the captivating story, horrifying and sometimes hilarious, about the contradictory demands placed on our men in uniform by an American public that's at war with itself. A great read!"

> Bruce Porter, *New York Times best-selling author of "Blow," made into the hit movie starring Johnny Depp, and co-author of "Crossing the Bounds," about the deadly Miami Riot of 1980.*

"Set in Ecuador in the 1980s, Peter Cook's *Bootleg Heroes* brilliantly engages the reader from the first line to the last. The masterful dialog snaps, crackles and pops, and moves between being a hoot, to a profound view of Marines in foreign lands. Cook's novel belongs in the company of great novels exploring the American Empire of the 20th Century."

> Paul Cummins *Co-Founder The 5 Gyres Institute, Leap Lab and author of Dachau Song.*

"Human, hungry for life, full of wonder… In his first novel, with excitement and soul, Peter Cook touches the magic of literature and memory, and what else is there that moves the Earth?"

> Eva Lustigová, *Director/ Screenwriter, The Presence of Arnošt Lustig and Co-founder, The Arnošt Lustig Foundation.*

BOOTLEG HEROES

BOOTLEG HEROES

PETER DANIEL COOK

ONWARDPRESS.ORG

LOS ANGELES, CALIFORNIA

Copyright © 2024 by Peter Daniel Cook

All rights reserved. No part of this publication may be reproduced or transmitted in any form or by any means electronic or mechanical, including photocopy, recording or any other information storage and retrieval system now known or to be invented, without permission in writing from the publisher, except by a reviewer who wishes to quote brief passages in connection with a review written for inclusion in a magazine, newspaper, website or broadcast.

This book is a work of fiction. Names, characters, places and incidents are the product of the author's imagination or are used fictitiously. Any resemblance to actual events, persons, living or dead, is coincidental.

Onward Press is an imprint of the United States Veterans' Artists Alliance, a nonprofit 501c3 educational organization.

www.onwardpress.org
www.usvaa.org

Edited by Timothy Wurtz
Art by Trevor Denham
Cover design by Teddi Black
Formatted by Megan McCullough

ISBN Hard Cover: 978-1-954988-18-7
ISBN Paperback: 978-1-954988-19-4
ISBN eBook: 978-1-954988-20-0

Tie A Yellow Ribbon Round The Ole Oak Tree
Copyright © 1972 by Peermusic III, Ltd. and Irwin Levine Music
Copyright Renewed
All Rights for Irwin Levine Music Administered by Spirit One Music Crescendo
International Copyright Secured All Rights Reserved
Reprinted by Permission of Hal Leonard LLC

Thanks, Jerry –

Special and sincere thanks to

Trevor Denham, Keith Jeffreys, Tim Wurtz

Alice Tasman Morris

and

The Members of Team 54!

USVAA/Onward Press would like to thank the following organizations for their support in publishing this book and their support of the USVAA/Onward Press Veteran Writers Workshop, held monthly since 2013, free of charge to military veterans and personnel.

- The Nathan Cummings Foundation
- Sony Pictures Entertainment
- Warner Bros. Discovery
- The Golden Globes Foundation
- The Los Angeles County Department of Arts and Culture

Thanks to Timothy Wurtz on behalf of USVAA/Onward Press for his tireless work in getting all of our books to publication.

CHAPTER One

"Buckwheat's dead," Curtis said as he read *The Washington Post*. "Heart attack. Died in Los Angeles yesterday." He read a bit more. "Poor bastard was only forty-nine, and Darla didn't fare a whole helluva lot better. Died of a botched appendectomy, followed by goddamn hepatitis from a bum blood transfusion. She kicked the bucket last year. Forty-seven years old."

Sergeant Gamboa said, "No shit."

He was pissed off. His flight didn't leave for nine hours.

"Holy smokes," Curtis said when he got to the details on Carl Switzer. "Alfalfa's been dead for two decades already. He was shot to death in 1959 and get this - he caught it in the nuts for Christ's sake. Age thirty-one. None of 'em made it to fifty."

Curtis was two weeks shy of his own birthday. His twentieth.

"Doesn't say about Spanky," he said. "Probably alive."

He folded the paper in half. Read the front page.

'October 11, 1980 – Today marks day three hundred and forty-three of the Hostage Crisis in Iran. Iranian President Abolhassan Banisadr has revealed additional conditions for the release of the fifty-two American Hostages being held in Tehran...'

"Yikes. Want some of the paper, Sergeant Gamboa?"

Gamboa declined. He was irritated. Didn't want to spend the night at the airport.

Plus, his ass was chapped over where he was headed in the morning. Friggin' Africa.

Ouagadougou, Upper Volta. Gamboa had put in for Paris.

Curtis whistled. "Three hundred and forty-three days and counting."

"We ought to nuke 'em till they glow," Gamboa said, "Turn that place into a parking lot."

Curtis thought Sergeant Gamboa was the type of Marine who'd say 'Nuke 'em till they glow' only when he was having a bad day. Had he been on his way to France, like he'd hoped, he'd be acting diplomatic as hell.

"You know Gunny Tibbitts from S-1?" Curtis said.

"With the purple shit on his face?" Gamboa said.

"Before Vietnam he was a teacher in Pennsylvania. Claims people retain *images* better than words. They think in pictures. He told me, 'It's spelled Q-U-I-T-O, but it's pronounced *Key-Toe*, and he drew a key and then he drew a big toe. It's a good way to memorize odd words. Tibbetts must've been a good teacher."

Curtis wondered if his students gave him crap about his birthmark.

Sergeant Gamboa stood. Grumbled. "Mental pictures."

Back at Quantico, Gamboa was famous for saying, "That is one handsome negro," every time he passed a mirror. He was gonna drive the French women crazy. "I hear *Ouagadougou* and not one single, solitary mental picture forms what-so-fucking-ever," he said. "You say 'Paris,' I see the Eiffel Tower, man. You say *'Upper-fucking-Volta,'* my mind goes blank."

A loudspeaker called for passengers traveling to Quito, Ecuador.

"Key Toe," Curtis said. "That's me, Sergeant Gamboa."

They exchanged Semper Fi and good luck.

Curtis left the lounge and crossed the tarmac toward the plane.

He was taller than everyone else. Short passengers crowded close, unconcerned with personal space. The group included an oily-haired man who held a wire cage with a rooster inside. He made cluck-cluck noises and swung the cage to and fro.

A corner of the coop slammed into Curtis's knee.

The guy with the greasy hair grinned and showed gold teeth. *"Lo siento, Señor."*

Curtis rubbed his knee. He whispered, *"Dick..."* and limped on.

The *Aerolínea Ecuatoriana* logo was navy blue over white. It ran the entire length of the dirty plane. People made the sign of the cross as they climbed the portable stairs. Curtis thought of his mother, an unstable Catholic. He crossed himself as he reached the top step.

A twenty-something stewardess said, "Bienvenidos." She was nervous. Her eyes darted from Curtis to a gaggle of policemen who milled around on the tarmac. She flashed them a thumbs up.

Curtis presented his ticket.

He regretted checking his seabag. Should have carried it on. He'd left his copy of *Little Big Man* in it. The newest issue of *American Film* was in there, too, with an update on Greta Garbo at seventy-five and an article on Michael Cimino's latest movie, *Heaven's Gate*. Curtis couldn't wait to read it.

The stewardess swiped at her brow and said, "You may sit at any place."

Inside the aircraft, a tiny woman with jet-black hair that fell to her waist held a bulging cardboard box tied together with green and yellow strips of cloth. She looked up at the overhead bin.

"Let me get that for you, yeah?" Curtis said. He popped open her unit and took the box. The woman smiled, then turned just enough for Curtis to see a bright-eyed infant strapped to her back with a wrap-around sash.

The guy with the rooster tried to shove past.

Curtis said, "Quit pushing, man. I'm helping this mother." He jammed the box into the bin, then moved to the last available window seat. He slid in and massaged his knee. A racket started at the front of the plane.

The three D.C. cops made their way down the aisle. They nudged people aside with black batons and parted the sea of South Americans who clamored to fly home. The trio made their way to a man in a pin-striped suit. He looked out of place amidst the serapes and straw hats. The head policeman leaned down. Got in the guy's face.

He demanded something, then snapped his fingers.

The man jerked his head. "I am not the one."

The cop yanked him to his feet, then twisted the guy's wrist hard and high behind his back. Curtis recognized it as a Marine Corps "technique of the week." He'd been taught that move at Quantico. It was designed to limit mobility. His close combat instructors said it could make the meanest men beg and squeal.

The man in the fancy suit neither begged nor squealed.

He stayed bent and looked scared as the cops hustled him toward the exit.

As they moved him out, passengers whistled and clapped.

Curtis looked at the man's empty seat and pursed his lips.

Aerolínea Ecuatoriana apologized in Spanish and English for the disturbance. Then they amped up the music. Gloria Gaynor sang about being afraid and petrified. An appropriate choice, all things considered.

Curtis looked out the window at the group of cops outside the plane. They joked, and one did a slow-motion karate kick that brought laughs. Curtis wondered what the bad guy had done. The officers departed. He leaned back and listened to the song. It conjured memories.

He'd seen his first naked lady up close and well-lit while listening to Gloria Gaynor. His father had taken him to Pokin' Porky's on Route 20. Curtis loved his dad but thought he was vulgar – not for taking him to a strip joint but because of his father's diction. His South Boston accent appalled Curtis. Every time Ronald said *car*, it came out *cahhh*. When he'd say *paper*, it sounded like *pay-pahhh*.

At Pokin' Porky's, Ronald handed the cashier a twenty and asked for singles. He explained to Curtis, "We'll need a fist full-ahh doll-ahhs fah tonight's en-tah-tay-ment, Sam." He'd sounded ignorant. All night long, Ronald slid his dollar bills to one lovely stripper. Thirteen in all, one after another, to stay on display and from time to time wink. She wore nothing but a ten-gallon hat and tasseled boots and positioned herself at eye level, knees wide, right in front of Curtis.

The naked cowgirl lip-synced while she toyed with herself. Curtis had been a Gloria Gaynor fan ever since.

After the show, Ronald climbed behind the wheel of his Monte Carlo, lit a Chesterfield, and looked at his son.

"Geez, Dad," Curtis said.

"Helluva look-ah, that one was."

"She was so talented. Lookin' at a lady gets you mesmerized. You get curious."

Ronald nodded. "Wonder pie will do that."

Wonder came out *won-duhhh*. Pie was pie.

On the plane, the man with the rooster sat next to Curtis.

He held the cage in his lap. It reeked of sulfurous bird shit. Curtis opened an airline mag as the filthy rooster clucked and scratched. He read, "Quito is the second highest capital city in South America, located some 9300 feet above sea level. Only La Paz, Bolivia is higher. Ecuador sits in a triangular wedge, bordered by Colombia to the north and Peru to the south." Curtis glanced at the rooster.

Its pink eye drew a bead. The owner shrugged.

Curtis returned to his magazine and read, "The western part of the country meets the Pacific Ocean." He flinched. "Hey, man. Watchit." The rooster's head and neck craned through the wires. Its ugly beak cocked at the ready. The man jiggled the cage, and the rooster retreated.

"That bird's a nuisance. Can you get a blanket? Cover him up?"

The man waved his hands. "No blank. No blank. He crying, 'Cock-a-deucey.'"

The rooster eyed Curtis out of the side of its head. Clark Gable had led a horse through fire by putting blinders on the animal in *Gone with the Wind*. Curtis knew where the vomit bags were stowed from the one other time he'd flown. That was from Boston to boot camp. He'd puked over Delaware. He took out his barf bag and motioned his neighbor to pass his over. Curtis fastened both bags to the cage with twister seals and secured a waxy shield against the aggressive cock.

As the plane flew south, the sullen bird flapped at the scrim a few times with ruffled feathers but didn't think to use its beak. Curtis ignored the rooster as best he could and dozed when he was able. He tossed and turned, his sleep fitful and erratic.

A short time later, the rooster let loose a shrill cock-a-deucey.

At thirty thousand feet, the goddamn bird recognized sunrise. Curtis looked out over the Andes. Morning sun kissed the snow-capped mountains. It turned the rugged peaks from purple to green. Then came the valley. The colonial city of Quito was white-washed, tile-roofed and sleepy-looking. It seemed ripe and peaceful.

He thought of Henry and the pact they'd made at the Shrewsbury Drive-In while watching *Taxi Driver*. Travis Bickle interviewed for his cabbie job, and Joe Spinell asked if he'd been in the Army. Travis said, "Marines." Curtis had leaned in and said, "Uh oh." Later, Travis sprang into a bad ass karate stance that had so intimidated Albert Brooks that Albert screamed for the cops.

Henry said, "That Albert's a real puss."

Curtis said, "Puss? Who's gonna fuck with Travis Bickle?"

After Robert De Niro rescued little Jodie Foster, Curtis knew.

He told Henry straight up, "I'm joining the Marines."

"What about the Coast Guard?"

"Marines, Baygo. I'm gonna learn karate and save girls."

"Man, I'm in. Screw the Coast Guard," Henry said, and they shook on it.

A week later, the boys were at the Marine recruiter's office on Front Street, a few doors down from *The Fine Arts Theatre*, Worcester's sleaziest porn palace. The Gunny had taken their info and told them to return in the spring. Curtis wanted to sign up on the spot, but the Gunny said no, they had to be eighteen or have parental consent.

He gave them glossy pamphlets.

On the cover, Marines leaped over ditches and swung from ropes, and they shouted and sweated. The best photo was on the back. A square-jawed Marine in Dress Blues sat outside a European café. He looked stern and preoccupied, and beside him was a very pretty blonde girl who was clearly enamored of the Marine.

She caressed his forearm. She was totally smitten.

To be ignored by a man so macho must have been thrilling.

All through senior year of high school, Curtis imagined himself in Dress Blues with a beautiful babe of his own and here he was, his dream come true, about to land in a foreign country with foreign women - eager to express foreign desires. He looked out the window at the city below and grinned. Curtis felt nothing but lucky and totally charmed.

A massive jolt caused the plane to shudder. The passengers froze. The aircraft lurched and the engines quit. Curtis's smile disappeared. The airplane plummeted in a jaw dropping free fall. The cock crowed loud and long. Curtis gasped and pulled his knees to his chest.

He filled his lungs, prepared to let loose a cock-a-deucey of his own.

Curtis would have deuceyed good and plenty had the plunge lasted a single second longer, but the plane jerked skyward like a yo-yo on the rebound, stutter-stepped and choked, and began to level out.

Everywhere Curtis looked, people genuflected, wrung their hands, kissed their thumbs, and hugged their children. The plane waggled and groaned. The cock crowed a third time, then four sharp, loud cracks boomed through the cabin. They sounded like God playing snap-ass with a towel. The cracks caused ear-splitting lamentations from the passengers. One hapless man who'd shit his pants careened toward the restroom.

The plane went into a hard, wild bank. The pilot spun into a woozy descent. Curtis forced swallows over and over. A gurgling sensation pulsed up from his guts into the back of his throat. He groped for the vomit bag still stuck to the rooster cage.

"Ouch! You goddamn son of a bitch!"

The malevolent bird had slashed a gash in Curtis's middle finger.

He bent over the cage and spewed what used to be coffee and doughnuts on the cringing bantam's head. The bird shrieked. Curtis wiped the tears from his eyes and turned to the window. He saw fire trucks on the landing strip. They lumbered past the skeletal remains of previous failed landings.

Seat belt signs flashed in haywire blinks. Oxygen masks dropped, bobbed, and twirled without any takers. Curtis felt cold sweat on the back of his neck and waited for the world to go black.

The drop stopped with a brutal thud and the plane bounced.

It hung a moment, bounced again, and for Christ's sake once more after that.

The aircraft skidded. The loud screech of tires on asphalt was matched by a unified human wail that lasted until the plane came to a hot, stinking, seared rubber stop. The plane rocked gently and hissed.

Absolute stillness pervaded the cabin.

Somebody farted slow and long. Sounded to Curtis like an appraisal of the flight. Sniffles and whispers broke out. There was no sign nor word of encouragement from the cockpit. The young stewardess coughed, then stood on shaky legs. She released the emergency lever on the rear exit door. The door folded back.

A rubber slide hung from the plane like a banner of defeat, limp and useless. Curtis was two seats from the exit. He couldn't think of a good reason to remain seated. He stepped over the splashed cage, walked straight to the oval hatch and high-fived the bewildered stewardess. He glanced behind and saw the little woman with the baby. The chubby infant was sound asleep. Curtis winked at the woman, then looked out the hatch. He faced the stewardess and stated the obvious.

"That rescue slide is totally fucked."

He considered his options. No one was gonna get anywhere safe on the tattered-ass slide. Gene Hackman had fashioned an emergency net with Ernest Borgnine in *The Poseidon Adventure*. Maybe he could do that - grab some guys on the ground and catch kids with a blanket. He turned to the desperate stewardess. A tear ran down her cheek.

It inspired Curtis.

"I'm gonna find us some help, really quick."

She nodded and said, "*Si, por favor.* You find help."

Curtis shimmied down and out to a swinging position, then pushed back from the hatch and twisted free. He hit the ground and sprang forward. He came still on all fours in a grassy knoll beside the runway.

A tiny brush fire fueled by sparks tried to grow.

Curtis stood, clapped his hands clean, and tamped out the flame with spit shined shoes. He gave the stewardess a wave then jogged toward the front of the plane. Liquid leaked in streaks from ruptured seams. Passengers' bags were scattered across the tarmac, ejected from the cargo bay that had sprung open. Several complacent firemen dragged a stubborn set of mobile steps toward the nose of the plane.

A sign fluttered at the top of the rolling staircase.

It read, "*¡Bienvenidos a Quito - El Centro Del Mundo!*"

"You all have a net? A blanket or something?" Curtis said.

His suggestion had no impact at all. Perhaps it wasn't understood. Curtis leaned in with the other men and helped push the steps under the nose. A middle-aged stewardess was at the door. The fireman closest to Curtis belched as they positioned the steps. Smelled like beer.

Curtis spotted his seabag under the plane. He grabbed it, hoisted it and double- timed back to the rear. A ground crew of *Aerolinea* employees had fashioned a pump for the deflated slide and had begun resurrecting it. The production looked iffy at best. Curtis raised his palms toward the weepy young stewardess. He called, "What gives?"

The pretty girl gave him a bewildered shrug.

The woman with the baby appeared.

The infant squealed in her arms.

Curtis kicked the slide.

He then plopped down on it and bounced back up.

It was firm enough. He waved and shouted, "Come on, then!"

The mom kicked her cardboard box forward. It bounded ass over tea-kettle in a downward tumble until the straps burst. The contents spilled out on the slide. There was a snow globe, coloring books, jeans and bulky souvenir sweatshirts. A fat member of the ground crew chose a *Maryland is for Crabs* hoodie and discreetly tucked it beneath the slide. He made a separate pile of the little woman's less-desirable goods.

The tiny mother inched forward into a sitting position and adjusted her skirt.

She held her baby tight and scooched over the edge.

They slid to safety without incident.

Curtis and the firemen helped at the end of the slide. The mom glared at the thieving fat man, who feigned innocence. The baby kicked and screamed. The fat guy stuffed the hoodie under his shirt, turned quick and wandered off. Curtis looked towards the terminal building, where three Ecuadorian men emerged from the heat haze mirage that blistered off the tarmac. Two wore tiger striped fatigues and carried Uzis. The third man wore a suit.

They reached Curtis. Stood close.

"Policia," the third man said. *"¿Hablas Espanol?"*

Curtis shook his head and said, "English, Sir."

There was something about the third man he didn't like.

"Bueno, pues, entonces," the third man said. He clasped his hands and raised them so that his index fingers rested against his thin lips. He tapped them, then asked in heavily accented English, "Why you jumping from the plane?" Curtis realized the third man wasn't handing out *attaboys.*

"Are you serious?"

"Yes, very much. *¿Porque saltaste?*" he said, interrogation style.

"Because the plane was un-fucking-safe." Curtis pointed skyward. "Didn't you see us bounce the fuck in here?" He looked over at the slide. A pair of Ecuadorian kids glided down. They held hands and giggled. At the bottom of the ramp, the pair paddy-caked and hooted, then jumped up and performed a playful little jig. Passengers on the ground drank from paper cups and toasted their shared experience. It looked more like a kindergartener's pool party than any kind of brush with death. The man holding the dirty rooster spotted Curtis and raised his cage.

Curtis shrugged, aware that he was nobody's hero.

As if on cue, a military Jeep peeled into view.

Two U.S. Marines rode in the Jeep. The driver was white, the co-pilot black. Both sported high and tights, which matched Curtis's own mandatory buzz-cut. Curtis knew Marine guards weren't authorized to wear full uniforms outside the embassy compound, but the identical navy blue windbreakers and matching mirrored sunglasses made an I.D. easy enough. The Jeep rolled up fast. The driver braked hard.

The eagle, globe, and anchor, and the words "U.S. Embassy Marine Guard," emblazoned across their chests confirmed what Curtis already knew. These two had come for him. He looked to the third man. The white Marine said to the third man, "He's with us, *Jefe*." He held up his Official Passport. Maroon in color as opposed to the blue for a U.S. tourist.

The third man turned to Curtis. "You have passport?"

Curtis handed it over. All Marines carried Official Passports -a step below Diplomatic, but better than nothing. The third man pressed it open on the hood of the jeep and looked to his soldiers. He snapped his fingers, then tapped the passport twice with his index finger. The tiger striped soldiers shifted their weapons. They laid out a rubber stamp and an ink pad. The third man did the stamping, and said, "We don't need no gringo heroes."

Curtis said, "Just trying to help," and took his passport.

The black Marine whistled and said to Curtis, "You have permission to come aboard, son." He grinned. Curtis climbed into the Jeep. He asked the third man, "You need feedback on the flight?" But the guy wasn't interested. Curtis's jaw was tight with superfluous adrenaline. He thumbed his knuckle where the rooster had pecked him. He looked at the third man and they locked eyes.

The cop blinked, then turned to his men.

The tiger stripers waved go with their Uzi's.

The white Marine said, "You good back there, Jarhead?"

"Fine, Sir. Lance Corporal Curtis B. Dark reporting for duty."

The white Marine smiled. "Closest officer is in Panama City, Panama. No 'Sirs' required south of the border." The black Marine waved a pack of gum.

"It's cinnamon. Take two."

"Thanks." Curtis put the extra stick in his shirt pocket.

"Dan Sherman. Call me D.L. Happen to be a Corporal," said the white Marine. He turned and put out his fist, friendly. Curtis tagged it. Sherman said, "And say hello to our dusky brethren. This is Pops Dillard. He's a private. A real underachiever."

"Not even," Pops said, "Three stripes up, man. We saw you come in. That was some Mr. Toad's Wild Ride shit. You got all your gear?"

Curtis raised and lowered his seabag. The gum helped to loosen his jaw. He said, "That landing was a complete clusterfuck. Do I report anything to anybody?"

"Say cheese, man," Pops said. "Whole country is bubble gum and band-aids."

"But it beats the Fleet," said D.L. Sherman. He put the Jeep in gear and drove.

CHAPTER
Two

Pops swatted at something as the Jeep circled a roundabout. "I wonder what in a bee's body helps it dig in sand?" he shouted.

Curtis listened to a cacophonous and continuous *On Any Sunday* soundtrack of grinding gears and blaring horns that played under a smash up derby swirl of rust and primary colors. Red lights, green lights and occasional yellows acted as suggestions. Traffic roared, screeched, skidded, and slid... then bucketed forward and lurched on.

"Christ on a crutch," D.L. called, "They drive like they fly."

He hit the brake. Downshifted.

"Hold on to your butts, boys," he said.

D.L. swerved left and shot into a faster lane.

Taxis were smashed all to hell. Cars, trucks, and mule wagons kissed in motion. Passengers clung to the backs of buses. Some rode on rooftops. Automobile frames, broken bikes and wagon wheels were at left, right, and center - heaps of evidence against weak-willed vehicles that had given up the ghost.

A sallow dog trotted out from around a blind corner. It displayed a mangy snout and prominent ribs as it lugged a heavy-looking grey-green rat in its scrawny jaws. The animal lumbered into the street. A dull brown Toyota truck sped up and turned into the cur's path. It clipped its canine target right upside its flea-bitten head.

The dog's body was punted high enough to complete a full three-sixty before it landed atop an inert oil drum. The truck jostled on. Its driver's honky-tonk horn sounded a tin pan victory of man over beast.

Mountains towered above the city on all sides and hemmed in the energy. Curtis saw two llamas, more stray cats than he could count and something dead covered in flies. At a stoplight, he watched a leather-faced woman in a black fedora hike her dark green skirt above her thighs. She tucked it in under a tri-colored vest and squatted atop a rock pile. The woman let free a vigorous stream. She splashed stones.

In Curtis's world, girls went tinkle.

Here, he learned the truth. Women pissed and meant it.

He was astonished by the street beggars. Little kids rode on the backs of bigger kids. The rag-tag army of children held unclean palms up and open. The piggy-backed young ones were a mass of twisted limbs. Legs and arms appeared snapped, crackled, or popped out of place. Some bones looked twice or three times broken - distorted angles of impossible trauma. Most of the faces were bruised. One was handsome.

Curtis chomped his gum. He was awed by the spectacle.

D.L. turned right and cruised to a halt. A female security guard stepped out of her booth and raised a boom barrier. The Jeep accelerated up a steep hill.

At the top, there were gardens and lilacs. The sun was brighter and it was quiet. A few sheep roamed. Gentle bells hung around their necks and rang their presence. A sign read, "*Quito Tenis.*" Statues dotted sprawling lawns. Pops said, "Welcome to the hood."

Curtis turned in his seat and looked back at the valley. He saw a stadium and asked, "Who plays there?" The air had turned fresh, and they no longer had to shout. Pops said, "Rookie matadors tryin' out for Spain."

The Jeep crunched over gravel in a driveway and stopped at a wooden gate.

D.L. tapped the horn three times quick, then lit a Marlboro red. He turned to Curtis, lowered his mirrored sunglasses, and said, "'Swimmin' pools. Movie stars.'" His eyes were bright blue. His grin was reckless. The arched doors were opened from within by a boy with curly black hair who smiled, then saluted. He looked about sixteen.

"Well, *muchisimas gracias*, Zhak," D.L. said.

D.L. fixed his sunglasses and tossed the boy a Marlboro, but it was an end-over- end flick, the kind you can't really catch. It bounced off the kid's chest. The boy's eyes dimmed. He bent to pick it up, and D.L. continued along the winding drive. Curtis heard a recording of a twangy Tammy Wynette tune. Over Tammy's guitar picking, someone shouted, "Change it up, Okie!"

The music stopped. Pops snickered and said, "Cracker ass."

An aria began: *La donna è mobile* from Verdi's *Rigoletto*. It was familiar to Curtis. He'd heard Tom and Jerry singing it. After they passed a copse of tall trees, the Marine House came into view. Curtis said, "Holy smokes." The Marine House was no house. It was a mansion that stood like a massive layer cake of clean, sugar-white bricks tucked in under waves of interlocking burnt orange tiles. There was a matched set of external spiral staircases. Each led to a wrought iron balcony. A come-hither widow's walk was front and center just above the roofline.

D.L. pointed. "When you get laid up there, you'll have arrived."

Curtis was eager to get laid *anywhere*. His next time would be his first time.

Hinda Cohen, his white-sweatered sweetheart up until boot camp, had allowed Curtis to gently explore under her skirt, but Hinda refused to take her panties all the way down. Ever. Henry had teased Curtis about Hinda's reticence. "I looked it up in the library," he said. "In Hebrew, Hinda means blue. Cohen means balls."

Henry had been Curtis's best friend longer than Hinda had been his girl.

One afternoon, he and Henry had slipped the buck-toothed ticket vendor at The Fine Arts an extra five bucks to worm their way into a Triple X double bill. During *The Other Side of Julie,* they'd elbowed each other and glanced at the busy paying customers - disheveled members of the raincoat crowd. After *Taboo* began, they forgot all about the surreptitious masturbators. They were totally enthralled by Kay Parker as she hungrily seduced her "teenaged" son. Henry had whispered, "That guy is a motherfucker."

Their eyes stayed glued to the screen in the pornographic dark.

On the bus ride home, Curtis said, "That was one sweet-ass babe and a very rare type of mom."

"Kay Parker is something," Henry said, "but I'd never hump my own mother."

Curtis said, "Well, your mom is no Kay Parker." That hurt Henry.

After an embarrassed silence, Curtis attempted to make amends. He asked, "Whose mom would you?"

"Drea DeMello's," said Henry.

Curtis agreed and suggested, "Lauren Landry's, too."

"Lauren Landry's so pretty, I'd fuck her dad," said Henry. Their laughter healed the rift, though a tension remained. When they returned to Curtis's house, they found no one else at home. They listened to a train pass. Then they listened to the silence.

Curtis said, "We could…"

"Yeah, but…"

"Come on. Let's just see…"

They walked through the dining room, past the framed print that advertised Pepe Lopez Tequila. Lila-Ruth had presented it to Ronald Dark when he'd been promoted to foreman at Bell System. Pepe, a poncho-clad Mexican, head canted to the side in a jovial loll, smiled from under his sombrero. Curtis climbed halfway up the carpeted stairs, then turned. He pulled open his jeans and offered himself to Henry.

Henry stood and gawked.

"How do I do it?"

"Like Kay Parker," said Curtis. "Do *Taboo.*"

Henry knelt on the stairs. "I'm nervous, Curt."

"Don't be. Who cares? Just pretend you're a girl."

Henry leaned forward. He chewed his lip. Then he puffed out his cheeks.

"Don't just breathe on it. Do like in the movie, so I can see what it feels like." Curtis thrust his hips forward. Henry backed away. "Come on, Baygo. Give it a try. You should bob."

Henry sighed, then bobbed.

"Yeah. Like that," said Curtis.

"Wait," mumbled Henry, his mouth full.

"No talking. You're wreckin' it. Just be quiet and work it like the mom," said Curtis. Henry put his head down. Curtis experienced a twinge of glad feelings and almost laughed. Henry had his eyes shut tight. Curtis felt giddy. Henry stopped.

"What are you doing?" Curtis said.

"Something feels funny."

"There's nothin' funny. You're doin' great."

Henry frowned. "I'm Catholic."

"So go to confession."

"Not doin' it," Henry said.

He rose from the stairs and clumped down to the dining room.

Curtis sighed, tucked himself into his jeans and hustled down the stairs. His best friend had his arms crossed and was staring out the dining room window. He watched a mailman stick envelopes into the Aljoe's mailbox across the street.

Curtis took two green apples from the fruit bowl.

He offered one to Henry. "I'm Catholic, too. Big deal."

Henry took the apple. "Nah, man. Forget it." He bit the fruit.

Curtis grinned as he craned his neck and looked up at the Marine House.

It was a cross between fortress and frat house. He figured if a guy was gonna get laid anywhere, this had to be the place. A black Marine stepped onto the balcony. From the Jeep, Curtis saw Sergeant stripes. The Sergeant shouted, "That's better," to a cowboy in the driveway.

The cowboy wore brown boots, faded jeans, a plaid shirt, and a stained Stetson that looked too big for his head. He twisted a loop of rough rope and yelled over Verdi's aria, "I got you, Sergeant Baxter!"

Baxter yelled, "Classical. Good for the brain."

D.L. parked the Jeep beside a fountain in the side yard.

Three flowing tiers were crowned by a flying naked cherub.

A droplet christened Curtis's forehead as he climbed out of the vehicle.

Sergeant Baxter called again to the cowboy, "Got your juice cup, Okie?"

"Sure do, Sergeant Baxter." He shifted his lasso, grabbed the cup, and held it up, like a big kid showing off.

Baxter turned his attention to the Marines standing beside the Jeep. "Lance Corporal Dark arrive in one piece?"

"One piece," Pops Dillard said.

"Outstanding," Baxter said. "Be right down."

Curtis, Pops and D.L. walked toward the cowboy.

The cowboy set his cup down, whirled his lasso over his head, and tossed it hard at the wooden practice pony stationed beside a boom box. The rope whacked against the crude T-shaped head fashioned from two-by-fours. The lasso slid to the ground.

"Bitch and bad news," the cowboy said.

He picked up his juice cup and spat into it.

"An elusive stallion," said D.L., as the cowboy retracted his rope. "Okie bye-bye, this here's Curtis B. Dark," D.L. twanged.

The cowboy tipped his hat and said, "Billy Ray Poore. Call me Okie. Good to know you."

Curtis nodded. The boy from the gate trotted up and stood near the group.

D.L.'s Marlboro was tucked behind his ear.

"What's your name, man? I'm Curt."

"Guillermo."

Curtis took the extra stick of cinnamon gum out of his shirt pocket and offered it to the boy. Guillermo took it and said, "I prefer the spearmint."

Sergeant Baxter opened the front door of the Marine House.

"You a chess player yet, Lance Corporal?" he called.

"No. But I'd like to learn."

"That's the spirit. You coming up, Billy Ray?"

"I gotta finish my fifty," Okie said.

He launched his lariat yet again.

Guillermo grabbed Curtis's seabag. They walked up to the house.

Baxter stood at the top of the stairs, feet spread twelve inches, hands on hips. "Butch Baxter," the Sergeant said. "Welcome aboard, Marine." He was the same height as Curtis and smelled of soap and English Leather. His skin was black coffee black. They shook hands. Baxter crossed his arms as they entered the Marine House.

Curtis gaped at the interior.

High ceilings.

Iron chandeliers.

White stucco walls.

A leather couch and love seats.

Ornate rugs over hardwood floors.

"Holy smokes," Curtis said.

"Pops, you'll need to quarter our Lance Corporal," Sergeant Baxter said.

"Quarter our Lance Corporal. Aye-aye, Sergeant Baxter."

"Got a swimming pool and a weight room, too," D.L. Sherman said. He shook a smoke out of his pack and flipped it between his lips. He grinned but didn't light it. "The Marine House bar is stocked and operational twenty-four seven, offering an endless array of libations. There're no fees, no dues, no tipping required. Just show up thirsty." Dan lit his cigarette, crossed the living room, and climbed steps towards the bar.

Butch Baxter looked at his watch, then set his arms akimbo. He stood eye-to-eye with Curtis and said, "Listen up, Dark. The Gunny lives two hills from here. He's new. He's eager to make his bones. We don't need to give him any reasons to come sniffing around. Enjoy the life, but be smart." There was an edge to the advice.

"Will do," Curtis said.

He studied Baxter's face.

There were no bumps like you sometimes see.

A shrill whistle came from the bar area, followed by, "Here's lookin' up your old address." It was D.L. Someone responded, "Beware the hungry llama." Glasses clinked.

Butch picked up his briefcase and called, "Shorty, *nos vamos.*"

A very short, very fat man squeezed in from a side door and said, "*Si, Jefe.*" He bowed, then shuffled down the steps toward a large, white Econoline van. Butch said, "Adios, boys," and left.

D.L. yelled from the bar, "Gunny's a real peach. We feel better when he's not around. Go stow your shit, man, and join us for a *cerveza* or two. Pops, take him by and rattle Square Head for kicks."

Pops said, "Rattle Square Head," and laughed. "Yeah, yeah."

The polished floorboards gleamed, and large, square patches of sunlight spilled in from outside. Curtis heard birds singing.

Pops said, "Hold up, man," to Guillermo, then waved Curtis down a short flight of stairs. Pops dug for keys and said, "Check this." He opened a padlocked door. "Private stash." He flipped a light switch. "Detachment bodega."

It was like a convenience store.

Curtis saw Campbell's Soup, Kraft Mac n' Cheese, Frosted Pop-Tarts, A-1 Steak Sauce and case after case of Coca-Cola. "The State Department brings everything in on allowance. Even got Pringles," Pops said. He hit the light, then re-locked the bodega.

"We get access to all that?" Curtis said.

"Hell, yeah. Come on, man." Pops waved Curtis down another set of steps. "This should be real fun." He rapped against a door. "Down here is supposed to be storage." They waited, then Pops pounded again and said, "Hey, Corporal Brick!"

A groan came from inside. Curtis heard a thump followed by footsteps. The door opened a crack.

Curtis saw a mattress on the floor. A green blanket was wadded on one end.

Brick stood stock still in skivvies, fists clenched, head bowed, as if he expected something awful to happen. He stood sideways and looked at a distant point on the floor. A Harley-Davidson logo was tattooed on his right shoulder. He seemed at home down here, like some creepy troll living under a bridge.

"I had the mid-watch, Dillard," Brick said.

"We got a new Marine out here."

Brick opened the door three inches wider.

"Corporal Brick," he said. Didn't offer a hand. Didn't say anything more.

"Go ahead and get your beauty sleep, Chief," Curtis said. The door closed.

Upstairs, Guillermo picked up Curtis's seabag again. Pops opened a linen closet and pulled a shower towel. He handed it to Curtis and shrugged. "Square Head's not a dummy, per se, but he ain't much fun. Afro-phobic, too, man."

"Did he pick that room? In the cellar?"

"Topside rooms were available. He's tricky. He was on consular section and didn't like the way the Ekwads were lining up one time, so he calls, 'Y'all *motherfuckers* need to make a straight fucking line!' In front of the DCM. He growled that shit all loud."

"DCM?" Curtis said. He glanced at Guillermo. Guillermo shrugged.

"Deputy Chief of Mission," Pops said. "Sergeant Baxter can maintain with just about anybody, but that kinda noise coming from some Alabama redneck, all loud? Flag forward and in uniform? Nah, nah, nah. Butch handles everything in house, but Gunny Alfred heard about it from the DCM, so Gunny let Panama know direct."

"Office hours?" Curtis guessed.

"Brick was in full dress that Monday. Major on speaker. Lost a stripe and a month's pay. Used to be *Sergeant* Brick. Major told him to think whatever the fuck he wants, but he's a guest in country and to keep his mouth shut, especially in uniform. Square Head's too goddamn thick to know he's in a sweet spot."

"You call him Square Head to his face?" Curtis said.

"We call him Bam-Bam."

"Bam-Bam," said Curtis.

"You get a look at that head?" Pops asked.

"I did. Like a cinder block with whiskers," said Curtis.

Pops chuckled. "Cinder block." He clapped his hands and said, "Jowly-ass motherfucker. Detachment problem child, man. Guillermo, let's show brother Dark his new bathroom." Near the end of the wing, Guillermo opened the penultimate door.

Room one had a double sink and full-length mirrors, all spotless. The second chamber sported a rose-colored carpet and a massive jacuzzi, with ample parking for six, maybe seven visitors. The third room had a glass-topped table with iron legs that held a sky-blue vase filled with yellow flowers. There was a shiny black throne trimmed with gold that looked as if it had never been used. The shower in the corner had a U-shaped bench built right in and it was tiled with swirly Chinese dragons.

All three rooms smelled of eucalyptus.

"You'll share with D.L. Sherman," Pops said.

"All this for two guys?" Curtis said.

"Asi es, Jefe," Guillermo said.

Restroom realities in the Fleet Marine Force had consisted of solid rows of free-standing crappers and no stalls. That was a shock to Curtis early on in boot camp. Trading magazines and bullshitting freely whilst sitting on the can hadn't come easy. None of it was pleasant. Even the most robust flatulence garnered very little attention - no more than a glance up and a bit of bitching before offended Marines returned to their periodicals.

It was like living with housebroken apes.

And like it or not, Curtis had been just another monkey.

He pondered his change in station as he walked with Pops and Guillermo to the end of the hall. Guillermo opened the door to what would be Curtis's bedroom. They'd saved the best for last. Beyond the four-poster bed with the satiny quilt, past the antique roll top desk, and after the leather lounge chair with a matching ottoman, for cryin' out loud, was *a floor-to-ceiling wall made entirely of glass*, with an astounding view of the snow-capped Andes mountains. Curtis touched his fingers to the sparkling glass.

Pops said, "The big one is Cotopaxi, man. It's a live volcano."

"Holy smokes," Curtis said. "Will you just look at that?"

The room with a view made one thing clear....

Curtis was no longer just another monkey.

CHAPTER
Three

It was midnight. A sleep deprived hooker in tattered panties sat on the edge of Curtis's bed. He stood next to her. They were both drunk. Curtis was mesmerized by her exhausted nipples. Her breasts were a lovely cocoa color, though her dark buds refused to bloom. "Some bashful beauties you got there," he said.

The girl yawned big and said, *"Yo tengo sueno."*

"Wait, I have an idea," Curtis said. He removed the Saint Christopher medal his mother had given him from around his neck and placed it on the bedside table, then took off the rest of his clothes. He steadied himself, then walked carefully to the roll top desk, where he opened a box of cassette tapes. He strummed his fingers before choosing *Make Your Move*, by Captain & Tennille. He slid it into the boom box and pressed play.

Curtis scurried back.

He planned to dance nude to excite the sleepy girl.

"Me and my friend Henry love to boogie." The music started.

Toni Tennille sang and Curtis started to spin. "You see me go?" he asked as he spun. Curtis paused in profile for the girl. He winked. Toni crooned, and Curtis worked several round revolutions into his ass parade. He hoped to stimulate some kind of response, but the girl didn't even crack a smile.

He did a double bicep flex at Toni's fade out.

The hooker blew a strand of hair from her face.

"Your turn," Curtis said. "You try!"

He grabbed the girl's wrists, pulled her up and sat down in her spot. Her butt had warmed the satiny sheets. The girl lifted her arm and scratched at her armpit. Captain & Tennille's next hit began, but the girl just stood there. Curtis felt like an ass, sitting there clapping his hands. He shouted, "Do something!"

"Yo siento ridiculo," the woman said. Finally, she did a sarcastic finger twinkle and then launched into an apathetic loop around the four-poster bed. She expressed her acute disinterest by way of a listless rabbit hop. It was fucking feeble. She wasn't even trying. Curtis thought her titties jiggled nicely despite her attitude.

He hummed. The girl hopped. The room spun.

When she was half-way around, he said, "Whoa," leaned in, and clutched her hips. He pressed his forehead against the small of her back. He mumbled, "I'm a little dizzy," and rested there. He pulled his head back, put his hands against the sides of her butt and appraised what was in front of him. He squeezed her buns and licked his lips.

Curtis wasn't used to being drunk.

He put his head against her cheeks again and said, "I admire everything about you." He began fingering the dime-sized holes in her gauzy underwear. He pressed his index finger against each exposed circle of coffee colored flesh.

The girl looked over her shoulder and down. Curtis looked up. "I'd really, a lot, appreciate," he whispered, "if you would bend over and touch your toes."

The girl rolled her eyes at his incomprehensible *Inglés*. *"Tengo mucho sueno,"* she whined and flopped on the bed. Curtis moved in beside her.

The girl yawned, her breath mulchy.

She watched him dance his fingers across her belly.

She said, *"Yo estoy cansado,"* whatever that meant and then she said, *"Vamos."* The hooker grabbed Curtis and gave him an aggressive set of three very rough tugs - boom-boom-boom. That did the trick. *"Bueno,"* the girl said, *"eso es."*

Curtis swallowed. "Geez, I wasn't expecting that," he said.

He fumbled for his tee-shirt. Found it under the pillow.

It was the sleeveless kind, like Rocky's in *Rocky*.

"Es sufficiente," she said and turned toward sleep.

Bluish moonlight played against her naked shoulder.

Curtis listened to her breathing, and then he heard a sheepdog bark.

He reached over and stroked her hip. The girl jostled onto her tummy. Her shopworn panties hugged her fanny. He knelt beside her and whispered, "Let me get these out of the way." He slipped his thumbs into the waistband and worked her panties all the way down her legs, then over her ankles. The girl snored. Curtis clutched the panties in both hands, like a mendicant friar might do with a valuable coin.

He hummed Captain & Tennille.

He brought the raggedy panties to his nose. They smelled beachy like the sea. Curtis moved into a push up position above the girl. His right arm held him up as he teased her shoulders with the undies that dangled from his left hand.

He chanted, *"Chica, chica, chica..."* The girl made no response.

He slid the silkies back and forth. There was no evidence of arousal, no matter how creatively he waved her panties around. Curtis sighed. He dropped the panties, rolled off the bed and went to sit in the Eames chair. At Lord Byron's Bar, Corporal Custer had said the chair style was named after a Ray Eames. Custer's nickname was Bighorn. His main interest was anthropology. Bighorn had filthy fingernails and spoke with a stutter. Curtis had asked if Bighorn wanted to dig around in caves.

Bighorn had said, "I, uh, tend to dig around in libraries."

The leather on the Eames chair was a little cold at night. Curtis got up and brought the ottoman over to the world map that hung by the window. He adjusted the ottoman so he could sit and look at the map.

Other Marines were awake.

He heard music and sometimes shouting.

Curtis stared at the map. In the moonlight, he could make out Cape Cod and Boston. Worcester might have been there too, in smaller type. His hometown, no way. Too tiny even if there was a light on. Hinda Cohen was still there, of course, but Curtis had wanted to see the world and *voilà*, here he was, seeing it. He moved the ottoman and faced the hooker. Curtis admired the girl in slumber. He looked at her legs. He could see all the way up, almost.

A completely unobstructed view was lost in nighttime shadow.

Curtis looked back at the map.

He thought about how small towns glorified homegrown heroes. Westborough, Massachusetts was no exception. The goddamn Historical Society celebrated Eli friggin' Whitney, for Christ's sake. They held a cotton gin parade every other year.

Curtis felt that inventing interchangeable parts for a flintlock rifle did not a hero make. He had always resented the excessive celebrity conferred upon Eli for contributing such who-gives-a-shit staples to the town's history. He'd met Henry the very day that Eli Whitney's landmark home had gone up in flames. Curtis stopped to ask Eddie Belder why he was laying out road flares. Eddie said, "There's been a fire."

"No shit," Curtis said. "What's that got to do with you?"

Belder puffed out his chest. "I'm a Police Explorer."

"So, what's that make you? Captain safety?" Curtis eyed the dirty white whistle that hung from a loop at Belder's shoulder and noted Eddie's rumply pants, saggy socks and scuffed up shoes. He'd have simply walked on if he hadn't heard someone snigger, "Somebody torched ol' Eli's ass, but good." It was Henry. He was fat in those days. He stood in a hydrant puddle munching a Milky Way. He waved a hand toward the smoking ruins and said, "Eli's flintlocks sucked. They only got off one round at a time. While you're messin' around trying to reload, some sneakin' Indian's gonna put an arrow in your ass, guaranteed."

"You're supposed to be assisting the injured," said Eddie Belder.

Henry stuffed the last of the Milky Way into his chubby face and said, "What injured, Beldo?" He'd looked toward Curtis and said, "Guy's a douche." Curtis nodded. The fat boy pitched his candy wrapper into the gutter and approached Curtis. He put out his sticky fingers and said, "I'm Henry Fonda." They shook.

"Get back on post, Fonda," Eddie shouted.

Henry yelled back and told Eddie to stick two flares up his ass and call him in the morning. Curtis thought Henry had balls, so he asked Henry if he wanted a pizza.

Henry said, "I don't have any money."

Curtis said, "Don't worry, man. I got dough…"

At Penny's Pizzeria, Curtis swigged from his coke and watched Henry shake parmesan onto a slice of pepperoni. "Did your parents name you Henry Fonda after the movie star?"

Henry chewed. "Coincidence," he said. "I got adopted. I was Henry already."

Curtis took a slice of the pie. "Do people give you shit about your name?"

"Why should they?"

"I know people who would,'" Curtis said.

"Yeah, maybe if they're assholes," Henry said.

"You got any plans after high school?" Curtis said.

"In five freakin' years? I ain't thinkin' that far ahead." Henry held up three fingers like a Boy Scout reciting an oath and said, "I'm thinkin' about getting these babies into Laura Nugent's twat. Can you imagine swirlin' around in that?"

"I'm thinking about joining the Coast Guard," Curtis said.

"What are you gonna do in the Coast Guard?" Henry said.

"Save people on the open seas. Rescue 'em if they suck at sailing."

"You ever been on a boat?" Henry belched.

"Who gives a fuck? They train you," Curtis said.

"Join the Police Explorers with me. We get brownies."

Curtis said, "And do what? Burn flares with Eddie Belder?"

Curtis waved to Penny for the check.

Henry claimed that Lisa and Valerie Van Dorn were Police Explorers. "Both of 'em got the jumpin' boobs," he said and he wagged his tongue. Penny brought the check to the table right then. Curtis remembered clearly because Penny had asked, "How's your mother doing?" and Curtis felt his face flush.

He said, "Fine," but never raised his eyes from the table.

Penny picked up the cash and left. Instead of acknowledging anything about Curtis's mother, Henry said, "Anyway, the Van Dorns. That's some set of sisters."

Curtis was goddamn grateful Henry had left his mother out of it.

The hooker in his bed whimpered and curled herself into the fetal position.

Curtis stood and walked over to her. He pulled the quilt from the foot of the bed and covered the girl. He went around to the other side, scootched in under the quilt, slid close and attempted to spoon her. She swatted him away in her sleep. He lay back and tapped his thumbs together.

Glass shattered.

The night dogs of Ecuador howled.

One of the Marines yelled, "Shut your asses!"

The hooker bolted upright, looked around in the dark and said, *¿Qué paso?*"

Curtis said, "You're awake!" The Bee Gees started to thump from another part of the Marine House. "Hear that? *Stayin' Alive!* Should we get down?"

The girl moaned and dove under the covers.

She sandwiched her head between two pillows.

"Gimme a break. It's the Bee Gees."

As far as Curtis was concerned, the night was still young. You only arrive in country once, yet here she was, his welcome wagon hooker, totally out of it. Henry Fonda had never been too tired to party, boy. Henry resembled his adoptive mom, but he didn't move like a fat kid. He was a smooth and confident dancer, albeit a pot-bellied one.

They'd dance together, snapping their fingers and moving as one, while lip-syncing lyrics. They'd spun and they'd gyrated. One time, Henry decided to drop his trousers and moon Curtis as a randy finale to *More Than a Woman*. When Henry started to pull up his pants, Curtis asked him to keep them down a little longer. "A girl's ass probably looks like that under a spotlight," he said.

Henry, who had his hands on his knees, looked over his shoulder. "If this was a girl's ass, would you think it was cute?"

Curtis whispered, "Yes."

He glanced at the hooker.

Her back was to him and a hint of her hip was exposed.

She snored. He gnawed his lip. He'd ask permission in the morning.

The Marine House quieted, the revelry slowed and Curtis drifted off.

At first light, a rooster crowed. Curtis jerked awake - a conditioned response to the cock-a-deucey. It took a few seconds to register where in the heck he was.

He turned toward the sleeping girl. She faced him now, her lips apart.

Curtis slid over close and rubbed gently at her chin with his knuckles.

The girl woke up. She blinked several times and pushed her hair from her face.

Curtis said, *"Buenas Dias."*

The girl lifted the quilt and glanced at his crotch. *"Ay dios mío,"* she said and dropped the blanket. She grabbed her purse and extracted a nearly flat yellow and white tube and lubricated three fingers. She reached under the quilt and after that she used the pillowcase to tidy her fingers. She said, *"Ya."*

Curtis climbed over. The girl slid under him and adjusted her hips.

She absorbed his virginity displaying no more enthusiasm than she might have done had she plugged in a radio. "Wow," Curtis puffed, "you're really warm." The girl employed a very sensuous squeeze and release maneuver. She used her virtuoso lady parts with rhythmic authority. Her talent made him shudder. He started to pant.

Right then, there was a quick knock at the door.

The bedroom door flew open and D.L. Sherman stood in the doorway.

"Goddamn Lance Corporal!" He raised his mug and said, "Well, here's to the whore behind the door!" He drained what was left in his cup. "Hot chow when you're done, Marine." Dan closed the door.

The dexterous lass made a final adjustment and played Curtis like a piano. In seconds the deed was done. *"Bueno, ya,"* she said. Curtis leaned down to kiss her but she turned his head away. He knew nothing of prostitute etiquette.

He wasn't sure what he was supposed to do next.

As if she were reading his mind, the girl placed her palms at his shoulders and shoved. Curtis rolled off. The girl scrounged around for his shirt and worked it under the covers. She said, *"Su camisa esta bien mojada,"* which Curtis didn't understand. When she put out her hand and said, "Me money?" he understood perfectly.

Curtis moved the Saint Christopher that was draped over his wallet.

He thought of his father. He once asked him, "Dad, when do I get an allowance?"

Ronald Dark said, "Every time you eat."

Curtis asked the hooker if dollars were okay. The girl took dollars.

D.L. had told Curtis, "You can buy a night for ten bucks."

Curtis felt the girl had done a bang-up job.

He plucked two twenties from his wallet and handed her those. "Are you hungry?" Curtis said. "Wanna have some breakfast with me?" He pantomimed eating with a spoon.

"No, gracias. Nada para me. Voy a dormir un poco mas." She took her purse from the nightstand, put the cash inside and rolled back into bed. She laid the bright red purse atop her breasts and tippy-tapped it with her fingers, then sang out in heavily accented English, *"Hey, beeg spender…"*

She had a wicked laugh.

CHAPTER Four

Curtis strode into the Marine House kitchen.

D.L. Sherman said, "Caught the newbie on the down stroke, fellas. He's been baggin' the beave all night." Curtis smiled and pulled out a chair next to Sherman's.

Bighorn held a ceramic bowl against his lips with dirty fingers. He said, "That's, uh, real nice work if you can get it." He chugged from the bowl. Milk ran down his neck and seeped into his lime green bathrobe.

A king-size platter of scrambled eggs and a silver tray of bacon were on the kitchen counter. Down the line, next to the plates and silverware was a large bowl full of fresh fruit and two pitchers of juice - one tomato red, the other pale yellow.

Billy Ray kicked back his Stetson. "That there is Zoila. Chief cook and bottle washer. She ain't bad, either." Zoila carried a basket of toast to the table. She was short, squat, and bandy-legged. She tipped side to side when she walked. Curtis smiled at her and Zoila changed course toward his seat.

She held out the toast basket.

Curtis selected a dark piece and Zoila nodded.

"You were diddlin' till dawn, am I right, Lance Corporal?" D.L. said.

Sherman grabbed an end-slice and looked to Curtis for confirmation.

By staying silent and grinning wide, Curtis transformed his inauspicious first night performance from embarrassing quickie into an all-night marathon worthy of uber-macho accolades. When Billy Ray asked if he was hungry, Curtis's simple, "Heck, yeah," produced whoops of support.

Curtis, the erstwhile virgin, was now a certified stud.

"Put your feet up, newbie, you need the rest," Pops said.

Curtis winked counterfeit confidence and spread honey on his toast.

"Hey, if it feels good, go for it," said Chetbo. He scrubbed his hand through his crew cut. He appeared more or less sober. He'd been drunk the last time Curtis saw him. Curtis had a foggy memory of Chetbo lumbering under a disco ball. His head bobbed and his arms pumped. Sweat soaked his too-tight Panama shirt. He danced with a woman in a hot pink halter and slugged whiskey straight from a bottle. Late in the evening, Chetbo pulled open his shirt and flashed the leprechaun tattoo that covered his chest. Chetbo's lucky charmer was naked from the waist down.

It stood atop a shamrock, waving a swollen penis.

His dance partner was not amused.

Chetbo croaked, "It's magically delicious," and moved in close against the girl's breasts. She reared back and slapped him hard across the face. That tickled the shit out of the Marines who saw it happen. "What the fuck," Chetbo said. He rubbed his cheek and slapped her back. The Marines ejected him from the disco.

They made Chetbo sit in the van.

In the kitchen, Zoila placed a mug of black coffee and a plate of bacon and eggs in front of Curtis. He said, "Thank you so much."

"You, uh, need milk?" Bighorn said. A stream dribbled down his chin.

"Nah, man, I'm good," Curtis said.

Duke Sweetzer ambled in. He wore sweatpants, sandals, and shades. He had on headphones attached to his Walkman. A large envelope was tucked under his right arm. "Hello, gentlemen. Madame Zoila," he said. Duke sat down and pulled off the headphones. "What did I miss?"

Zoila waddled over. *"Buenos días, Señor Duke."*

D.L. reached into his windbreaker and pulled out his Marlboro reds. "Anybody mind if I smoke?" He immediately lit a cigarette.

Bighorn lifted a haunch from his chair and let one go. Curtis looked to Zoila, who was either hard of hearing or pretending to be. Zoila poured coffee for Sweetzer as Billy Ray placed his Stetson over his face and said, "C'mon' Bighorn."

"Uh, the stomach's a little sour," Bighorn said. "Sorry, boys."

D.L. said, "Lovely," then raised his mug. "I would like to propose a fitting moniker for our newest arrival and my fellow Masshole. Any guy who heaves on a rooster has pretty much christened himself. I submit '*Yardbird*' for the vomitous Lance Corporal Dark."

"I'll take it," Curtis said and he clinked cups with D.L.

Bighorn farted again and Zoila winced. She'd heard him that time for sure.

Duke pulled a *Playboy* from the brown envelope and held it up for all to see. "Miss October has arrived. She was pilfered from the diplomatic pouch, Yardbird. She'll have to go back in that pouch by Thursday, so the DCM can have her for the weekend."

On the cover was a sweet looking Mountie in a red tunic seated on a patent leather saddle. She wore thigh-high boots with bunny spurs. The Mountie wore no pants.

Bighorn asked, "Who, uh, who's the interview?"

"Let's see. We've got, 'A candid conversation with the former sphinx of Watergate about patriotism, Nazi Germany, willpower and the virtues of being ruthless.' Mr. G. Gordon Liddy," said Duke.

He laid the mag in the center of the table.

Bighorn said, "Let's, uh, let's take a gander."

"I got first dibs," said Duke. He put on his headphones and pressed play.

D.L. leaned over and gave Curtis the scoop. "Craig Sweetzer, a.k.a. 'The Duke,' does not partake of the ladies of the evening. A bit of a mystery, there. Good fuckin' guy, though. When Sweetzer first got here, we rode donkeys around a base camp at Cotopaxi. One of the Gunny's brilliant ideas. Ol' Sweetzer didn't have his boots on for some reason, and he was trying to ride this belligerent mule that wouldn't listen for shit."

"More of a surfboard type?" said Curtis.

"Good guess. Duke is from Vero Beach, Florida. At one point the donkey went crashin' off into the woods with Craigger huggin' like a bastard around its neck, trying to hold on. Duke and donk just disappeared."

"Duke and donk," Curtis chuckled.

Zoila poured more coffee. Curtis thanked her. Dan didn't.

"Fifteen minutes down trail, we hear a scream and here comes Craigger blastin' outta the underbrush still hangin' onto the donkey, way back by its ass end, all wild-eyed and terrified, and they launched right across the bridle path with Craigger kickin' his heels into the donkey's ribs and screamin' at it to whoa the fuck down. All to no avail. They just thrashed around in a circle, all *Urban Cowboy*," D.L. said.

Curtis spit coffee and laughed.

"Gets worse," D.L. said. "They fly off into the woods again, boss donk totally in charge. The miserable beast eventually bucks Duke into a lovely patch of poison oak."

"Holy smokes," said Curtis.

Sweetzer looked up, oblivious due to the Walkman. He winked at Curtis.

"The sorry fucker had to walk back barefoot," D.L. said. "He comes into camp, feet lacerated all to hell, ears all swollen, all thick and bigger than normal. Guy had bright red welts of poison oak everywhere. I took one look and said, 'John Wayne Sweetzer. Howdy-do, Duke?' We all fell the fuck over. Never saw that donkey again."

Bighorn knocked on the table.

Sweetzer pulled off his earphones. The guy was skinny as hell.

"Let me, uh, see what G. Gordon Liddy has to say, Duke," Bighorn said.

"Sporting a moustache only a mother could love," Sweetzer said. He slid the magazine toward Bighorn. "Page sixty-five. Did you all ever notice how the Playmate data sheet has pictures of the girl at like seven and like nine and like twelve? What's that about? That's a little uncomfortable."

"Not for Corporal Brick," D.L. said.

"Bam-Bam's an idiot, not a pedophile," Duke said.

Bighorn farted a third time. Curtis saw Zoila frown.

It was apparent that Bighorn disgusted Zoila, and he baffled Curtis.

Training for the Marine Security Guard Battalion was like attending a finishing school. English tutorials helped free Marines from atrocious grammar use and cursing in public. There were etiquette lessons, too. Marines learned which fork was the salad fork and not to chew with their mouths open. The MSGs also received specific training that emphasized the importance of meticulous personal hygiene and how to maintain it on a daily basis.

At Quantico, an MSG candidate stood at the position of attention to Curtis's right. He was asked a question by the inspecting Sergeant. Sergeant Owen McBride had served as a Marine Security Guard, first in Ankara and then in Abidjan. At the embassy in the Ivory Coast, he'd won a citation for wrestling a jagged Coca-Cola bottle away from a deranged West African, who kicked and screamed in vain for a visa.

Sergeant McBride asked the would-be MSG, "How come you have Irish pennants dangling at your collar, Candidate?" The candidate began to respond. He managed to spit out, "I didn't see..." before McBride brought his hand up, the one with Coke bottle scars, and fanned it under his nose. "Your breath smells like a salami," McBride whispered ominously. "One that's been plucked out of somebody's ass."

That candidate had been summarily dismissed – dropped from MSG school and recycled back to his infantry unit at Camp Lejeune within twenty-four hours. How in the hell, Curtis wondered, had Bighorn been able to fly under McBride's radar and make it to Ecuador acting so unrefined? Lila-Ruth had raised Curtis to say please and thank you, and Ronald Dark had taught his sons the meaning of clean.

It was against Curtis's nature to chew food with his mouth open.

And for pity's sake, farting at the table à la Bighorn made no sense at all.

Pops said, "Screw G. Gordon Liddy, Bighorn. I wanna see some titties." He snatched the *Playboy*. Bighorn tried to grab it back, but Pops said, "Uh, uh, uh," and pulled it out of Bighorn's reach. Pops then raised his coffee mug and called, *"Zoila, café especial por favor!"*

"Si, Señor Pops," said Zoila, and she shuffled out of the room.

Bighorn made another play for the magazine.

"Hey, take it easy meathead," Pops said.

"Don't soil the pages, boys," Duke said, "I have to give that back."

"Goddamn it, Custer, your dirty ass fingers are tearin' her tits," said Pops.

Bighorn reluctantly let go of the magazine. Pops pressed the centerfold flat and laid it out for the Marines. He made a big show of his disdain for Bighorn's crease marks. Miss October's denim vest was wide open, and a bolo tie dangled between her sweet breasts. She held a loop of tightly coiled rope against her naked thigh.

Her lips formed a melancholy pout.

The Marines leaned in.

"What's she got to be sad about?" D.L. said.

"Even cowgirls get the blues," said Duke Sweetzer.

"I do like that," Billy Ray said, "Her pretending to be a cowgirl."

Zoila returned with a bottle of Maker's Mark and topped off Pops's mug.

He took a long slug. Slammed the mug on the table. "Rootin' tootin' raspberry!" He belched, then read, "Miss Mardi Jacquet. Our Miss October. Get this. She likes kisses in the palms of her hands. Behind her ears, too. Hmmm. Says, 'I could watch *The Sound of Music* every day for the rest of my life.' Yardbird, you're a movie guy. How does that grab you?"

"Seems excessive," Curtis said.

Billy Ray sang out, "If I were a rich man..." He looked around for approval.

"That's fuckin' *Fiddler*, dumb ass," Chetbo said, "What else she digs on, Popsy?"

"Mas café," Pops said. *"Fuerte!"*

Zoila reappeared and tipped the bottle.

"Give me a hit of that, will you please, Zee-mama?" Chetbo said.

Zoila poured him a generous splash while Pops raised his mug for more.

Curtis was astonished. They'd been drunk last night. They were still at it.

Zoila peeked at Miss October's manicured muff as she poured booze for Pops. Curtis noticed a little kid standing in the corner of the kitchen. He wondered how long she'd been there. The girl had black opal eyes that didn't blink, and she stood stock still and totally silent. Curtis had read in *Little Big Man* that in certain tribes, babies were put in cradleboards and then those were hung out on bushes far away from camp, so that the Indian infants would learn that crying didn't do 'em any good. That way, children of the Cheyenne grew up pretty stoic. Curtis tapped D.L. and pointed at the girl.

"Zoila's granddaughter. Paulina," Sherman said.

Curtis guessed she was five or six.

He twinkled his fingers at her.

She turned her back on him.

Sergeant Baxter arrived in uniform carrying a clipboard. Around the table, the Marines sat up a little straighter. "Morning, Gents," said Butch, "I'll be brief. Only word over the wire is that the Iranians and the Iraqis are really going to town in the Gulf, which is bound to make things even more dicey for the hostages. Make double sure you have a beeper whenever you're off post."

Zoila handed Butch a cup of fresh coffee.

Baxter said, "Thank you, Doña Zoila," then waved to Paulina.

The girl kept her hands tight to her sides but didn't turn her back.

"That fuckin' peanut farmer has his thumb up his ass," said Chetbo.

"He's, uh, afraid to make any kind of move at all after that mess in Tabas. Gotta wait until after the election." In Quantico they'd learned about the eight guys who'd died in the desert debacle. Five of the dead were Airforce. Three were Marines.

"Operation Eagle Claw," D.L. said.

"Operation Eagle Flaw," Duke said.

"Operation clusterfuck," Chetbo said.

Butch Baxter put his clipboard in his briefcase. "What's really ironic," he said "is that after a year of denouncing the U.S. as Satan's playground, Khomeini's now got Iranian pilots schooled at Pensacola doing flyovers and making ready to rain down American ordinance all over Baghdad."

Curtis watched the other Marines quietly swirl near empty mugs.

"The joke's gonna be on Khomeini," Bighorn said. "He's gonna end up having to free the, uh, free the hostages outright, if he ever wants to end the embargo and collect any hardware for his troops to use against the Iraqis."

"The fuck a big ass Ayatollah care about any of that?" Pops said.

His words were slurred. He listed to the left.

"Unconditional, Pops," Bighorn said. "Goddamn Banisadr can't beat the Iraqi ragheads without imperialist American heathens selling him the, uh, the spare parts they need. Any materiel they have was bought under the Shah..."

"They all some raggedy Nazi-ass-Communist fucks," Pops said.

"Nazi-ass-Communists?" Bighorn said. "There were no Nazi-Communists, you half-wit. Stalin and Hitler hated each other."

"Oh, ho, and you're all that, Custer?" said Pops.

Sergeant Baxter stepped in and stopped the argument.

"We're done here. Corporal Sherman, if you've got any meter maids in the Marine House in need of transportation, get 'em taken downtown before zero eight, please. Sergeant Dillard, you hit the rack. Your last one was your last one."

Pops looked into his empty coffee mug and licked his lips.

"You squared away, Dark?" asked Sergeant Baxter. "You're down for a walk-through at thirteen hundred. You'll meet Gunny, and Sergeant Trumbo will snap you in."

"I'm set, Sergeant Baxter," Curtis said.

"Deltas. Trumbo's gonna pace you out." Baxter left the kitchen.

D.L. said to Curtis, "B. is one of the good ones. Says please and thank you."

Pops belched and gave Bighorn the finger, but he did it behind Bighorn's back.

"Who has hookers that need rides?" D.L. said.

Pops raised his hand. Curtis said, "I have a girl." D.L. counted, "Got one, got two." He jerked his thumb at his chest. "So, three. Three whores on wheels. How about you, Sergeant Boseovski? Where's that slap-happy chick with the pink tits?"

"Not a prostie," Chetbo said.

"She cuffed your ass just for askin'?" D.L. chuckled. "Ooooof."

D.L. turned to Zoila and held up three fingers. "*¿Comida para tres chicas, OK, Zoila?*" Zoila handed three plates to Paulina and said, "*Si, Señor Dan, platos para tres amiguitas.*" Paulina began to set the breakfast plates for the working girls' end of shift.

Bighorn Custer grabbed the Playboy and said, "Mine, now."

Curtis needed a shower. He left the kitchen.

He thought his girl looked nice coming out of his bedroom.

Her pretty red sweater was long-sleeved and there were five silver buttons that decorated her plunging neckline, two of which looked like they'd sprung open. Her slick red purse had a black strap. The strap matched her black vinyl mini-skirt. The girl waved, all smiles. Curtis thought she was excited to see him but she was waving at the woman who had just come out of D.L.'s room.

"*¿Esta casa está bacán, verdad?*" His girl whistled appreciatively at the Marines' incredible house and Dan's girl responded, "*Si, esta bien bonita.*" She rubbed her thumb against her two forefingers, presumably calculating costs.

The three converged in the hallway.

"I never got your name. What is it?" Curtis said.

His girl put her tongue in her cheek and swung her red purse.

"*Mi nombre es 'Zorra Hembra,'*" she said. Curtis could tell her answer was meant more for the other hooker's benefit than for Curtis's own because he, of course, had no idea what *Zorra Hembra* meant.

The second hooker got the joke and giggled.

D.L.'s whore said, "And you name?"

"Curtis Dark. Nice to meet you."

"Your name is not Cur-tease," Zorra said. "I give him nicky name; 'Beeg Spender.'" Zorra Hembra punched Curtis playfully on the arm and said to the other girl, "*El vino muy rapido. Fue un buen negocio.*" She tapped her purse and then the two girls locked arms.

D.L.'s hooker said, "Bye-bye."

Zorra said, "See you later, money man."

They tramped off down the hall toward breakfast.

Curtis went to his room and grabbed his shaving kit.

He also checked his Spanish/English dictionary.

Zorra meant *Fox*. *Hembra* meant *Chick*.

Foxy Chick. Clever girl, that *Zorra Hembra*.

The shower ran warm as he pondered sex with the fox.

It seemed impossible to do what the guy in Taboo had done.

The actor who'd made love with Kay Parker had lasted forever.

Curtis had hardly moved at all. Wham. Bam. Thank you, Ma'am.

He'd have to train. The first time Curtis played ice hockey, his ankles were all bent in and he'd fallen on his ass every five seconds. Eventually, he became a pretty decent skater. By the time he reached Bantams, he made All-Stars.

Improving his hockey skills had required some serious rink time.

Tapping ass...

Doing the nasty...

Shrimpin' the Barbie...

Call it what you will, he wanted to get better at it.

In his bedroom, he put on fresh skivvies, a clean sweatshirt and jeans and then unpacked more of his seabag. He took out his personnel file and laid it on the bed. Kris Kristofferson was on the cover of his *American Film* magazine along with Isabelle Huppert. He put the mag on his bedside table and put *Little Big Man* beside that.

Curtis took his out spit-shine rag and polished his shoes.

Next, he pulled a manila envelope from his seabag.

He removed his poster of *The Poseidon Adventure* that was folded flat between two pieces of cardboard. There were brass tacks in the pencil drawer of the roll top desk. Curtis stood on the ottoman and tacked it up. He sat on his bed and read the tag line for the thousandth time; *"HELL, UPSIDE DOWN."* He thought of his brother.

Paulie wasn't allowed to see *The Poseidon Adventure*. Lila-Ruth decided he was too young. However, Paulie knew how badly Curtis wanted to see the movie, so he said, "Have a great time, guys!" and waved. The kid never sulked. That's the kind of brother Paulie was. He never ruined things for the other guy.

Marilyn Ritacco, the theatre manager, gave Curtis the poster to take home.

Curtis told Paulie it was the greatest escape adventure of all time. Excited, Paulie said, "Let's put her up and see." He got a roll of masking tape from the top drawer of his desk.

"Use tacks, Paulie," Curtis said. "Tape bleeds."

"Tacks it is." They hung up the poster together.

This poster. The one he took to *Key-Toe*.

Paulie might not have liked the movie that much, had he ever seen it.

He preferred movies where no one got hurt. Paulie was that kind of kid.

The hookers left the Marine House after breakfast. Curtis watched Shorty escort the three down the driveway to the van. He held a black umbrella against the rain. The girls huddled underneath and shared a cigarette.

"How you rate those babes, Yardbird?" D.L. said.

"Right up there," Curtis said, as if he had actual points of comparison.

"You'll find the Ecuadorian strumpet can be quite accommodating," D.L. said.

Shorty drove off with *Zorra Hembra* and her friends. Curtis's virginity went with them. He felt wistful. He never got Zorra's real name. He remembered asking his father, "Did you ever meet any really special girl in the Army, Dad?"

Ronald Dark thought a moment.

"Met one once who could blow out a pack of matches with her pussy."

As special as that may have been, it wasn't at all what Curtis had meant.

CHAPTER
Five

Curtis hunted for an iron.

Halfway from his room to the Marine House bar, he heard movie music. He followed the beat, opened a door, and saw images from a 16mm projector flicker on a pulldown screen. *The Warriors* was playing to an audience of one. Bam-Bam Brick sat dead center in the front row. He munched Pringles out of a red tube. Film canisters and an open shipping case were at Bam-Bam's bare feet.

Had it been anyone but Brick, Curtis would have asked who oversaw the requisitioning of movies. Instead, he left without a peep.

Bighorn was downstairs at the house bar. Curtis asked him where the kit closet was and where the Detachment kept their ironing boards and spray starch. Bighorn threw his head back and tipped a box of Cocoa Puffs toward his mouth. He rattled the box and then began to lick and chew. Looking at Bighorn, one might assume that not one single iron existed in all of Ecuador.

"Closet there," Bighorn said with his mouth full of cereal. He pointed. Even in uniform the guy looked as if he'd just crawled out of a hamper.

Gobs of cereal, now paste, fell from his lips and landed in a pile atop the bar.

Being close to Bighorn, Curtis saw that his teeth were in lousy shape. He guessed their shady tint was not the result of the Cocoa Puffs. Bighorn poured again and gnashed away with his mouth wide open. "The guy you're gonna replace," he said, "is, uh, Kent Trumbo." Curtis had heard that name. A Dalton Trumbo had written *Spartacus*. "Uh, Gunny's gonna run the same drill on you he runs on everybody."

Curtis opened the closet and silently set up the ironing board.

"Gunny'll have you run a PFT today, is, uh, my guess. Bring running shoes. You'll recite your general orders. Blah, blah, blah." Bighorn sniffed and asked, "You a reader?" Bighorn appeared to know a thing or two about history and current events, so there was that, but Curtis could have explained in rich detail which movies over the past ten years were superior to which novels - and vice versa, for that matter - had he been so inclined. But Bighorn had just tipped his head to accommodate the box of Cocoa Puffs yet again and the cant of his head revealed exactly how dirty his ear canal was.

The view extinguished any desire to share.

Bighorn said, "Need some milk. Uh, back in a sec."

Curtis looked at the slop on the bar. "Bring a napkin, man. Bring several." In a minute, Bighorn tromped back to the bar with a bottle of milk and no napkins. Curtis pressed flat a clean white towel with the hot iron, then laid his uniform shirt on top of that. He pressed the collar, the yoke, and the hem gussets, then cut in five precise, vertical creases - three down the back and two down the front, exactly where they belonged. The pair in front split the breast pockets right down the middle. Curtis placed the shirt on a hanger. It was a thing of beauty.

"So, what, uh, what are you reading now?" Bighorn said.

"*Little Big Man*. Thomas Berger."

"Why do you, uh, read fiction?"

Even Bighorn's tee-shirt, which was exposed at the neck of his khaki shirt, was more goddamned gray than white. It made no fucking sense. Curtis popped the yellow top on the spray starch and said, "Back up, Bighorn. I read whatever I feel like reading."

"I, uh, pretty much only read history."

"Well, bully for you," Curtis said.

Bighorn turned silent.

He sat down on a bar stool and his shoulders slumped forward a little. "I'm not, uh, giving you shit. I get, uh, a little tongue tied, but, uh, uh, I enjoy talkin' books, and, uh, don't get too much of a chance." He scratched his head like he'd conjured a crystal-clear idea, but was perplexed as to how he could best articulate it. He exhaled slowly, then said, "Sergeant Trumbo reads fiction and non-fiction both, but he's, uh, he's, uh, shipping out. I always wonder what fiction provides, uh, for a person who reads it."

Curtis had to admit it was a pretty good question.

He strummed his fingers against the ironing board, then looked up and locked eyes with Bighorn. He looked like somebody's overgrown and really fucking grubby kid.

Curtis had seen this type of thing before.

Back in Westborough there was a boy named Ricky Malone. He moved in from Texas in seventh grade. Everybody called him *"Dirty Tex,"* because Ricky always had a finger up his nose, never washed his hair, and his clothes were always filthy. When it came to school work, Ricky aced problem after problem in Miss Shapiro's math class, but nobody gave a damn.

One time, Timmy Foley and Wally Powers, an awful pair of shitbag bullies, hung Dirty Tex over the third-floor balcony by his ankles. Ricky blubbered and begged, and he screamed and cried until Foley and Powers finally relented, pulled him back up again, and set him on his feet. Ricky was all red-faced and goddamn hysterical.

It was terrible, and it was true. Even if a kid was the smartest kid in the room, if he came to school dirty, he'd get fucked around without mercy and end up lonely.

"Gimme your shirt, Bighorn. I'll show you how to iron the damn thing," Curtis said. "Then we can talk fiction." After he'd pressed Bighorn's shirt, Curtis went back to his room, placed his personnel file in his kit bag along with his Adidas, his shorts, socks, and *MSG Battalion* tee-shirt. He tossed in his jock, too.

Done packing and in uniform, he walked outside to the van with Bighorn.

He noted that Bighorn's shoes were as dull as dishwater.

Curtis called shotgun.

Bighorn settled into the back seat and said, "The embassy is about eleven miles from here, about sixteen klicks north. Takes, uh, thirty-five minutes depending on traffic and Shorty. Drivers gotta take different routes every day. Been that way since Tehran. No exceptions. Whole Battalion, pure rotation and, uh, change-ups. No discernible patterns."

Bighorn yawned as Shorty started the van.

Curtis shot a quick look back at Bighorn.

He didn't look too bad in his freshly pressed shirt.

At the gate, Curtis waved to Guillermo. The kid waved back.

They drove to a triangular kiosk at the bottom of the hill. It supported a black and red boom barrier. A female guard wore a yellow vest over her blue blouse. She raised the barricade with a rope pulley. A sign above her shack read, *"Alerta - Comité de Seguridad Ciudadana."* The word *Conococto* was embroidered on her cap. As Shorty rolled past, Curtis said, "Check that out," and pointed at the tree behind the security lady.

A shaggy-assed creature with beige fur rested in it.

It had a cute, mauve colored face and a shit-eating grin.

"Tree sloth," Bighorn said. "They're everywhere out here."

"What's *'Conococto'* mean?" Curtis said.

Bighorn shrugged. "No clue."

This route was rural as hell. The vegetation on either side of the road was thick. Enormous leaves were wet and sweaty and there were ponds and vines and lumps of what looked like yellow candy stuck to trees. Everything was damp and lush.

Shorty turned onto *Avenida Simón Bolívar* and picked up speed.

A few minutes later, it started to rain.

A huge steel angel stood on a hill to the west.

Curtis was going to ask Bighorn about it, but Custer had dozed off.

The right hand of the angel showed a Christ like open palm. Her left hand held a chain. The angel stood atop a snake. That seemed like something Curtis's mother would try to do, stand on a snake. Lila-Ruth had always been a little strange.

She wasn't dangerous, exactly. She was just kind of dippy, a sort of benevolent cuckoo. Paulie had once asked Lila-Ruth if she loved having two boys for kids and she'd said, "Mothers love their children. They must. It's a biological imperative."

Lila-Ruth was extremely articulate and precise with her words. She couched her phrases in the jargon of a psychologist. She used lingo she'd picked up in her behavioral science classes at Lake Quinsigamond Community College. Neighborhood housewives were impressed and came to her with their social-emotional concerns. If life were a comic strip, she'd have been Charlie Brown's Lucy.

All that changed when Paulie died.

Lila-Ruth hadn't been healthy since.

Her theories about mental health had fallen apart.

She wasn't even able to get her makeup on straight.

In Curtis's senior year, Lila-Ruth decided she was going to take the bus to work. Mr. Garvey from the Worcester Greyhound Terminal had to call Curtis's dad to pick her up. Mr. Garvey wouldn't sell her a ticket. He knew she didn't work in Minneapolis, plus Lila-Ruth forgot to put a skirt on. She just had pantyhose on.

The last time Curtis ever talked to Paulie, his kid brother rode up on his bike in the driveway and said, "Wanna do loops around Juniper Circle?" Curtis said he didn't feel like it. That was five years ago. Paulie said, "Kay, I'll see you later," and rode off.

It was June 20th, 1975.

The same day that *Jaws* came out.

"Kay, I'll see you later," and he was gone.

Paulie had a massive stroke and never woke up. He was eleven.

Shorty passed *El Teatro Atahualpa*. *Ben-Hur* was on the marquee.

Paulie loved Charlton Heston in *Planet of the Apes*, but in *Ben-Hur*, not so much. He didn't enjoy the scenes in which Stephen Boyd got all messed up and maimed during the chariot race.

In the cinema courtyard there was a huge poster of Robert De Niro's battered face. A banner read, *"El Toro Salvaje – ¡diciembre!"* Curtis removed his notepad from his shirt pocket. Marine Guards were required to have a pad at all times and to carry a writing utensil. They issued notepads and golf pencils at Quantico.

Curtis wrote, *"At the Atahualpa, in December, Raging Bull opens."*

Bighorn glanced at the poster and said, "That oughta be good."

Curtis said, "De Niro and Scorsese? Oughta be great."

Traffic slowed and they stopped for a red light.

A street urchin in a torn serape staggered to Shorty's window. He toted a broken-down little girl on his back. The poor kid waved shattered arms that were disfigured and bent beyond belief. Shorty screamed at them. *"¡Vete! ¡Fuera de aqui! ¡Indios! ¡Sucios!"*

Curtis shot Shorty a *what the fuck is your problem* look and Shorty flinched, then chuckled and offered a shrug.

"Human, uh, hierarchies," Bighorn said. "Ecuadorians treat the obvious Indians like dirt. Won't give 'em jobs. Dominant society insists on, uh, creating a 'nigger class.' Ethnographic reality. Malignant human truth. In Ecuador, it's the Indians." The urchin turned toward the median strip. Curtis winced.

The girl on his back was an awful mess.

"You know how they get twisted up like that?" Bighorn said.

"No idea. Not enough milk? Maybe a calcium deficiency?"

"Not even. Parents break their kids' arms and then, uh, they set 'em bent. Mangled kids get more sympathy and collect more dough as beggars. That's, uh, that's the system. Poverty is brutal. The father makes the kid grotesque."

"Christ," Curtis said.

He gazed out the window.

They passed a park. There were swings.

He stayed quiet and thought about his father.

Once, Ronald drove Curtis and Paulie through Roxbury en route to a cub scout event in Boston. Paulie watched all the black faces go by. Grownups on stoops. Kids out playing. "Which ones are the niggers, Dad?" Paulie said.

"Hey! I don't wanna hear that bullshit business comin' outta you."

"He didn't mean it mean, Dad," Curtis said.

"Stay out of it. I ain't talkin' to you." Ronald glanced at Paulie from the driver's seat. "I knew some in Korea. They did okay."

"What are you thinking about, Yardbird?" Bighorn said.

Curtis snapped back to the present.

"Nothing really. *Jaws*, I guess..."

"The movie?"

"The book," said Curtis.

"*Tiburon,*" Shorty said. He clacked his teeth together as if he were biting something and offered another lame chuckle. Curtis could tell he was trying to be cute as a way back in. "Light's green," Curtis said. Shorty drove on.

"Never, uh, read the book," Bighorn said. "Great movie. Uh, 'Smile, you son of a bitch!' Great line."

"See, that line was courtesy of Carl Gottlieb," Curtis said. "He wrote the script. None of the really great stuff that's in the movie is in the book. In the novel, when the shark's closing in on Brody, and has like nine harpoons up its ass and is comin' in for the kill, the fucking thing just runs outta gas. It just fucking sinks. Peter Benchley wrote the book and he tagged on a line that was so remarkably lame, I memorized it. Get this; '*It seemed to fall away, an apparition evanescing into darkness.*' I've got *evanescing* branded into my brain." Bighorn laughed as Shorty pulled up to the front gate.

"*Aquí estamos, Señores,*" Shorty said.

"Home turf," Bighorn said.

The Embassy of the United States of America was four stories high - a perfect, whitewashed rectangle. Fifteen windows spanned each floor. That totaled sixty front facing windows. Every window panel held a protective concrete slab in the center. Nine horizontal and fourteen vertical holes were bored in each slab. They looked like empty wine racks. Curtis did the math. Each of the would-be racks had a one hundred and twenty-six bottle capacity.

There were two sets of Jersey barriers on either side of the embassy's entryway. There was enough space for one vehicle to enter at a time. A cinder block wall to the left of the auto entrance stood twelve feet high. Colored bits of sharp glass were embedded in the cement crust that ran across the top.

"That is some anemic security..." Curtis said.

Further on, cinder blocks were stacked about four feet high as a base for a flimsy looking metal fence. "Throw a rubber mat over those phony spikes and you're in," Curtis said. Large trees grew within the compound. Leafy limbs jutted over the fence and hung above the sidewalk. "Or fuck, man, somebody gets a ten-fingers and just swings in like Tarzan."

"It's, uh, kind of a sleepy hollow," Bighorn said. "I appreciate the quietude."

Curtis and Bighorn stepped out of the van. In the corner of the courtyard, three men in blue jumpsuits were washing a limo. The Marines passed under a huge flag pole. An enormous American flag hung limp. No wind. Two shorter flag poles stood beside it. The Ecuadorian National flag dangled from one and on the other, a flag of blue and red. Curtis didn't recognize the third flag.

Inside the embassy it was cool and dark.

In the center of the lobby was Post One. It reminded Curtis of Kirk's bridge aboard *The U.S.S. Enterprise*. He hadn't yet met the Marine who stood post at modified parade rest. "Sergeant Trumbo," Bighorn said, as he and Curtis crossed the lobby. The Marine raised his right hand – not a salute, just an acknowledgement.

Trumbo then tapped his watch and said, "On time every time, Corporal Custer. Come on around, fellas." Trumbo buzzed the two past the waist high door. They circled back and entered the elevated guard booth. The Marine said, "Kent Trumbo," and smiled. He had great teeth and green eyes like Faye Dunaway's green - in the neighborhood of blue. A reporter had once asked Faye what made her eyes so captivating. She'd said that her particular shade of jade was the most *persuasive* color human eyes could be.

Kent Trumbo's eyes had that kind of sincerity.

He nodded to Curtis and flicked an intercom switch.

"Gunny Alfred, Corporal Custer's here with the new Marine."

They heard the Gunny say, "Send him in. Corporal Custer as well."

Kent put his hand on Bighorn's shoulder and whispered, "Better you than me." Bighorn sighed and shook his head. Trumbo stamped the guard log and signed out. He passed the duty belt to Bighorn and he cinched it around his waist, drew the .38 caliber pistol from its holster, opened the cylinder, checked the ammo, snapped it closed, and re-holstered the weapon. Bighorn looked into the security cameras, panned the parking lot and frowned. He watched the workers soap the limo, scratched his chin and said, "The Gunny is, uh, gonna gimmie shit about something. You watch."

"Look at it this way," Trumbo said. "Only five days till T.G.I.F."

"Provided the Gunny, uh, doesn't come hounding us," Bighorn said.

Trumbo turned to Curtis. In a low voice he said, "Gunny just picked up his rocker."

"Sergeant Baxter says he's an eager beaver," Curtis said.

"He's, uh, got alpha-dog delusions," Bighorn said.

"Where were you prior?" asked Trumbo.

"Cherry Point," Curtis said. "This ain't that."

"Craven County, North Carolina. Spent a month, TDY."

"Pits, man," Curtis said. "Hey, is Dalton Trumbo any relation?"

"He was. Dalton was my second cousin, twice removed," said Kent.

"Holy smokes. *Spartacus* was the greatest. You ever meet Dalton?"

"Once, at a wedding," Trumbo said. "You'd better get on in there."

Curtis grabbed his orders from his kit bag. He and Bighorn left the bridge.

They crossed the lobby and marched into the Gunny's office.

Gunny Alfred was at his desk, his nose stuck in a magazine.

Curtis and Bighorn approached the desk. Curtis came to the position of attention. Bighorn was right beside him. "Lance Corporal Dark reporting as ordered, Gunny."

The Gunny took a long beat and turned the page.

Whatever the fuck he was reading must have been really important.

Shellacked strands of rust-red hair sprouted from his pale scalp. They created an orangish hue. The buttery smell of Murray's Original Pomade wafted off the Gunny's noggin as he continued to fuck with his magazine. Eventually, he closed it.

Time Magazine.

A cartoon on the cover showed President Carter and Ronald Reagan as they played high-stakes poker. A pile of golden chips was stacked in the middle of the table. The chips were labeled Ohio, Texas, and California. Curtis read the lead story snipe upside down. *The Jackpot States.*

The Gunny looked up.

Behind rimless glasses, his eyes were a watery blue.

His scarlet pelt, blue peepers and milky skin reminded Curtis of Lucille Ball. Not the zany Lucy who'd wolfed chocolates off a conveyor belt with Ethel Mertz and not the spot-on Lucy who'd done the mirror-mirror skit with Harpo Marx. Alfred was like the lame Lucy who'd slogged her knackered way through *Mame*, warbling her dissonant rendition of *Bosom Buddies* whilst yoked to Bea Arthur.

That Lucy. The one in the dud.

Gunny said, "Lance Corporal..." He let it hang like a question.

Curtis was the only new Marine reporting for duty in the entire goddamn country.

"Dark, Gunny. Lance Corporal Curtis B. Dark, reporting as ordered."

Bighorn stepped forward and planted himself beside Curtis. "Corporal Custer, reporting to, uh, take the, uh, watch Gunny." He thrust out his chest. Bighorn's buoyant posture accentuated the well-pressed and very tidy shirt he wore.

Gunny Alfred stood. He ignored the shirt and peered over his desk. "What the hell did you, uh, uh, polish those shoes with?" mocked the Gunny, "Uh, uh, a Hershey bar?"

Bighorn's face fell. He looked like Ricky Malone when the bully boys closed in and chanted Dirty Tex. Curtis wondered what kind of a goddamn Gunny mocks a guy with a speech impediment? Alfred looked at Curtis and said, "General Orders, Lance Corporal Dark." Curtis decided *fuck this Lucy*, and stayed quiet.

The Gunny waited – the silence awkward.

Bighorn shifted his feet and coughed.

Finally, the Gunny said, "Well?"

"Yeah, Gunny?"

"Your General Orders..."

"There's eleven of 'em," Curtis said, smarmy as hell.

One notch short of a shout, Gunny said, "I know that. Don't tell me. Recite your General Orders, Marine."

Curtis decided to annoy the Gunny further.

In a tedious, lifeless, mechanical monotone he recited, "To take charge of this post and all government property in view. To walk my post in a military manner keeping always on alert and observing everything that takes place within sight or hearing. To report any and all violations of orders I am instructed to enforce. To repeat all calls from posts more distant from the guard house than my own. To quit my post only when properly relieved." Curtis rolled his tongue in his cheek.

The Gunny gnawed his lip.

Curtis brought his fist slowly to his lips, cleared his throat deliberately, then droned on. "To receive, obey, and pass on to the sentry who relieves me all orders from the commanding officer and officer of the day. To talk to no one except in line of duty. To give the alarm in case of fire or disorder. To call the officer of the watch in any case not covered by instructions. To salute all officers, colors and standards not cased."

Curtis puffed out his cheeks, then exhaled slowly.

"That's only ten." The Gunny's face was flushed. "Where's number eleven?"

"Gosh, Gunny, I must've lost it. It just seemed to fall away," Curtis shrugged.

"Goddamn it, Lance Corporal. General Orders do not just seem to fall away."

"This one did. It was like an apparition evanescing into darkness."

The Gunny snapped a pencil, grabbed another, and scrawled a note.

Curtis wagged his eyebrows at Bighorn. Bighorn winked back.

Trumbo's voice came over the intercom. "Gunny, I'm set to run Lance Corporal Dark through orientation just as soon as Corporal Custer is able to take the watch."

Curtis and Bighorn stood and waited at the position of attention. They did so as Gunny Alfred's eyes bounced side-to-side from one Marine to the other, then up and down, heads to toes.

"Lance Corporal..."

Curtis prepared himself.

"I want eleven the next time I see you. Leave your file."

Curtis was surprised he hadn't been ordered to pack his shit and return to the airport. "Aye-aye, Gunnery Sergeant," he said. He dropped the file on the Gunny's desk.

"You're dismissed," Gunny Alfred said.

That was the one thing Curtis loathed about being a Marine - the "You're dismissed" part. Especially when it was some half-assed Lucy doing the dismissing.

CHAPTER
Six

Curtis and Bighorn left the Gunny's office.
Bighorn said, "You gotta meet Pat."
They crossed the lobby and Curtis was introduced to the embassy librarian.
"In Quito," she said, "We dive."
She was tall and fifty, maybe, and she had on bracelets that had a filigree swirl. They were silver. Her earrings were gold with four little bells hanging from a crescent moon and a fifth bell dangling in the center. Her head looked like an art piece.
Most women were not nearly as tall as Curtis. The librarian was taller. She said, "I'm Pat Bartok." She offered her right hand. Curtis took it and shook it. Her fingers were long, her hands cool. She wasn't a hippy, but she had Katmandu Mountain energy.
"You'll come to class, yes? I'll certify you."
"Dive class? I'll come for sure," Curtis said.
"Saturday at nine at the DCM's residence," Pat said.
"Scuba diving. Holy smokes. I'm all in." They smiled at each other.
After Trumbo signed the duty log over to Bighorn, he turned to Curtis. "OK, Dark, let's show you what's what." They left Post One and stepped onto the elevator. They rode up quiet. The Ready Room was on the fourth floor of the embassy.

The windows were reinforced with steel mesh, not cemented like the wine racks on the front face of the building. Ready Room windows had handles and hinges so the Marines could climb in or out if they had to. Coils of rope fashioned with intermittent knots were bolted to the floor. Sergeant Trumbo said, "Rope drill."

Trumbo stripped his name from above his locker. He wadded up the athletic tape and tossed it in a wastebasket. "This'll be yours. Go ahead and pull a piece." He reached into the locker, grabbed his kit bag, and opened it. Curtis took the roll of tape, measured out the appropriate length, and cut it with his teeth. He pressed the blank tape where SGT. TRUMBO had been, and smoothed it down. He grabbed a magic marker from the bag, uncapped it, and wrote LCPL. DARK in all caps.

Trumbo packed up his boots and cammies.

Curtis left his own kit bag and running shoes on the boot bench. He didn't want to rush Sergeant Trumbo out of his locker. "That Miss Bartok seems pleasant," he said.

"Pat is not only pleasant, she's a fine librarian," Trumbo said.

That Trumbo called Pat 'Pat' and sounded all familiar didn't thrill Curtis. He felt a pang of jealousy. "I'm taking her scuba class. Did you do that? Did she certify you?"

"Wish I could have. I've got an inner ear problem. Pressurizing is too painful."

Curtis was relieved that Trumbo wasn't one of Pat's former dive students.

"That's too bad. You dug your tour, though? You enjoyed it here?"

"Six days and a wake-up," Trumbo said, "I loved every minute."

A blue ribbon was pinned to Trumbo's chest beside his Good Conduct Ribbon. Three years of "honorable and faithful" service earned any half-decent Marine the Good Conduct. It was a gimmie, like the Armed Forces Reserve Ribbon that reservists got just for being reservists. To get the Good Conduct no special action was required. The Gunny had his. You had to be a real turd not to get one.

Trumbo's blue ribbon was one Curtis hadn't seen before.

He jerked his chin at it and asked, "What's that one for?"

"Humanitarian Service. Not to be confused with the Medal of Honor," Trumbo dead panned. "Last year there was an earthquake in Columbia. Twelve December. 'The Great *Tumaco.*' The epicenter was at a fishing village on the Columbian coast. A seven point nine on the Richter scale."

"That's a big deal," said Curtis, "seven point nine."

"It was for the Columbians. Mostly we shoveled mud," Kent said. "The Major pulled Marines from Bogota and Quito. I flew from here with Sergeant Henrici. He was a good Marine. He broke his foot on the second day and had to rotate stateside. It was a nasty break." Trumbo didn't say anything more about his ribbon. He pulled a pair of books from his locker and said, "I heard you on the intercom with Gunny Alfred."

"Dickweed, that guy," Curtis said.

"No sense getting on his bad side," said Trumbo.

Curtis shrugged. He thought, 'No sense kissin' his ass either.'

He said, "What does *Conocoto* mean? I saw it on a guard's hat."

"Ecuador's cut into provinces. They're sub-divided into parishes," said Trumbo. "The Marine House is in *Conocoto* Parish." Trumbo crossed to the water barrel that was suspended from the ceiling. He slapped the tank's belly. "This is in case you get a splinter."

Curtis was aware that the contents of the tank were there to flush corrosive chemicals off skin and clothes. All MSG candidates were regularly doused after gas drills at Quantico. Trumbo stepped up to a secure, steel door. It had a combination lock.

"Weapons safe," Trumbo said, "You know how to spin it?"

Curtis walked to the safe and placed his fingers against the dial.

Trumbo said, "Just ten, twenty, thirty."

Curtis spun right three times, and then clicked through the keep-it-simple combination. He turned the handle which unlocked the heavy door and pulled it open.

Trumbo flicked a switch and they stepped inside. The safe smelled like oil and cleaning solvent. A pistol rack made of dark wood held a dozen revolvers, and Kel-lites hung from the wall. The flashlights were like iron pipes with bulbs. Fourteen Uzis, sixteen 870-P Shotguns and a dozen M-16 A-1 rifles were mounted further in.

Trumbo tapped a clipboard that dangled on a leather strap. "You sign here on nights you catch cleaning detail." Curtis nodded.

He didn't particularly like guns.

His only exposure to firearms before he joined the Marines was limited to plinking pigeons with Henry's twenty-two. One time a pair of crows were perched at the top of a leafless tree behind Baystate Abrasives. Curtis whipped Henry's twenty-two up to his shoulder and cranked off a round. Just as the shot cracked loud, one of the crows that had just begun to spread its wings made half a caw and tipped over backwards. The crow hung there upside down, it's talons clamped solid, almost like a bat.

Except the bird was dead.

The other crow shrieked and launched itself into the air.

Henry shouted, "You nailed him! Will you look at that?"

Curtis did look and it was awful, hanging upside down like that.

If the goddamned bird had fallen, Curtis might have felt differently about what he'd done, but it just hung there looking awkward and shocked and almost funny. His partner circled back, all frantic, as if it were trying to figure out whether the dead one was gonna be OK, or come to, or wake the fuck up, but it wasn't going anywhere.

Henry grabbed the twenty-two and fired twice at the distraught sidekick.

It got the message and fucked off someplace safer.

The dead one continued to hang up there - for three weeks, in fact. Its sleek feathers turned gray as the carcass decomposed. It was a goddamn shame is what it was. Then one day it was gone and Curtis was relieved that the factory workers from Baystate Abrasives wouldn't be pointing at it anymore during their smoke breaks.

Trumbo said, "You're gonna have to memorize the inventory in here and then recite the placements with Gunny. I'd advise you to sketch it all out when you stand Post Two and learn the stacks by heart. Be sure you turn 'em and burn 'em. Don't leave any notes lyin' around. Gunny gave Chetbo Office Hours for leaving a sketch in his locker."

Curtis felt a fresh wave of disdain for Gunny Alfred. He thought about Lucille Ball and Bea Arthur. "Did you know that Bea Arthur was a Marine?" Curtis asked.

"*Maude* was a Marine?" Trumbo said. "I had no idea."

"Yep. She was a Dispatcher at Cherry Point. Her picture's in the Motor Pool."

"Women Marines," Trumbo said, "I love it. 'Do I contradict myself? Very well, then I contradict myself, I am large, I contain multitudes,'" he quoted. "Can you manage those bags?" Curtis picked up two cloth sacks. They were stamped *Burn* and secured with yellow ties. Curtis lugged the bags out of the weapons safe.

"Ever read *Johnny Got His Gun?* That was Dalton Trumbo," Curtis said.

"Oh, yeah. Fantastic. Made me think twice about joining up," Trumbo said.

"You know what made me think twice? *Hair*, man. The musical." Curtis dropped the burn bags on the floor. "Hey, who requisitions movies? I'd like to volunteer for that."

Trumbo secured the weapons safe.

"Talk to Sergeant Baxter," he said. They crossed the Ready Room to a green door. Behind it was a sound proofed room that housed an enormous industrial shredder. There were two sets of neon orange earmuffs that hung on pegs sunk in the wall next to the door. A box cutter was beside them.

Trumbo said, "OK, let's make some money." He removed the box cutter from its peg and cut through the yellow ties on the burn bags. "When you go through, make sure that there's no staples or paper clips. Go slow. Gunny wants us to report submits that aren't stripped. Nobody does. Just pocket any metals you find."

"See, he's a clown," Curtis said, "Goddamn Gunny wants to squeal."

"Yeah, well, just throw away whatever you find," Trumbo said, "and don't put more than an inch of paper in at a time. Clogs the hose. On switch is here. Off there. Shake the hose free into the barrel when you're done, OK? You got it?"

"I got it."

Trumbo pointed at the earmuffs. "Put on your Honeywells."

Curtis slipped the earmuffs over his ears. Nodded to Trumbo. Trumbo stepped out of the burn room. Curtis punched the go button. Listened to the hum. He pulled the first burn bag wide open and took out a fist full of documents. He looked over a few pages, then thought who gives a fuck. He fed the machine and bent down for more.

The hum continued.

Curtis's mind skipped to his car. A Maverick.

He and Henry decided hot girls liked cool cars.

In high school, the two of them figured they'd have a better chance with babes if they pooled their resources and saved some dough for a kick ass vehicle that would act as a chick magnet. After six months they'd managed to squirrel away exactly nothing toward the purchase price of anything. On Henry's end, he was also saddled with a debt of fifteen dollars to his mother. He destroyed her blow dryer.

He'd used the goddamn thing to fluff his pubes. He took his eyes off the prize, and inadvertently touched the tip of the hot machine against his scrotum. In a rage, Henry yowled and smashed the hair dryer against his bedpost.

When Mrs. Fonda found out, she was none too happy. His mother insisted that Henry find a job and buy her a new hair dryer. Henry told her he already had a job. Mrs. Fonda argued that Henry had outgrown his once-a-week paper route, and long since.

Henry told her to stop giving him shit.

Meanwhile, Curtis had done some rough calculations in his head. Henry earned six bucks a week on the paper route. It would take him nearly a month to pay his mom the fifteen dollars.

New cars cost *fifteen thousand*.

That would take forever. Even a shitbox was way out of reach.

The next afternoon, Curtis waited for Henry at Ronald Dark's workbench. The garage door opened, and Henry waltzed into the basement without knocking. "What say, Darkie?" He offered up Juicy Fruit. Curtis took the gum and told Henry, "We gotta think up a radical score, Baygo." They chewed it over.

"What about doin' a yard sale?" Henry said.

Curtis glanced around the basement. There was a drop leaf table, some canned goods and a shelf in the corner that held terra cotta flower pots and a few neglected board games. He looked at Ronald's tools. Valuable, of course, but completely off limits.

"A yard sale's not radical, Henry, unless you got something better at your house."

Henry surveyed the room. "Same shit," he said. "Hey, wanna play Twister?"

"Nah, man. We gotta think. How in the heck are we gonna afford a car?"

Henry scrunched up his face, lifted his leg, and farted.

"Woo! Think we could sell that?" Henry said.

"Why don't you stop dickin' around?"

"I think I smell a bake sale," Henry said. "Hey, Darkie, what about that? We could claim the proceeds benefit the Police Explorers. You run the till. I skim the cash…"

"That's creative," Curtis said. "I like using the Explorers as a front, but how many loaves of goddamn banana bread could we sell? Not enough for a car. Not even a bike." Curtis pressed a finger to his lips. "Plus, we'd have to bake all that shit."

"*I don't like the panties drying on the rod.*" Henry quoted Richard Dreyfuss and used a goofy voice to do so. He said, "Hey, we could embezzle dues. How about that?"

Curtis stood. "Now you're talking," he said and he put his hands on his hips and began pacing back and forth in front of his dad's workbench. "You're definitely on the right track, Baygo, but if we embezzle funds, they might be able to trace it."

"Who? Eddie Belder? The freakin' FBI? They got more important shit to do."

"Wait." Curtis snapped his fingers. "I know. I got it." He turned to Henry and put his hand on his friend's shoulder. He pulled him close and whispered, "A raffle, my boy! Ho! Ho! A friggin' raffle, Henry!"

"Let's hear it, baby!" Henry said.

Curtis moved back to the workbench and sat down. He strummed his fingers. "OK. We print up a ream of tickets, see, and we get ready to sell them in front of Stop & Shop. It's almost Christmas. In a couple of weeks, the malls are gonna be packed. People will be putting out the cash anyway, so what's another buck for a good cause?"

"Maybe we do three tickets for a five-spot?" Henry said.

"Never get a fiver, but if they can get us off their backs for a single goddamn dollar, it'll work like a charm. We'll hook 'em large, like fish for a buck, Baygo!"

"Like fat carps!" Henry cried.

"Like fuckin' flounder!" Curtis grinned.

"Man, we'll be servin' up sweet ass in a bitchin' car by New Years." Henry danced around the basement while riffing on Donna Summer. "Someone left that freakin' cake out. So, the frosting's fuckin' sog-assed. I'm gonna kick somebody's dumb ass." He stopped and said, "Hold up, man. You don't have any shit to raffle, Darkie, and neither do I."

"That's the beauty," Curtis whispered. "We raffle nothing."

"Whose gonna fork for that? Nobody shells dough for nothin.' For nothin'?"

"The prizes are pretend!" Curtis yelped. "We totally make 'em up. There's nothing there! We promise 'em the world, but they can't win a goddamn thing! There are no prizes, Henry! It's a fantasy of our own creation!"

Henry raced to Curtis and said, "Oh, you're beautiful, man!" He grabbed Curtis by the hand, pulled him to his feet, and said, "You're an entrepreneur. A self-made man. Spin me. Spin me." They spun. "Could we raffle a T.V.?" Henry asked, as he fell into Curtis's arms.

"Sure."

"Alpine skis?"

"If you'd like."

"How 'bout a trip to Hawaii?"

"Whatever you say, old shoe," Curtis said. He dipped Henry.

They'd gazed warmly into one another's eyes. "OK," Curtis said. He raised Henry gently. "We gotta get back to work." Curtis took a pencil from the workbench and pulled a brown paper bag from the collection wedged behind Ronald's pliers.

"We'll do a mockup on this," Curtis said.

Henry leaned in. "Your hair smells nice," he said.

"Alright. 'Post 924 Raffle.' Wait. 'Westborough Police Explorer Post 924 - Annual Christmas Raffle.'" He looked at Henry. "Annual, see? That way all these saps think it's a tradition, so we look legit," Curtis said.

"Clever."

"First prize?"

"Trip to Hawaii."

"That's too enticing." Curtis said.

"Give 'em a T.V. then." Henry said.

"Black and white or color?" Curtis said.

"I'm thinking color, but a tiny asser," Henry said.

"Color," Curtis said. He sounded out the words; "Twelve - Inch - Color – Television." He wrote them on the side of the shopping bag. "That looks tempting. What thoughts on a second prize?"

"The Hawaiian vacation."

"No, man, I told you. It's too good."

"Up to you, then," Henry sulked.

"Fifty bucks, cash. Not too much, not too little. Cash'll catch the eye, but it's not huge dough, see?" Curtis said. Henry shrugged indifferently. "Come on, Fondue, stay focused," Curtis said. "You're good at this. What's a nice crappy third prize?"

"I don't know."

"Yes, you do. C'mon."

"A bag of groceries, maybe..."

"See now, that's perfect, Henry. That is perfect. It'll get the sympathy vote. Look, I'm writing it right here." Curtis showed the bag. "They'll think the Explorers chipped in together, like everybody brought a can. It's an inspired idea, Baygo. A killer third prize." Curtis showed Henry the mock-up of the raffle ticket. "How's she lookin'?"

"Authentic as hell," Henry said.

"Yup. People will fall for this any day."

"What about a date for the drawing?" Henry said.

"I'm thinking we leave that off," Curtis said. "Any hard ass comes along, we say, 'Drawing is Christmas Day.' If some loser finds his stub in January, he'll chuck it in the trash, no questions asked."

Every afternoon, Monday through Friday, and all day on Saturday, they sold raffle tickets in front of the Stop & Shop at West Meadow Plaza. They took Sunday mornings off because they had to go to church, but after communion, they were right back at it. The biggest single day tally came on Christmas Eve.

The crisp air was charged with good will toward men, which they worked to their advantage. Jolly shoppers peeled off dollar after dollar after dollar. Some didn't even take stubs. Curtis was happy as hell when he ran into his sexy cousin Sandy, decked out in her fluffy pom-pom boots and cotton candy snood.

He was happier still with Sandy's whopping ten-dollar contribution.

Before she skipped off, Curtis gave Sandy a grateful holiday hug. He said, "Holy smokes, Sandy. Tomorrow's the big draw. I sure hope you win. Say Merry Christmas to Auntie Lou!"

Only one hitch occurred. A Salvation Army Santa's suspicions were aroused by the boys' ascending glee. The Santa said, "What're you guys getting so worked up about? You dance around like cats catchin' canaries, every time you grab a dollar."

"Look, man, we're trying to do something nice over here," Henry said.

"Yeah? I'll take a ticket," Santa said, "and maybe I'll make a few inquiries."

Not one to be bullied, Curtis said, "No need, Nick. I got twenty bucks right here all ready for your bucket. You're not the only charitable guy on the block. We're happy to spread a little good cheer." Curtis felt sure the double sawbuck would end up lining the pockets of the leery Claus. He shrugged it off as the price of doing business.

That Christmas season, Curtis and Henry raked in twelve hundred dollars.

With the loot, Curtis bought a cherry red 1970 Ford Maverick, a veritable steal at nine hundred and fifty dollars. They christened the car *Darkie's Mavey*. Henry spent two hundred clams from what was left over to get his hands on Fatman Belder's black and red Kawasaki. They split the final fifty, twenty-five bucks each for walking around money.

Curtis shut down the shredder and grabbed the now empty burn bags.

Trumbo waited on the boot bench outside the burn room. He smiled and said, "Got something on the roof for you, Lance Corporal Dark. You'll dig it for sure."

CHAPTER
Seven

Heat roiled off nearby buildings. Traffic was loud even four stories up.

On the embassy roof there were four sandbag nests, one per corner. Each had a camouflaged footlocker squeezed in against the makeshift bunkers. A Quonset hut in the center of the roof was surrounded by a rusted railing. Rock piles slouched at awkward angles and peppered the roof with chaotic cairns.

"Looks like the set of a Sam Fuller movie," Curtis said.

He put his hands on his hips and kicked at one of the sandbags. Trumbo knelt at the first footlocker. His walkie-talkie squawked. It was Bighorn from the lobby. "Post Two. Post One. All quiet."

That was the extent of the transmission.

Trumbo adjusted the squelch and said, "Copy." He turned to Curtis. "OK, Dark, listen up. One key works in all of these lockers. You'll get a duty ring from the Gunny. Probably this one." Trumbo flipped open the footlocker lid. Inside were two flak vests, two helmets, one first aid kit, six cannisters marked 'CS GAS,' a short stack of white towels tied with string, a pair of binoculars and a couple baseball gloves.

"What's with the gloves?" Curtis said.

Trumbo tipped his chin toward the rock piles. "Catholic University is up the street. Students cast stones at ugly Americans." He pulled a canvas bag from the locker and said, *"Voilà."* He showed Curtis the chess pieces inside the bag, then started to close the footlocker.

"Hold on, man. Let me get those." Curtis pointed.

Trumbo handed him the binoculars. Curtis hung them around his neck.

They moved to the edge of the roof. Trumbo cranked open a rose-pink beach umbrella. They set up two campaign chairs and a folding table and placed them in the circle of shade. Trumbo fished around in the chess bag and grabbed a white pawn and a black one. He presented both fists and Curtis pointed to Trumbo's left hand. Kent opened his fingers and said, "You'll play black." The umbrella kept the sun off, though it was still hot as hell. "Takes an hour to learn and a lifetime to master," Trumbo said.

He set up the pieces. Trumbo waved his hand over the board. "There're more options in a single chess match than there are electrons in the observable universe. That's according to Boris Spassky."

Curtis gazed through the binoculars at two women. Twins maybe. They wore matching navy blue skirts and frilly turquoise blouses. Each had a yellow ribbon tied in a bow that held beautiful coal black hair in a ponytail. "Spassky's gotta be guessing," Curtis said. "How could a guy even know a thing like that?"

"Point is, when you see a good move, look for a better one," Trumbo said.

The twins strolled around a fountain in which four sculpted seals spat a continuous stream of water at a mermaid. A sunbaked drunk in tattered shorts sat in the mermaid's lap. He scooped water with a straw hat, and poured it over the mermaid's head and shoulders. "Some dickweed's down there messin' with the mermaid," Curtis said. He watched the boozehound canoodling the statue's breasts.

Two policemen in beige fatigues approached the fountain.

Curtis panned to the twins, who interlocked their arms and stood together. They looked toward the fountain. He panned the binoculars back to the mermaid. The shorter of the two cops leaned over the lip of the fountain with his billy club in the air. He swung in low and whacked the man across his shin. The drunk jerked his leg and yelped.

He lost his balance and tumbled over backward.

The cops dragged the poor guy from the fountain by his hair.

They dropped him face first onto the sidewalk. He rolled onto his back and gyrated around. He frantically massaged his shin. The pint-sized cop turned to holster his baton and the lush leapt up and took off like a shot. Curtis followed the fugitive in flight. The guy weaved in and out of traffic, bounced against the side of a slow moving bus, staggered to the far curb, rubbed his forehead, then hauled ass around a corner.

Curtis tracked back to the cops. They showed no interest in the great escape. Instead, they ambled over to the twins. The little cop pulled out his billy club again and he flipped it up and down in a perverse salute. He stood there and ticked the rod against the brim of his hat. The twins backed away and ducked into a taxi.

Curtis lowered the binoculars and looked at Trumbo.

"These local cops seem like a barrel of laughs," Curtis said.

"They're tons of fun," Trumbo said.

"Why do those fuckers harass nice girls? Assholes."

"Agreed. Alright, back to the matter at hand." He introduced the chess board and explained the role and functions of both king and queen.

"Ever see *A Man for All Seasons* with Robert Shaw?" Curtis said.

"No, man, I haven't," Trumbo said. He pointed to the board.

"Sergeant Trumbo, you got a special Señorita down here?"

Trumbo raised his right hand as though swearing an oath. "Nope. My fiancée lives in Fayetteville." Trumbo scooped up a bishop. "Consider the man in the mitre," he said. "Tactically, you want to use your bishops jointly, like two fists. Boom, then boom. They move diagonally."

There was a lot of action in the streets below.

It wasn't easy for Curtis to give the board his full attention.

"Hey," Curtis said. He pulled out his note pad. "Would this be easy to find? The Atahualpa Cinema?" He glanced over at Trumbo who looked preoccupied, as if he were formulating another news flash about the bishop. "They'll be showing *Raging Bull* in December," Curtis said.

"Big on movies, aren't you, Dark?"

"Heck, yeah."

"Shorty knows where it's at."

"I'm looking forward to it. Boy, am I," said Curtis.

"You've seen *The Empire Strikes Back,* have you not?" Trumbo tapped on his rook with his right index finger. "This guy has the same kill-square capabilities as a Jedi Knight with a light saber. He can shoot his laser both horizontally and vertically."

Even if Curtis hadn't been sweaty as hell, he wouldn't have cared very much about Trumbo's allusion to a Jedi Knight. He thought *Star Wars* was a goddamn bore and the second one was worse. "What's your all-time favorite movie, Sergeant Trumbo?"

Trumbo cracked his knuckles and continued to stare at the chess board.

*"*I really liked *The Sand Pebbles."*

Curtis thought that was a helluva pick.

He quoted Steve McQueen's last line in the movie. *"'I was home! What happened? What the hell happened?'"* Curtis raised the binoculars and zoomed in on the mountain angel. She wore a tiara made of silver stars. In the shimmering heat, she appeared to dance.

Curtis thought of Paulie. His heart broke a little, like it always did.

"What's the story on the steel angel up there?" Curtis said.

"Lance Corporal Dark," Trumbo said, "let's do this in three dimensions…"

Trumbo stood up and moved clear of the chess table. He placed his right leg straight back, locked it rigid, then leaned forward over his front facing knee. He got low. "Step over here, Dark. Try this. This is the ready position in Shotokan karate. You can think of the knight as a martial artist that can leap over any piece on the board and can strike in any direction."

Curtis stood up quick.

Jedi Knights were total horseshit.

Goddamn karate, however, was something else.

He attempted to replicate the stance. Trumbo kicked Curtis's feet wider apart.

The binoculars bounced against Curtis's chest.

"Keep both feet planted on the ground," Trumbo said. "Don't lift 'em up. To maintain proper balance, you slide and turn. Don't break contact with the ground when you move. That way you stay solid." They shuffled and pivoted in tandem and moved around the roof in a wide circle. "This way, no one gets in behind you, because you're like a snake. You strike fast." They finished the impromptu kata at the edge of the roof above the courtyard.

Winded, Curtis said, "How'd you get all Chuck Norris?"

"Sergeant Baxter. He's the black belt. He'll snap you in at Guard School."

Curtis lifted his foot and planted it on the corner flashing of the roof. He rubbed the ache out of his thigh. "Karate is mint, man. I wanna get in on that." Below in the courtyard the guys in blue jumpsuits waxed the Marine van.

Curtis had washed and waxed his fair share of vehicles.

On the day he came back from the recruiter, his father had already finished most of a wax job on his Monte Carlo. He tossed Curtis a chamois and said, "Help me out. I don't wanna see any spots."

Curtis buffed the hood.

He said, "You think it's good I joined?"

Ronald took a drag on his Chesterfield and exhaled slowly. He said, "You live and you die and it don't much make a fuck what you do in between." After that, he hosed the tires. He said, "Get on them whitewalls."

Curtis clamped his fingers around the binoculars.

He aimed them southwest, toward a mass of leafy green trees.

"You're lookin' at *El Ejido*," Trumbo said. "Quito's Central Park."

"They got some kind of acreage, don't they?" Curtis scanned the woods.

A crescent shaped building constructed of black glass stood at the center of the huge park. He could see a brass bell tower on the hill behind it. Indian peddlers manned wagon wheel carts. Most sold food, a few trafficked in hats and ponchos, and a couple more hawked flowers. Women walked the park in pairs. Men roamed the grounds alone. A dozen hoboes snoozed in the grass. One lay face down in the dirt.

Trucks and buses belched smoke and rumbled past the stone arch entrance.

A stoic hombre in a faded blue smock and tan fedora stood outside the gate. Beside him was a battered wooden sign. His face looked frozen, in spite of the heat and sunlight. Menu options in dull paint ran down an oblong piece of whitewashed plywood. *Coca - Cola Frio* was rendered in flat red. *Empanadas* were offered in a wilted green. *Ceviche* was scrawled at a slant, in faded purple.

"The hell is ceviche?" Curtis said.

"Shrimp, man, in lime juice with red onions and tomato. They put jumbo kernels of popcorn on top and serve it chilled," Trumbo said. "Sometimes they throw in cuts of raw fish, as well." He gave a thumbs up. "It's outta sight."

"You eat that shit raw?" Curtis winced. "All full of bacteria?"

"Citric acid denatures protein. The juice acts to cook the seafood."

"Oh. Well, that sounds alright, I guess. You put it like that..."

Curtis could imagine *chewing* a frigid hunk of slippery ass fish pickled in O. J.

He couldn't imagine swallowing it. "I feel like a hot dog," he said.

They heard sirens, and Trumbo asked for the glasses. After handing him the binoculars, Curtis took out his notepad and jotted down *denatures*.

Trumbo gazed through the eyepiece.

He whistled. "Presidential motorcade."

Curtis took the glasses and looked where Trumbo pointed at the *Avenida Patria*. Two motorcycles escorted a shiny black limo. A pair of colorful, triangular shaped pennants flapped on the corners of the hood.

"What's the blue and red one?" Curtis said.

"City flag," Trumbo said.

"And who, exactly, am I looking at?"

"Señor Jaime Roldós. The President of Ecuador, Brother."

"What's the skinny on him?" Curtis said. "Good guy, or what?"

Trumbo tapped Curtis on the shoulder, and Curtis lowered the glasses.

"He's the John F. Kennedy of South America, man. Locals love him. Particularly the younger crowd, the students and that. Guy took on three ranking Generals and he won seventy-seven percent of the vote." They walked toward the chess table. Trumbo raised his hands, as if he held a great big sign. "*Bread, Freedom, Democracy,*' is the Roldós doctrine. Everyplace else down here, a dictator runs the show. It's all military from Bogota to Buenos Aires."

Curtis had no point of reference for politics.

He sat in his chair. It was hot as hell on his side.

Trumbo adjusted the umbrella against the belligerent sun.

Curtis said, "I shook the Commandant of the Marine Corps' hand one time. General Barrow. He had a very soft hand, which was surprising. A pleasant guy. He reminded me of Jimmy Stewart in *Harvey*. I told him I was from Massachusetts, and he said he'd had a picnic with his wife at Tanglewood. People could do a heck of a lot worse than military rule. I mean, couldn't they? If they got a decent enough General?"

Trumbo looked at Curtis and blinked several times. He adjusted his king.

"These Generals down here aren't anything like Jimmy Stewart, Dark. You won't get the real dope outta *Time* or *Newsweek* magazine." Trumbo lowered his voice. "We're not *authorized* to read the burn, but I'll tell you something. I got hooked. I want to read the truth." Trumbo tapped the middle of the chess board. "Alright, now. So, these four squares here, this cluster, are key. Everything in chess is oriented though the center."

Trumbo brought his king's pawn out two spaces. The game was on.

Curtis brought out a pawn, the one from in front of his kingside bishop.

Trumbo said, "Can you imagine what the Ecuadorian people had to put up with before Roldós?" He chewed his lower lip. "Or what life is like in Argentina now, under Videla? I wanna know what's *really* going on. It's ridiculous, not being authorized to read the burn." Trumbo brought out his queen, two spaces on the diagonal.

"I can see your point," Curtis said, even though he couldn't see shit.

He had no clue what Ecuadorian people put up with before Roldós - beyond ceviche. And as for Argentina, did anyone give a flying fuck what went on way down there? He tried to make sense of the chess board. A lot to consider.

"How about us?" Curtis said, "Who are you thinking, next month?"

"Oof," Trumbo said. "Carter. Of course."

"Oh, yeah?" Curtis scratched his head and pondered the choices.

No doubt Ronald Reagan had made some dimwit fucking movies. Truly awful shit like *Cattle Queen of Montana* and *Tugboat Annie Sails Again*. But his final movie, *The Killers*, was a good one. That might have had more to do with Angie Dickinson than with Reagan. Goddamn Angie was terrific in just about everything, plus she was a total knockout in a sweater. Curtis remembered that when Ronald Reagan slapped Angie Dickinson across the face, Paulie said, "That guy looks like he likes to hit girls."

Reagan *had* looked as if he enjoyed smacking Angie around.

Of course, he'd been acting, so you couldn't really hold it against him.

Curtis had to admit Ronald Reagan had played a pretty convincing bad guy.

But what about the goddamn Gipper? Reagan was outstanding in *Knute Rockne, All American,* when he played football star George Gipp. All feverish and handsome, he looked up from his death bed and whispered his last wish to Pat O'Brien. He told Pat that if the team was ever up against it and getting their asses handed to them on the gridiron, Pat could tell the boys to go in and win one for the Gipper. Reagan said he wasn't sure where he'd be, but he was certain he'd know about it, and he would be really happy for the guys.

Curtis saw tears in his father's eyes. Paulie's too, or course.

Ronald said, "You hate to see that. Young fellow like that. Gotta hand it to Ronald Reagan, for Christ's sake. That's a very vivid portrayal."

You'd have to have a heart of stone not to vote for those kind of sentiments.

On the other hand, there was *Death Valley Days*, which was even more leaden than goddamn *Star Wars* and watching Ronald Reagan drone through the narration of that dusty ass show was like taking *Sominex*. Still, as far as Curtis knew, Jimmy Carter hadn't made any movies at all. Not even one.

Curtis said, "I'm still on the fence."

He moved out his second pawn and placed it right beside his first one.

Bighorn's voice came over the radio. "Gunny wants run times on record for the new Marine, and you'll need to log in five miles before end of shift. He wants an escort for Lance Corporal Dark until he gets familiar with the area."

Trumbo squinted at the radio and mopped his brow.

"It gets cooler later," he said, "but it's better to beat the rain."

"You want to hit that angel?" Curtis said. "How far away is she?"

"'Bout six miles, but those are serious hills. We're at nine thousand feet, man." Trumbo keyed the radio and replied, "Copy your last." He swiped his brow again. "OK. Shorty can meet us up at the crest of *El Panecillo*, if you want, but be advised, altitude'll kick your ass hard when you first try to run up here. First few days, especially."

"I been running since *Rocky*," Curtis said. "Let's just do it. Yo."

"It's your funeral, Buddy." Trumbo examined the chess board, cleared his throat, nodded to himself, then moved his queen again, a mere two spaces. "Checkmate."

Curtis felt his jaw drop.

"You kiddin'? In three moves, already?"

The quickness caused a wave of wonder.

Trumbo winked and said, "Well played."

Curtis took his hand. He sighed as they shook. They bagged the pieces and went below. In the fourth-floor hallway, Trumbo said, "You'll start to see a lot more of the board each time you play."

Curtis wasn't there to hear him. He'd become distracted.

He was down the hall by the water cooler. "I'm Curtis Dark. New Marine." A chubby woman holding a Dixie cup against her lower lip acknowledged him and flashed a wide smile over the tiny brim. Her eyes and long-lash mascara were jet black, as was her skin. Plum-colored lipstick left a mark on her paper cup. Curtis thought she was very pretty.

"*Soy Dominique,*" she said, "*Quizas que nos vemos este viernes en la casa suya.*"

He got that her name was Dominique but didn't catch the rest.

She dropped the cup into the waste basket, gave Curtis a throaty chuckle, then turned and walked away. Her inseams in retreat produced a scritch-scratch sound. After she'd turned the corner, Curtis sidled up to Trumbo and whispered, "Holy smokes, what's her story?"

Trumbo opened the Ready Room door.

Inside, he said, "Let me save you a little heartache, man. Keep your eyes locked from the neck up with any and all females you encounter here on Post." Trumbo lay the flat of his hand horizontally against his own Adam's apple. "From the neck up in the embassy, man. No elevator eyes, or Gunny'll have you standing tall."

Curtis felt sheepish for about ten seconds.

He unbuttoned his shirt.

"Pops was saying T.G.I.F.'s are pretty incredible. So, that's fine, right? I mean, its fair game at the Marine House. Am I right?" He unlaced his shoes. "I've been looking forward to Friday or is the goddamn Gunny gonna rain on that parade?"

"Like I said, man, my fiancée is waiting on me in Arkansas. Friday nights, I'm playing duty bartender." Trumbo opened his kit bag, pulled out a pair of books, and then continued to grope around for his sneakers.

Curtis clucked his tongue. "Ho, now, Sergeant Trumbo. Last time I checked, Arkansas was like two or three thousand miles from here." Curtis chuckled at his own clever reference to geography. He said, "Your girl ain't gonna know."

Trumbo was quiet. The guy seemed more interested in politics than in women.

Curtis found that even more mystifying than chess. Not to mention the fact that politically speaking, Curtis thought Trumbo was backing the wrong horse. Jimmy Carter didn't have a snowball's chance in hell of being re-elected with the fifty-two American hostages still sitting on their asses somewhere in Tehran.

Curtis took off his trousers and hung them up.

Then he asked Trumbo if he'd ever tried Billy Beer.

"No, I have not." He sounded annoyed.

It occurred to Curtis that Trumbo might think he'd taken a cheap shot bringing up Billy Carter's shitbird beverage, since everyone knew Jimmy Carter's brother was a total douche. That hadn't been his intention at all.

It was true that Curtis wasn't all that interested in politics, but he wasn't all that interested in making enemies either. He took a different tack. Standing in his jock strap and trying to be friendly, Curtis said, "What are those books you got there, Sergeant Trumbo? Anything interesting?"

"Stuff on Vietnam," Trumbo said. He pulled a tee-shirt over his head.

"Vietnam? No joke? That's a topic that fascinates me," Curtis lied.

"Is that right?" Trumbo said.

"Oh, sure. Can I take a look?"

"Help yourself," said Trumbo.

Curtis grabbed a book and read the cover.

"*Dispatches*, eh? Now that's interesting," Curtis said.

This time he more or less meant it. Curtis knew that Michael Herr, the guy who wrote *Dispatches*, also wrote Martin Sheen's narration for *Apocalypse Now*. He'd read all about Herr's collaboration with John Milius in *American Film Magazine*.

Curtis gave a few emphatic oohs and ahhs as he skimmed the flaps and cribbed a blurb. He paraphrased it for effect. "I remember hearing somewhere that *Dispatches* may be the best book ever written on men and war. Oh. See? It actually mentions that here…"

Curtis strummed the book thoughtfully as if deep in thought.

"I'd really like to study up, man, on our brothers in Nam…"

Trumbo double tied his sneaker and said, "I share your enthusiasm, Dark. Tell you what, man. *Dispatches* is a heck of a read, for sure, but if you really wanna be blown away, I've got something even better." Trumbo pulled on his USMC running cap, then slid a second book to Curtis. It was called *The Village of Ben Suc*, by somebody named Jonathan Schell, and Trumbo's copy had an inscription on the title page.

"To Kent – Find peace with both eyes open. Thanks for the eggrolls
- Marty Munson"

"Who's this? Who's Marty Munson?" Curtis said.

"Vietnam vet," Trumbo said. "We did Meals-on-Wheels through my church as a service to Vets, and Marty and I really hit it off. I'll see him when I get home. He lost his legs, man. He's in a chair." Trumbo shrugged. "My fiancée checks in on him."

"What's your fiancée's name?" asked Curtis.

"Amber," said Trumbo.

Curtis could tell Trumbo loved her by how he said her name.

"This book *Dispatches* looks compelling. I'd definitely like to read it," Curtis said. He wanted to add, 'and that's the truth,' but decided against it.

"Take 'em both, man. I gotta have *Ben Suc* back before I leave, though," Trumbo said. His innocent ears protruded wide from under his runner's cap. Out of uniform, he looked boyish and a little bit vulnerable.

Curtis stashed the books in his kit bag.

"Your Amber sounds nice, man. I'm happy for you," he said.

In the courtyard, they dropped their gear at the van.

"Encuéntranos en la montaña junto a la estatua del ángel," Trumbo said to Shorty. He and Curtis headed out the embassy gate and trotted right on to the street *12 de octubre*. Twenty minutes into the run, Curtis's head spun. Sergeant Trumbo hadn't been wrong about the altitude. Curtis wanted to puke. He kept his gaze fixed on the ring of sweat that had developed on Trumbo's back as he slogged

along. He panted like hell. It got even worse once they cleared the city and started on the hills.

Trumbo jogged in place or ran switchbacks while he waited on Curtis. He never said, 'I told you so.' For the final push, Kent advised, "The quickest way to the top is to go by the Plaza Grande on the Palace side. It's steeper, but we won't drag it out so long."

Curtis managed a weak thumbs up. They passed through a broken-down gate and crossed an open field that was home to a motley crew of skinny dogs and listless puppies and then started up cinder block steps that went on forever.

The last stretch was cobblestone.

When they reached the angel, it started to rain. Curtis staggered and spit. He put his hands on his hips and circled the base. He worked to catch his breath. When he came around to where he could finally see the face of the angel, the Angel of the Apocalypse, it took away what little breath he'd managed to retain.

He knew her.

It was her posture of loss that was so familiar. The way she held her right arm high, in a feckless attempt to ward off the inevitable, while her left arm was brought in tight across her churned belly - her form bent in a self-protective wince against an eternal body blow that had rendered her soul so damaged - so totally and completely impaired - that any whisper of rehabilitation or recovery would be an insult to her agony.

That same shattered pose had been adopted by his mother at the close of Paulie's funeral. Curtis turned from the angel and looked out through sheets of rain that drenched the city. Two boys, obviously brothers, waved from below.

Trumbo shouted, *"¡Hola, chicos!"*

The little one yelled, *"¡Saludos, Americanos! ¿Usteds son soldados, verdad?"*

Trumbo grinned and bellowed, "Marines!" and then, just like that, he pulled off his cap, and hurled it over the fence toward the boys. It tumbled down the wet hill. The bigger boy ran over and picked it up.

He did a kind of hop and waved the cap. Then he jogged it back to the smaller boy. He placed the cap on his little brother's head.

The small one stood with rain on his face.

He grinned, stood at attention, and saluted.

CHAPTER
Eight

Curtis's father said, "What the fuck is a troglodyte?"

That was in reference to a TV show he and his boys watched. *Hawaii Five-O*.

"It's a cave dweller," Paulie said.

Ronald looked annoyed. "How do you know?"

Paulie shrugged. "My dictionary, Dad. I like to find words." He'd won the dictionary in a spelling bee. Mrs. Foss told him *The Chambers Dictionary* had a real personality. Ronald asked Curtis to take care of it after Paulie died.

It was with Curtis in Quito.

He looked up *denature* in Paulie's dictionary and wrote, '*Denature means to destroy the properties of a protein, or other biological macromolecules, by heat.*' After that, he looked up *macromolecule*. '*A macromolecule is a very large molecule such as in protein.*' Then he started his homework.

He read Trumbo's Vietnam book in one sitting.

It was a true story, but not a nice one.

Curtis decided that *The Village of Ben Suc* would have *sucked* if it were made into a movie because it didn't have any heroes. Not a one. In the story, the goddamn U.S. Army developed a knucklehead plan to relocate an entire village of Vietnamese people to a kind of ersatz internment camp, ostensibly for their own good.

The plan turned out to be a horrendous fucking failure.

Anyone who watched those events unfold on a movie screen would walk out.

The problem was, everybody who lived in the village *liked* living in the village. They didn't want to relocate to an internment camp or to anywhere else for that matter. The Army, in its infinite wisdom, sent in, like, sixty helicopters to surround the village. Then the American soldiers shoved everybody on trucks, like it or not. A lot of the soldiers grew edgy as they did the shoving.

On top of that, a lot of the villagers refused to cooperate.

A few of the jumpier Army guys started to shout at all these hapless goddamn villagers. They yelled at them to move their asses, or screamed at them to slow the fuck down or to just plain halt if, say, some girl rode her bicycle in the wrong direction or if, say, some guy started to wander off on his own somewhere. Then, if that girl or that guy didn't come to an immediate goddamn halt, the soldiers shot them dead. The logic was they didn't stop because they were V. C.

That was the argument.

As for the internment camp, it was a lousy place with just cots and a few big top tents the Army threw up. They didn't have bathrooms and the latrine pits were too hard for old people to get to, plus the chow was standard American. The Vietnamese couldn't stand that kind of food. As for drinks, all they had was Kool-Aid, which the Vietnamese detested.

So, the book ends with all these thirsty people who need to go to the bathroom, lying around all bloated and sick, and worried as hell because their kids have no place to play. The worst part was they could never go back to *Ben Suc*, because their empty-ass village was fire-bombed and didn't even exist anymore.

Apparently, the U.S. Army didn't want the Viet Cong to hang out in the vacant *Ben Suc*, so they *denatured* the place. The Army brought on total fucking destruction by heat. Curtis made a mental note to discuss the book with Trumbo, first chance he got.

He turned his attention back to *Little Big Man*, and finished that, too. Dustin Hoffman's wheeze and cackle delivery underscored all the Jack Crabb dialogue in Curtis's head, since Hoffman had played Jack Crabb in the movie. When Curtis thought about it, the Indians in *Little Big Man* hadn't fared a whole helluva lot better than the Vietnamese in *Ben Suc*, when it came to encounters with the U.S. Military.

But Thomas Berger had a hilarious way with Indians.

There were all sorts of internment camps, and tons of murderous soldiers, and goddamn villages being denatured all over the place in *Little Big Man*. However, Berger made you laugh out loud. Curtis made another mental note, this one for Bighorn, to discuss how ugliness and goddamn depravity can be funny as fuck in fiction.

On Friday mornings the Marines did Karate.

Sergeant Baxter said, "When things get ugly, you're gonna fall back. You're gonna be prepared. You'll step outside that adrenaline rush. When that ignorant S.O.B. comes at you swinging wild, you'll step back, you'll think, and then you'll end it with just one punch. Focus just beyond the point of impact. Punch through."

Butch stood square, placed his fist against his hip and said, "Torque is the measure of the turning force on an object, like on a flywheel. You get me?" He rotated his hip to and fro, real slow. "With that force you get a full hundred and ninety pounds or what have you, behind the strike. When you drive with full body torque, you'll ring some bells." Baxter snapped his hip forward and launched his fist into the heavy bag.

The impact rattled the suspension chains.

"When you're out there dancing for real," he said, "you're gonna hear two sounds. You hittin' that sucker, and that sucker hittin' the deck." He sprang backward, then forward again. He rattled the chains once more. He performed a roundhouse kick that landed a high smack on the bag.

Pops said, "You the black *Billy Jack*."

Sergeant Baxter nodded. "Alright then," he said.

The Marines practiced. They hit the bags and each other.

They wore baseball catcher pads for protection. Baxter coached.

An hour after Guard School ended, the recall alarm sounded, shrill and loud.

The Marines raced to the van double quick. They had to wait forever for Billy Ray. He flew down the front steps as he worked to hitch up his pants. Toilet paper trailed from the heel of his boot.

Sergeant Baxter was not pleased.

"You cost us four minutes, hillbilly boy. Next time you get left."

D.L. Sherman drove the van. It was a white-knuckle ride.

He used the wrong lane or the median strip or a hill on the side of the road if it wasn't too steep, to get around anyone in their way as fast as possible. At the embassy, the Marines jumped out of the vehicle. They ran up the stairs, two at a time. In the Ready Room, they donned flak vests and riot gear, then hauled ass to their assigned posts. On the roof, Curtis could see the Angel of the Apocalypse from where he knelt against a sandbag. His job was to watch and wait. That was the job of all Embassy Marines.

Exactly nothing happened.

After all posts had radioed in that they were secure, Sergeant Baxter told Bam-Bam Brick and Trumbo to let everyone know it was just a drill. They were ordered to stow their gear and to report to the Gunny's office.

In Gunnery Sergeant Alfred's domain, Curtis must've heard, "It is not my job..." about fifty goddamn times in the next five minutes. The Gunny whined about the Marines' recall response time. "Forty-four minutes does not cut it. It's not my job to figure out how to get it done faster. It's not my job to find a better route." Then Alfred added, "It's not my job to motivate Marines I cannot see." It was obvious that he meant Sergeant Butch Baxter, the Senior Sergeant at the Marine House, had dropped the ball.

Curtis looked to D.L. then Chetbo, to Sweetzer and Billy Ray, then to Pops and Bighorn. Their eyes were locked straight ahead, but they weren't listening. Butch Baxter, however, gave the Gunny his full, albeit stone-faced, attention.

The rest of the Marines sniffed the air and rolled their tongues.

When the Gunny was done bitching and moaning, the only thing Sergeant Baxter said was, "Aye-aye, Gunny." That was it. He didn't say word one about Billy Ray Poore taking forever to wipe his ass. Nor did he mention anything about the impossible patches of bumper-to-bumper traffic that D.L. had to negotiate while driving in. Instead, Sergeant Baxter silently distributed the absentee ballots that had arrived in the diplomatic pouch, so the Marines could go ahead and vote in the Presidential Election. That was the real reason the Gunny had sounded the recall in the first place.

Curtis figured if the Gunny pushed Baxter too far, he'd regret it.

Baxter's stoic expression did not come across as bitter – but it came across.

The Marines filed into the embassy library which was the acting polling place.

As Curtis waited his turn to vote, he sidled over to Pat Bartok.

He told her he was looking forward to dive class.

Pat said she was, too.

Curtis asked if she had anything lying around that might help him cast a more informed vote. Pat offered him the current issue of *Life*. On the cover was a chubby Asian kid in a bib. Curtis couldn't tell if the youngster was a boy or a girl. Under the child's chin a caption read, *"Faces of an Unexpected China."*

He sat across from D.L. and opened the magazine.

D.L. lit a cigarette, glanced at the cover photo, and said, "I spy a Chinese dumpling." He exhaled smoke and watched it waft up toward the ceiling.

Curtis read the table of contents. He turned to an article entitled *Reagan Versus Carter: a Showdown Between Scrappy Country Boys*. Curtis decided he wasn't interested in politics after all. Instead, he grabbed *Time* off the rack and read about Larry Holmes and Muhammad Ali.

A week before he'd left the States, Curtis saw on TV that Larry Holmes had handed Muhammad Ali his ass in the tenth round of a heavy-weight championship bout in Las Vegas. What he hadn't heard was that for years, Larry Holmes traveled the world with Muhammed Ali as his sparring partner and that the two of them were pals. In the article, *Requiem for a Heavyweight,* Holmes said, "When you fight a friend - to me, a brother - and you do what you have to do, you can't get any happiness from it."

Curtis removed his note pad from his pocket and wrote down *Requiem*.

Then he read that Henry Winkler's wife had a baby girl and about Steve McQueen, who was reported to be sick in Mexico, but not from food poisoning like everyone said. Whatever Steve had was way more serious.

At that point, Pat Bartok waved Curtis over.

She showed him where he could fill in his ballot.

He said, "It's nice being able to vote ahead of time. Absentee and all."

Pat said, "I remember the first time I voted. I've never missed an election." She smiled. "Let me tell you your options. There are three choices for President on the ballot. Jimmy Carter is a Democrat. Ronald Reagan is a Republican. John Anderson is running as an Independent."

Curtis had a vague recollection of the TV news anchor-lady Natalie Jacobson mentioning *the Anderson difference* on one of her newscasts back in Boston. He couldn't remember what that difference was supposed to be. As for Jimmy Carter, he knew Carter was big on human rights, but the guy seemed vague. He wasn't exciting. He wasn't *vivid,* not like Reagan in *Knute Rockne, All American.* Christ, Reagan stole the whole goddamn movie from Pat O'Brien, because he was way more vivid. Bruce Dern did the same damn thing when he shot John Wayne in the back in *The Cowboys.*

You gotta admire the vivid guys...

Dern in *The Cowboys*...

De Niro in *Taxi Driver*...

Hackman in *The Poseidon Adventure*...

On the strength of Ronald Reagan's performance in *Knute Rockne, All American,* Curtis decided to vote for the goddamn Gipper.

Back at the Marine House, Curtis moved furniture from the front room into the garage with Bam-Bam Brick in preparation for the T.G.I.F. Brick would jerk his chin or grunt or point. They cleared the entire room and didn't exchange a word. Butch Baxter came out to the garage, thanked them for their efforts and said, "Corporal Brick, I don't want you leaving that heap of clutter on the front lawn. Stow that mess in here."

Brick said, "It's not a heap, Sergeant Baxter, it's a Harley. I'm gonna restore it and add a side car to it. It'll match the Wehrmacht model. It's an original."

Butch put his hands on his hips and pursed his lips.

"You heard me, right? In here, under a tarp." He left.

Bam-Bam dug out a clean canvas.

He muttered, "Bitch-ass motherfucker," as he stomped out of the garage.

Curtis joined D.L. in the weight room and asked if he thought Brick was dangerous. D.L. shrugged. "I don't know that he's dangerous, but I do seem to feel better when he's not around."

Curtis did super curls and D.L. worked the bench.

They played Springsteen and bobbed their heads between sets.

Dan sat up on the bench. He wore a headband like Björn Borg's.

"See, with Brick, he's arrogant. Bam-Bam shows no humility. None." D.L flexed his bicep and kissed it. "He's an American chauvinist, totally unwilling to pretend he's no better than anyone else." He pulled a denim jacket over his bare torso. He stood before the mirror, adjusted his collar, and ran his fingers over his chin. He checked his teeth. "Pearly," he said. "See, as a proud Anglo-Saxon, I acknowledge my inherent superiority, though I am wise enough to do so discreetly."

D.L. chuckled and lit a Marlboro.

Curtis pulled on the Ecuadorian tribal vest of blue, black, and tan that D.L. loaned him. He flexed double and held the pose. "Quite imposing," D.L. said. Curtis lowered his arms and buttoned the vest.

He'd never been a bouncer before. D.L. slid his watch onto his wrist and checked the time. He said, "*Studio 54* opens in ten, Yardbird."

"Let's do this," Curtis said and they left the gym.

He'd seen pictures of the real *Studio 54* - the long lines out the door.

One photo showed a topless woman riding a white horse inside the club.

In the Marine House living room, Chetbo stood on a ladder. Pops held up a mirrored disco ball. He struggled to hand it off to Chetbo. "Take this thing already. You got a hook right there, Chetwit." Both dripped sweat. Chetbo's Panama shirt hung open and Curtis saw his wiseass tattoo of the donkey-dicked leprechaun.

Trumbo polished beer glasses at the upper bar.

He flashed Curtis a thumbs up and said, "What, no tie?"

Duke Sweetzer combed his hair. Bighorn was still in his bathrobe.

D.L. flicked his cigarette out the front door. He took a handful of candy from a glass bowl and shoved it in his jacket pocket.

Outside, the evening air smelled like a campfire. Billy Ray Poore stood near the garage. He swirled his lasso. Brick's heap was nowhere to be seen. As they strolled past Billy Ray, D.L said, "How're the lil' doggies gittin' along?"

He offered Curtis a Tootsie Roll.

"Not right now," Curtis said, so D.L. scarfed it himself.

At the fountain, a bird flitted from the cherub's head. Curtis thought of Henry and of Henry's twenty-two. He turned to D. L., who chewed his chocolate. "I told you about my buddy, Henry Fonda?"

D.L. nodded the affirmative and slurped at the candy.

He tweaked his headband and said, "That's his real name? Henry Fonda?"

"I mean, technically. He was adopted. You ever see *Rolling Thunder?*"

"No. This is the fat kid? The one you stole the Maverick with?"

"Well, it was a raffle. We didn't steal it."

"Tell it to the Judge."

"But you never saw *Rolling Thunder?*"

"I don't go to movies very much," said D.L.

Curtis couldn't imagine what that was like, not going to movies very much.

"I got a Henry story from before the Maverick. The guy's unbelievable. He's wild. See, we'd been dying to see *Rolling Thunder*, which was playing at the Shrewsbury Drive-In. So, we asked Eddie Belder if he'd be willing to drive and Belder says, 'Sure, what the hell,' but at the ticket booth, the bastard insists we pay not just for admission, but for the goddamn gas, too. He dreams up this outrageous price tag and demands twenty-five bucks, which left us fucked for concessions."

They walked the driveway toward the gate.

"What a prick," D.L. said.

Devo blasted from the Marine House.

"So, Eddie immediately skips off to the snack bar, and he makes an elaborate goddamn purchase. He comes back sporting cheeseburgers and fries, plus goddamn clam cakes, a massive bucket of popcorn, huge Coke, and he won't share shit. He just chows down solo through *Rolling Thunder* doing this finger lickin' good routine and making boatloads of noise, while refusing to offer up a single bite of anything..."

"Sounds like an asshole, this Eddie," D.L. said.

"Yeah. So, at intermission Eddie announces, 'I gotta go to the can. Too much Coke.' As soon as he slams the door, Henry says, 'Where's the chocolate rabbit Beldo was waving around?' This long-eared bunny is on the dash, lying right beside Eddie's statue of the Virgin Mary with *Yum-Yum Bunny* scrawled across the cellophane."

"Henry eats the fuckin' thing?" D.L. said.

"Wait, man, I'm telling you," Curtis said. "Henry tells me to pass it back, so I do and I hear goddamn Henry mumbling, 'Oof,' and 'Ah,' and he's saying, 'Is he coming? Is he coming?' And Henry finally taps me on the shoulder and says, 'Take this fucking thing and put it back.' He'd rewrapped the rabbit, so I laid it down next to the Virgin."

"What did he do? Lick it? Spit on it?"

"I thought he musta licked it. Henry makes this high-pitched giggle noise, like, 'Dee-hee-hee...' and I'm like, 'What, man, what'd you do?' and Henry goes, 'I shoved the ears up my ass! Right up my ass!' Can you imagine? I like to have died!"

"That's disgusting," D.L. said. "I admire it."

Somebody changed the music and put on Queen. Curtis and D.L. paused at the foot of the driveway and posted themselves under the archway. Guillermo was in the street below, along with several Ecuadorian cops. They directed traffic toward a sandlot at the end of the road, which the Marines used for spillover parking.

"Let's do some diamonds," D.L. said. "Get a pump for the ladies."

They dropped and hammered out a set of close grip push-ups and then stood to admire one another's triceps. D.L. looked at his watch. He said, "To be punctual is to be virtuous," and gave Guillermo the high sign. They drew open the gates. D.L. wagged his flaxen eyebrows and said, "South of the border, fortune favors the blond."

First in line was an American.

She was maybe five feet tall, if that.

A mane of tousled brown hair cascaded down to her waist.

"Christy Keane, as I live and breathe," D.L. said.

Christy grinned. She licked her thumb, as if she were about to count money, then waved the moist digit in the air. She laughed at nothing and stumbled slightly.

"Christy, meet our new Marine. He's a Masshole, too," D.L. said.

Christy slapped Curtis on his bare shoulder and said, "Natick, myself. See you inside, fellow Masshole," and she staggered off.

"Lance Corporal Dark, hold on to your hat," D.L. said.

"She's already drunk," Curtis said.

"Yeah," D.L. kept his voice low. "Keane-oh is a kind of a mascot. Conceals a helluva heinie under her skirt. A massive and very loose caboose. Entirely unblemished and milky-white. Suitable for framing, if one were in possession of a large enough frame. Christy Keane is extremely charitable toward Embassy Marines. She collects hats."

"Holy smokes," Curtis said. "Hats, huh?"

"Yeah. She does a neat trick with her opposable thumb."

Middle-aged diplomats, mostly male, high-fived the Marines as they entered. They said things like, "Semper Fi, boys," and "Looking good, fellas." Pat Bartok didn't show. In fact, very few American women did. Dominique Castro came with her older sister, a cheerful woman named Pierrette.

Curtis smiled and kissed them both, cheek by cheek.

Louise Bennett, the Ambassador's secretary, arrived at 19:30.

After the embassy employees were let in, the locals approached.

D.L. made a big show with the girls who strutted up in flashy clothes that accentuated their breasts. He'd jam his thumb into his chest and call himself *Dancito*. D.L. said, *"Entra, por favor, mi cariño, guarda me una bebida,"* which meant, "Come on in, sweetheart, and save a drink for me." He ogled each set of winning breasts. He'd sling a possessive arm over each girl's shoulder and guide her though the gate, and to each he'd whisper, "Don't forget about ol' Dancito, heh, heh."

If a girl didn't saunter up all boobs-on-parade and sporting a salacious grin, or if her sweater was only tight in the upper arms, or she looked kinda dumpy, Dancito would wave her through, but he'd do so with an exasperated expression as if he were doing her a big favor. He fluttered his fingers and said, "Come on, chickee." You could tell that every girl in the wallflower contingent knew she was just barely being tolerated.

Curtis didn't like that shit at all.

Plain girls had feelings, too, for Christ's sake....

Plus, he guessed that the homely girls participated in this uniquely American humiliation in the first place, only because their hopeless moms or stupid dads forced them into it and filled them full of half-baked fantasies about some wealthy prince of a goddamn gringo who'd be certain to spot her inner beauty and then whisk her away from whatever it was she needed to be whisked away from. That the girls themselves harbored no such illusions was obvious. It was painful to watch.

Curtis decided that being a bouncer had its drawbacks.

A final group of six Ecuadorian men stepped forward with no girls at all.

D.L. said, *"Buenas noches, amigos,"* and he nodded his head slowly with sham sincerity. He said, "Listen, fellas," and he cupped his hand to his ear. They could all hear the thump, thump, thump of Kool and the Gang's music blasting from the Marine House dance floor. D.L. sang along with *Ladies Night* and turned a disco shuffle.

The amigos smiled. They felt lucky.

Then Dan pulled a hard guy face and said, *"Estamos llenos por dentro. "*

He exhaled smoke into the half-dozen dark faces that expected they would soon be admitted. Their leader scowled at D.L. and mumbled, *"Puto,"* then looked to the local police - all of whom were armed - before he threw his arms in the air and walked away disgusted.

"I have placed a moratorium on the *Penis Latinis,"* D.L. said. "A few jackass dudes show up every week trying to squeeze by. Like the song says, it's ladies' night."

Curtis was embarrassed. D.L. could have been nicer about it.

If that wasn't bad enough - right then - the Gunny pulled up in a Jeep.

He was the only slap dick in the entire embassy who couldn't enter the T.G.I.F. on his own two feet. The Gunny had to turn up in a Jeep and demand the gate be sprung so he could ride in like some half-assed commando. In *Little Big Man,* Jack Crabb talked about an arrogant chief from a rival tribe who tooted his brass bugle every goddamn time he showed up someplace. Crabb had said, *"There is a snobbery among all people who run things, White or Indian."*

Goddamn Gunny.

At exactly 19:45, D.L. closed the gates behind a final group of U.S. diplomats. The Americans arrived three sheets to the wind. D.L. told the Ecuadorian guards, *"Nadia mas, sin cedula de identidad,"* and they secured the gate.

"What about Guillermo?" Curtis said. "He's still outside."

"Fuck 'em, if he can't take a joke," D.L. said. He offered Curtis another Tootsie Roll. Curtis waved it away. He thought of Henry, who waited through three quarters of *Rolling Thunder* for Eddie Belder to pick up the rabbit. When Eddie nibbled the rabbit's ears, Henry exploded in a triumphant peal of hiccupping laughter.

Eddie bellowed, "Shut the fuck up, you!" He wheeled around to glower at Henry. All Henry could manage to do was thump his head against the window and wheeze joy. At that point, Eddie tried to kick him out of the car for ruining the movie.

Curtis said, "Shut up you greedy bastard. Henry ain't goin' anywhere."

Henry was now stuck at Marine Base Twentynine Palms out in the Mojave Desert, somewhere in California. Every time Curtis called him from Cherry Point, Henry complained about how Twentynine Palms was wall-to-wall Marines with no single women in sight.

Curtis watched strobe lights flash as he approached the Marine House. He was aware that inside, the place was chock-full of girls, some wildly attractive and some not. He decided he should count his blessings. Since nobody ever came to a party to just stand around or take up space or feel lonely, Curtis planned to ask every single girl in the place to dance. There would be no goddamn wallflowers on his watch.

CHAPTER
Nine

Curtis lay at the bottom of the DCM's pool.

He breathed hard through a SCUBA regulator.

Every breath rumbled and hissed like Darth Vader. He looked up and saw Pat Bartok's legs as she paced the pool and checked on her dive students. She had taught everyone that *SCUBA* was the abbreviation for *self-contained underwater breathing apparatus*. The air from the tank made his throat dry.

Curtis looked to his right. A few divers down sat Louise Bennett.

On the sly, Louise twinkled her fingers at Curtis. He twinkled back.

He nursed a monster hangover. Resting in the deep end felt pretty good, except for his parched windpipe. The cool water helped his head. He closed his eyes and sucked from the tank.

The T.G.I.F. had been a real eye-opener.

Curtis had worn D.L. Sherman's vest. He rolled his fists in concentric circles and flexed his triceps to every third thump of the disco beat. He danced with all the girls who stood alone. Everybody he asked said yes. Curtis did the bump with the Castro sisters, both at once, all three of them together.

He drank beer after beer from a ceramic mug and gyrated to the music as he offered icy *Cuba-Libres* to any dehydrated female who glanced his way. It was a helluva party. Nobody was lonely for long.

Two hours in, Christy Keane grabbed his arm.

"Let me check out your room," she said.

Curtis obliged lickety-split. Once there, Keane-oh strode up to the window and eyed Mount Cotopaxi. She appreciated the mountain in twilight. "It's just spectacular," she said, "Man, you copped yourself the best view in the house." She turned and examined his *Poseidon Adventure* poster.

"Well, that's new," she said.

"I brought it from home," said Curtis.

"How 'bout that part where the fat lady sings?" Keane-oh said.

Keane-oh's mockery of Shelly Winters' epic death scene irked Curtis.

"I'm shit-faced, man," she said.

"Do you want to sit down or something?"

Keane-oh sat on his bed and swigged beer from a bottle.

"You have those dressy hats with white and gold, don't cha?"

"Dress Blues Covers?" Curtis pointed at his closet. "I got a pair."

"You got a pair?" Keane-oh smirked. "What else you got? A helmet? Or an anteater? Or are you just happy to see me? Ha! Ha! Ha!"

Curtis didn't pick up on what Keane-oh was alluding to. "Come again?"

Still on the bottom of the pool, Curtis opened his eyes and looked at Louise Bennett. Bubbles rose around her face and raced to the surface. Her legs were long. Her fins were crossed. He saw swatches of her blue and yellow bathing suit. He closed his eyes, gulped more oxygen, and returned to thoughts of Keane-oh.

As she sat on his bed, she grinned and said, "So, anyway, let's bet." She raised her thumb and winked it up and down, confident in the challenge she proposed. Curtis balked. "You gotta be outta your cotton-pickin' mind," he said. "Your hands are way too tiny, sister." He held up his own thumb, massive by comparison.

"I'd crush you," Curtis said.

Keane-oh frowned. "We're not going to *thumb wrestle,* you goose."

Curtis had lowered his hand and asked, "Well, what then?"

Keane-oh spelled it out for him; "Here's the bet. I put up my thumb and you put up your hat. If I can put a smile on your face using just my thumb, I get to keep the hat."

In the pool, Curtis opened his eyes. Pat Bartok extended a paddle underwater with a message for the divers to read - "Two minutes till we surface." He looked from the note to Louise Bennett. She gave him a thumbs up.

Curtis waved to Louise, then closed his eyes again.

In his room, Keane-oh said, "Don't be bashful, Curtis. I've already trounced Sweetzer, Pops and Custer." She had three fingers in the air and continued to count. "Plus Boseovski, Billy-Ray, and um, D.L. Sherman. That's almost every guy in the group." She crinkled her nose. "Custer is a dirty dingus Magee. Phewff." She took another swig, put her bottle on the bedside table, drew her legs up under her chin and said, "Get the hat."

Pat Bartok dropped a second signal - a checkered flag.

That was the sign to surface.

Curtis exhaled into his regulator.

He inflated his buoyancy compensator device.

As he floated upward his mind drifted back to Christy Keane.

He placed the Dress Blues cover on the pillow beside Keane-oh. She pointed at his pants. "You gotta zip it out, friend, cause I'm all thumbs." When he did, she smiled knowingly. She moistened her thumb. "Right under here," Keane-oh said, "is the jingle bell spot."

Curtis came out of the pool.

Pat Bartok stepped onto the diving board.

Curtis slumped into a deck chair, happy to drip dry.

Pat didn't look at all awkward as she stood on the diving board.

She taught class while wearing a string bikini. Pat looked like she belonged in charge - even almost naked. Curtis could tell she didn't want to spend forever doling out advice as she stood around a pool. Pat was eager for open water.

"Before you know it, we'll be at Darwin's Arch. The diving in the Galápagos is unparalleled, but we've got some work to do before we get there. One thing that typically causes student divers a great deal of anxiety is the need to clear the face mask, should the mask leak or begin to fog. Your first ocean dive will be only twenty feet from the shore and in very calm water, and not more than thirty feet deep. I'll be right beside you as dive-master, but if you need more practice clearing for confidence, now is the time."

Curtis didn't need to overdo it with the face mask.

Plus, he was only halfway interested because he was still hungover.

Besides, Pat had shown them how to clear the mask in the shallow end. It was a small potatoes maneuver. All you had to do was tilt the mask up and exhale though your nose. Big deal. Two would-be divers got weird about their faces getting wet under their SCUBA masks. Another one had whined about getting water up her nose.

Pat gave a last call for clearing practice.

Louise Bennett opted to join in alongside a fat guy named Rudy.

So did Dominique and Pierrette Castro. They were the only Ecuadorians in the dive class, which made them stand out. That they were the only black people in the pool made them stand out even more. When the sisters joined the circle next to Louise, fat ass Rudy let out a groan. He rolled his eyes and crossed his arms. His hammy shoulders were pink. His neck was red.

The Castro sisters stayed focused on Pat.

Their stoic expressions gave away nothing.

Louise looked like an older version of Sally Kellerman. She was tall like Sally, and her hair was long, down to her hips, and straight. She had that same kind of second-string, put-upon quality that Sally Kellerman had in *Rafferty and the Gold Dust Twins,* as if she'd tolerated a whole bunch of shit in her life. Curtis was a huge Sally Kellerman fan because she wasn't all Dentyne smiles in her movies. Farrah Fawcett-Majors was no slouch, he'd never say that, but her perpetual Cheshire grin was pretty one-note.

In real life, nobody that Curtis had ever met looked Farrah Fawcett gleeful.

He found sad actresses way more intriguing than the happy-go-lucky ones. If Sally goddamn Kellerman decided to smile, boy, you wanted to know why. When Curtis got to kiss Louise Bennett for the first time, right inside her front door, he pretended he was kissing Sally Kellerman, tongues and all.

That made him hungry all over.

Close to midnight at the T.G.I.F., Louise Bennett glanced his way with a look he couldn't ignore. It was a plea. He shuffled his way past Keane-oh - goddamn adorable in his Dress Blues Cover - and sidled up to Louise Bennett.

She was trapped between Chetbo and Pops and appeared to be doing *The Hustle* against her will. They knocked her all over the goddamn dance floor, out of sync with the music. Chetbo was drunk off his ass and Pops was at least two-thirds blitzed.

Louise was less than thrilled to be buffeted between two morons. She grimaced every time one of them stomped on her toes.

Curtis had spent the summer of '76 doing *The Hustle* with Henry. They'd loved the Van McCoy hit and practiced all the moves that the *Disco Step-by-Step* dancers did on TV, so it was a breeze for Curtis to swoop in and sweep Louise off her feet.

He pulled her away from the two clumsy mooks she'd been saddled with. He was delighted that Louise not only followed his lead, but executed several classy moves of her own. The music went *woo – oh - woo – woo...*

Louise was no spring chicken, but the woman was born to disco.

They paddy-caked themselves into a quiet corner where Louise credited *Pan's People* as the greatest influence on her charming performance. "I learned all of this from those girls," Louise said. "I was stationed in London with my ex-husband. We just loved Pan's People. All five were so incredible."

"I don't know Pan's People," Curtis said.

"British. Female dance troupe. Top of the Pops. Big on the BBC. We used to watch 'em perform in nightclubs and cabarets, too. Follow me, now." She bucked her hips backward and waved at Curtis.

He bucked his, too, and waved back.

"This may not be the hustle, according to Hoyle," Louise said. "But I saw 'em do it on *The Two Ronnie's* show. Babs Lord, Cherry

Gillespie, Dee-Dee Wilde, and two others I forget. Great hair. They called it the hip-hugger."

Side-by-side, Curtis and Louise did more than just stay in step.

They mirrored one another's moves better and with even more precision than he and Henry did by the end of their big disco summer. Their compatibility was surprising. Curtis and Henry were the same age. The age spread with Louise was much more significant. In a week, Curtis turned twenty.

Louise Bennett was two months shy of fifty.

That made her a decade older than Sally Kellerman and eight years older than Curtis's mother. Yet they'd appeared so simpatico as partners, several drunk diplomats applauded when they finished their set. Before Louise left the Marine House, she passed Curtis a note with her address on it.

"Come by later. Be discreet." She squeezed his hand.

At the DCM's pool, Curtis toweled off and thanked Pat Bartok for the scuba lesson. He smiled at the Castro sisters, then nodded to Louise in a cordial way. None of the other divers would have guessed that he and Louise had spent last night together and that they'd made love four times and had plans to meet up again soon. Curtis gathered his gear and left by the back gate.

On the way home, he slept in the cab.

At the Marine House an American diplomat was passed out on the front lawn near the fountain. His arms were folded across his chest. He wore his shoes on his hands. Guillermo stooped and picked up beer bottles and cigar butts scattered around the diplo's stockinged feet. Curtis waved to Guillermo, who stood and saluted.

"Muy buen dia, Jefe," he said.

Bam-Bam Brick wore a welder's mask in the driveway. Sparks flew from his forthcoming sidecar. The motorcycle half of the World War Two Harley stood in the shade. The open garage was still crammed with the living room furniture.

Curtis acknowledged Bam-Bam by jerking his chin in Brick's direction. Brick didn't bother to look up. Curtis climbed the steps to the Marine House, fished the keys from his pants pocket and opened the door.

Inside on the floor, a sodden brassiere lay in a puddle of beer.

Zoila stood by with a bucket and mop. The row of ashtrays on the shelf behind her were already sparkling clean. Curtis said hello and Zoila grunted.

At the foot of the bar, Pops and Chetbo lay huddled together, out cold.

Curtis had watched the Gunny take copious notes on Pops Dillard's alcohol consumption during the T.G.I.F. At zero-one thirty on the nose, Pops had drained to the dregs a final sloe gin fizz. He smacked his lips together, grinned goofy, and took a short step to the left before he froze. Pops swayed, dropped his glass, and without further ado, pitched forward and crashed face first into the polished hardwood floor.

That was the first time Curtis ever saw a drop dead drunk.

The plunge seemed almost lyrical. It occurred in a kind of strange slow-motion. Some peckerhead had shouted, "Timber," as Pops fell. His face planted with so definitive a crunch that Curtis had winced. Chetbo lurched over to Pops, plopped himself squarely on to the floor, swept aside the shattered glass with the back of his hand and lowered his ear as close to Pops's face as he could manage.

"He's still breathing," Chetbo said, and belched.

The Gunny slapped his notebook closed and put his hands on his hips. He shook his head in disgust and said, "Goddamn it, you two," and he marched out of the Marine House. The T.G.I.F. continued apace and not long thereafter, Curtis snuck off to meet Louise.

Pops's swollen face rested atop Chetbo's chest.

He wheezed and drooled all over Chetbo's leprechaun.

Chetbo snored. Both wore nothing but grungy boxer shorts and black socks.

Duke Sweetzer shouted "Aloha!" from the kitchen. Sweetzer was in partial uniform, halfway dressed for shift. Bighorn sat beside him in his bathrobe, appearing wholly unwashed. Right beside Bighorn sat a disheveled D.L. Sherman. The Marines hoisted one thumb each and hooted, "Aaayyyy!!!" The trio looked like a degenerate blend of uncouth Fonzarellis.

Curtis walked to them. He felt tiny shards of glass crackle underfoot.

D.L. drummed the table and altered a few lines from The Rolling Stones.

"The change has come, my friend. You've been under her thumb," he said.

Curtis blushed. "Well," he said. "Keane-oh came as a complete surprise."

"Wacky wahine," Sweetzer said, as he tugged on one of his jughead ears.

"Uh, Keane-oh does that," stammered Bighorn. "She, uh, uses the element of surprise." Bighorn nodded reflectively, then touched himself gingerly on the chin. He sighed and said, "Dang it. I, uh, I got a bitchin' hot zit."

Trumbo entered the kitchen.

He took a bow.

"Good morning, boys," he said.

He grabbed a mug and poured coffee.

"Last survivor signing off. It's been real, Jarheads."

The Marines gave out with an enthusiastic chorus of *"Urah!"*

"Today's, uh, today's the big day, Sergeant Trumbo?"

"Today *is* the big day, Corporal Custer," Trumbo smiled.

Duke Sweetzer waggled his thumb and pinkie, saying, *"A hui hou kakou."*

"Hey, Trumbo," D.L. said. "Yardbird got himself on Keane-oh's hat-trick list last night. His first T.G.I.F., and the bird's already on the boards. How you like them apples?"

"Not my cup of tea," Trumbo said. "No offense, Dark. I remain engaged."

"I gotta give you back your book, Kent. I dug it, man," Curtis said.

Trumbo raised his mug and winked one of his Faye Dunaway eyes.

The goddamn guy was charming as hell. Curtis was sorry to see him go.

Duke Sweetzer said, "I wonder if Keane-oh worked her magic on every eligible Marine in the Detachment. She must've by now, right? That chick maintains one cunning commitment."

Curtis knew that Brick and Baxter hadn't yet been counted amongst the thumb-trippers. "She skipped Butch and Bam-Bam," he said, "and those guys aren't engaged or anything, are they?"

D.L. Sherman stirred his coffee and shook his head. "Bam-Bam's a sociopath. Keane-oh wants nothing to do with him. As for brother Baxter, our sable Sergeant holds no truck with white women. Correct me if I'm wrong, Sergeant Trumbo."

"That is my understanding," Trumbo said.

"To each his own," D.L. said. "Not entirely unwise."

Bighorn plucked a tissue from the pink box on the table.

"Where's, uh, Sergeant Baxter from? Is he from the South?"

"Butch? He's an Air Force brat," Trumbo said. "High-schooled in Miami."

"You're from Miami, aren't you Duke?" Curtis said. "What's that like?"

Sweetzer said, "Heck no. I'm from Vero Beach, Bro. Winter home of the Los Angeles Dodgers. Indian River County ain't nothing like Dade County. I steer clear of Magic City. Miami can get a little too freaky deakey."

Curtis saw a door open and heard a faint rumble of voices from the garage.

"Winter home of the Dodgers, eh?" D.L. sniggered.

"That's what Vero's famous for, Dude."

"Vero Beach baseball?" D.L. said. He made a ding-ding noise with his spoon. Played it off his coffee cup. "Good folks were rather inhospitable to the Negro leagues back in the day, were they not? Some remain so. Just saying."

Bighorn held a blood blotched napkin to his chin.

"Uh, historically speaking, that's correct," he said.

"I'm not casting aspersions, Duke," D.L. said. "I'll call a spade a spade in any season. Believe that. You saw what those fucking burr heads did in Liberty City, right? Torched their own hoods? Their own businesses? Fuckin' idiots. Burn, baby, burn. Left twenty innocent people dead. Half of 'em white. The good half..."

Butch Baxter stepped through the doorway. He surprised everyone.

Bam-Bam trudged in behind him, carrying his welder's mask.

D.L. Sherman was first to redirect the conversation.

"You a fan of baseball, Sergeant B?" D.L. said.

"Not my game," Baxter said. There was an edge in his voice.

Brick walked to the back of the room and stood alone.

D.L. lit a Marlboro red.

Butch and D.L. locked eyes. Sherman spit a flake of tobacco. Baxter's face gave nothing away. His expression remained stoic. Curtis thought the look was similar to that of the Castro sisters, back in the DCM's pool.

Dan sniffed and cut his eyes to his cigarette.

Baxter looked towards the bar. "Let's go, Pops. Double quick, man."

He refocused his attention on the Marines in the kitchen.

Pops shuffled in, followed by Chetbo. Both were filthy.

Neither one struck Curtis as particularly bright.

Pops stumbled as he tried to sit. Trumbo reached out and gave him a hand.

Chetbo found a spot next to Curtis. His breath was rank. Dirt and grime were smudged on his arms and shoulders. Little bits of paper, pieces of lint and errant strands of hair clung to his back. A circular pattern was pressed into his left cheek. Curtis guessed that Chetbo had passed out with his face on top of something round.

Baxter stepped to the center space in the kitchen.

"Sergeant Dillard, you're currently in the hot seat."

Pops cocked his head to the side, the way a dog does when it only halfway comprehends its master's command. Pops glanced at Chet Boseovski, his partner in crime.

Chetbo was now absorbed in pondering his lint laden bellybutton.

Pops's mouth fell open. He turned his gaze toward Baxter.

"Just me?" He was mystified. "I'm the only one in the hot seat?"

Curtis saw a half-dozen examples of interracial clusterfucks back at Cherry Point. Black Marines tended to get fucked under first while white Marines often got to skate. On base in North Carolina, it played out like a precept of the Uniform Code of Military Justice, though it was seldom acknowledged out loud.

Sergeant Baxter said, "You've got exactly no wiggle room, Pops. Gunny has you on deck for un-suit relief. I'm going to make a recommendation that you commit to *Antabuse*. If we can get Panama's approval for a medical intervention, you might still have a shot at staying on Post. At the moment, it doesn't look good."

Pops dropped his head.

Chetbo moaned. *"Antabuse* tastes like shit-ass garlic."

Sergeant Baxter held up a hand and twitched an index finger.

"You don't get an opinion, Sergeant Boseovski. You've got enough troubles of your own. The Gunny is putting you on a scale, first thing Monday morning." Baxter looked hard at Chetbo's bulging gut. "You hear what I'm saying, Marine?"

Boseovski crossed his arms defensively over the flab.

"Hell, Sergeant Baxter, Gunny has to give me a couple weeks."

Baxter shook his head and said, "He doesn't have to give you a day."

Baxter surveyed the silent Marines. He looked from one to the next. He stayed quiet a moment and gnawed his lower lip. "Okay, Dillard and Boseovski, you gotta get out in front of this. Shower and shave. Polish your brass. Be in full dress at fourteen hundred. I'll accompany you to the Gunny's residence. You best be contrite."

"Contrite?" Pops mumbled the word like a question.

"'*So sorry, Mistah Charlie,*'" Baxter said. "You get me, Pops?"

Bewildered, Pops's head rotated in a circle. He licked his lips and nodded.

Baxter turned to Trumbo. "Can you put together a remedial PT program before you jump ship, Kent? Lay it out on butcher paper, so it's ready to roll up and let Chetbo bring it along to present to the Gunny?" Baxter cracked his knuckles.

"Absolutely," said Trumbo. "Single sheet of thirty by forty?"

"Outstanding." Baxter switched hands and continued to crack his finger joints. He turned to Chetbo and pointed. "Whatever Trumbo puts together, you're gonna follow it chapter and verse like you're training for the Olympics. You understand, Boseovski?"

Bam-Bam said, "Lard ass," from the rear of the kitchen.

Chetbo stood and said, "Aye-aye." You could tell he was sucking in his gut.

"Dark, Brick, Sherman, and Custer, you'll need to Field Day this house, stem to stern, in case the Gunny gets a wild hair and comes by for inspection. Anyone in shower shoes, put on steel toes, cammie trousers and boots. There's glass on the floor. Sweetzer, you'll drop us at the Gunny's before you take the watch. Dismissed."

Curtis walked to his quarters with D.L Sherman.

On the way, Sherman said, "Damn spook gave me the evil eye."

In his room, Curtis kicked off his flip-flops and thought about Charlton Heston.

The star told an interesting story in his autobiography, *The Actor's Life*. Heston wrote that he went to the craft services table for lunch when he was shooting *Planet of the Apes*.

He took his tray and went to find a seat.

What he saw surprised him.

All the gorillas sat with other gorillas, all the chimps sat with other chimps, and all the orangutans sat with other orangutans. None of the ape tables were integrated. All the humans sat together, too, but all the humans were white. There were no black people on the *Planet of the Apes*, except for Dodge, the astronaut who crash landed with Heston.

Dodge got killed right off the bat.

Negroes couldn't catch a break.

Not even in science fiction.

CHAPTER
Ten

They hoisted the love-seat and humped it out of the garage. D.L. Sherman bitched about taking orders from minorities.

Curtis didn't think *uppity* was an appropriate adjective for Sergeant Baxter.

"How do you figure a guy is uppity when he outranks everybody?"

"Who are you, now? Martin Luther King?" D.L. said.

"Baxter's trying to save Chetbo's fat ass and Pops, too."

"I'm not convinced their asses are worth saving."

"Well, that's a different story," Curtis said.

"Fuck 'em anyway," D.L. said. "My discharge date is 30 June of 1981. I'm not gonna sweat it for Chetbo nor Pops. I'll come back here as an emancipated civilian and full-time entrepreneur." They positioned the love-seat by the bar and clapped the dust off their hands. "I'm telling you, there's not one single automated carwash in this entire country. Just slobs with buckets," D.L. said.

Curtis said, "It's good to have goals, I guess."

"You should give serious thought to coming in with me. There's big money to be made. I shit you not." D.L. had gone into detail about his potential goldmine many times.

He and Curtis hustled down the front steps.

Curtis flipped his fingers through the fountain.

The notion of launching a carwash was repugnant to him.

He'd had enough Motor Pool experience back in the Fleet.

After Henry's orders were changed and the Marine Corps sent him to Twentynine Palms instead of Cherry Point, Henry called and said, "Those bastards told me that orders get changed based on the needs of the Marine Corps. Then they said, *'Get used to it.'* Dicks!"

After the phone call, Curtis had wandered back to the Motor Pool.

The recruiters had promised he and Henry would be stationed together. Curtis washed and waxed his truck in silence. He brooded and buffed all afternoon. He was surprised by the recognition he received the next morning, so for the next few days, he washed and waxed his truck with a vengeance. His Staff Sergeant started calling him Private Turtle Wax. Eventually, his C.O. took note of his spotless vehicle.

The Major called Curtis to attention.

"Fine-looking deuce and a half, Marine."

The Major asked Curtis his name.

"Private Curtis B. Dark, Sir."

"Son," the Major winked, "It's Private First Class, now."

At the promotion ceremony, Curtis's citation of merit read, *"For service in keeping with the highest traditions of the United States Marine Corps."*

Henry couldn't believe Curtis was promoted for wipin' down a dirty ass bumper.

From that day forward, Curtis jogged under the Major's window and performed calisthenics where his C.O. was certain to see him. It was peacetime and Curtis figured the Major must have been short on heroes and had plenty of time to stare out a window.

He figured right.

Henry was more than astonished at Curtis's *second* promotion. "Lance fuckin' Corporal for chasin' after your C.O.? These bastards strapped my balls on mess duty for a month." Curtis received a photo of Henry scouring a soup pot.

On the back, he'd scrawled, "Semper Fi, my ass!"

The Major and his Executive Officer approached Curtis a few days after he'd been promoted to Lance Corporal. "I'm out shopping for a new driver," the Major said.

Curtis eyed the Major and then turned his gaze toward the flight line.

The Major shifted his weight. He was uncomfortable. He'd expected Curtis to jump at the chance to be his driver. Curtis squinted into the distance, as if he were deep in thought. He decided that this was the perfect time to make his play.

"I think, Sir, I could best serve my country on embassy duty," he said.

Curtis received his orders and was headed to MSG school at Quantico.

He phoned Henry with the news. Henry, alas, had been extended on mess duty for an additional ninety days. When Curtis asked, "Why you?" Henry replied, "That's exactly what I said! 'Why me?' And you know what they said? They said, *'Why not you?'* Dicks!"

Curtis hadn't escaped from Cherry Point and traveled all the way down to South America to wash and wax more goddamn cars.

He and D.L. placed the big couch in the living room.

Sherman fired up a smoke. "I'm not going back to Massachusetts, no matter what. Just the thought causes acute consternation. It strikes me as a regressive step. You know the area, do you not? Chester? Agawam? Chicopee? Any of those places? Or the lovely Springfield, which is wall to wall kinks now?"

Curtis knew the area.

D.L. dragged on his Marlboro. He blew smoke rings, then exhaled fully and looked to Curtis. "My old man works in a plastics factory in Blandford. *EPI Plastics*. I labored there myself, one entire summer, before joining the suck. I worked as a press and stacker. My sister, a teacher, mind you, is *married* to a press and stacker. Hopeless moron, name of Jim. You'd think she'd have known better."

"Let's get this shit done," Curtis said. "I got other things to do."

They trotted to the garage, and D.L. ground out his cigarette.

They grabbed the last love-seat. As they carried it in, D.L. rattled off more blue-collar woes of plastics factory employment. "For eight hours a day he uses a scoop made from a Clorox bottle to catch plastic granules, then pours said granules into the yawning maw of a melding machine and then he jerks a lever, producing donuts the size of half dollars. He stacks said donuts on ten little spindles, all day long."

"That's the job?" Curtis said. "Sounds awful."

"With two ten-minute breaks and thirty for lunch."

"Holy smokes," Curtis said. He had to admit a carwash would be a step up by comparison. Curtis got into a half-squat and raised the love-seat to his hip. He started up the stairs backwards.

"I went to get my old man at work once, when I was like ten," D.L. said. "He was in someplace called *The Fisk Building*. I went through the main gate, and opened the first door I saw. There was this crusty son of a bitch leaning over a lathe, so I go up to the old geezer. 'Can you tell me where *The Fisk Building* is?' The guy says, 'Boy, you see that door there?' and he points to the door I just came through. I say, 'Yeah, I see it.' Then he says, 'Do you see this machine here?' and I say, 'Well, yeah, Mister, of course I see it,' and he tells me; *'Forty-one years, I been coming through that door and walking straight over to this machine. I don't know one goddamn thing about any Fisk Building.'*"

They plunked the love-seat down catty-corner from the couch.

"Made an indelible impression," D.L. said. "I'd fuckin' kill myself." He ran his fingers through his hair. "My old man has been there twenty-six years. Not me. No way." He put his thumb to his chest. "'*Sherma-Clean!*' Quito's King of the Carwash."

Curtis nodded. "I'm sure you'll do great."

In his room, he took out his notepad and retrieved Paulie's dictionary from the roll top desk. The *Time* article was called *Requiem for a Heavyweight*. Curtis looked up *requiem*. *Requiem Mass* came from the Latin *'Missa defunctorum.'* He copied, "A Mass for the dead," into his notepad. Muhammad Ali wasn't dead, of course, but his career was, thanks to Larry Holmes and Father Time.

Curtis had written another word when he was in Louise Bennett's bedroom.

She mentioned he had a short *refractory* before they'd made love for the fourth time. Curtis wondered if maybe Louise's ex-husband had had some kind of a goddamn horse cock or something, that might be dwarfing him by comparison.

Their intimate evening started off with a bang.

Louise waited at the door. She wore a see-through nightie that came down to the tops of her thighs. She held a glass of wine in one hand and a cigarette in the other. Curtis had never kissed a woman who drank and smoked at the same time, and never one who looked so much like Sally Kellerman. Louise's mouth tasted wonderful, like vanilla icing on a goddamn cupcake. Her lips were crazy soft and oh so warm, yet her tongue was chilly from the wine. Her kisses were long and soft. Much more stimulating than Hinda Cohen's had ever been, and he didn't bump up against braces with Louise, boy.

Curtis wondered if he might be in love with Louise.

Without a doubt, he loved kissing her.

Curtis was pleased to discover that where *refractory* was concerned, the shorter the better. He wrote: *"The refractory period is the time span after an orgasm, during which an individual is not sexually responsive."* He smiled. They'd managed four at-bats together in one night. Just before she'd dozed off, Louise called her ex *"Mr. One n' Done."* The comment about her former spouse now made complete sense.

Curtis re-read his *refractory* definition. He felt proud of himself.

Paulie's dictionary had originally belonged to Paulie's fourth-grade English teacher, Shirley Foss. She'd presented it to him after Paulie had won a spelling bee and inscribed; *"Well done, Mr. Dark! Dictionaries have personalities and this one is most amusing. You shall find much enjoyment here! Warmest regards, Shirley Foss."*

Mrs. Foss gave him an example of the warmhearted definitions within.

Paulie looked up *éclair,* as Mrs. Foss directed and he chuckled. The dictionary defined *éclair* as *"a cake, long in shape but short in duration, with cream filling and chocolate or vanilla icing."*

Ever the teacher, Mrs. Foss asked him, "Why is that amusing to you?"

Paulie said, "Well, it's funny because they tell you what an *éclair* is, and then they let you know its yummy on the sly."

Mrs. Foss surprised the class with a box of French pastries that she baked at home. A smudge from Paulie's finger was still there, right next to *éclair* on page 302. Curtis turned to the world map printed inside the front cover of the dictionary.

He tapped the star at Boston, then slid his finger a skosh further north to New Hampshire. That's where his dad took him and Paulie to visit the White Mountains. They explored the Polar Caves, and went spelunking through two rock formation mazes. One was called the lemon squeeze and the other was the orange crush. They saw stalagmites and stalactites, which were wet and had rainbow ring striations when they'd visited an underground waterway. Curtis remembered how the river gurgled in the dark. The conductor drew the vessel along on a suspended stretch of rope.

They'd heard his voice ring out from the pitch-black of the bow.

"This is the deepest and darkest part of the cave, folks! Can anyone see the handkerchief I'm waving?" To Curtis it looked like maybe a small puff of white was dancing up and down near where the tour guide's voice was coming from, or maybe his eyes were playing tricks on him. Paulie had whispered, "I think I can see it, Dad."

Ronald said, "I can't see squat."

"I can see your hanky, Mister!" Paulie said with pride.

His child's voice resonated over the black of the subterranean lake.

The guide hollered back, "Well, my boy, you must have really special x-ray vision!" He lowered his voice, and in a mock conspiracy, snickered and said, "See, I don't own a hanky, folks, and right now my hands are in my pockets."

The blind boat swayed with adult laughter.

Curtis had been holding Paulie's hand at the time.

His father reached down and gave a squeeze to their two small hands.

He enveloped both within his much larger one. After that, in a booming voice that drowned out the giggles of all the complicit tourists, Ronald shouted in the dark, "Teasin' kids ain't funny, fucko!" Curtis had patted his dad's broad back.

Just for kicks, he looked up *fucko*.

It wasn't listed in Paulie's dictionary.

Curtis grabbed *The Village of Ben Suc* and *Little Big Man* and headed up to Trumbo's room. He knocked at the open door. "Hey, come on in, Dark," Trumbo said.

He was tying a black tie over a white button-down shirt.

"I brought your book back," Curtis said.

"Why, thank you *muchisimo.*"

Trumbo made eyes toward his open suitcase on top of the bed. He said, "Governor Reagan appears to be gaining ground in his pursuit of the big casino. It's bizarre. Reagan doesn't talk about policy issues. It's all populist nonsense, and Carter is completely frustrated that no one else is calling him out on it, but whenever Carter does, it backfires on him."

"Maybe he should clam up," Curtis said.

"Maybe. Carter says Reagan is ignoring the real issues, like his SALT II stance, and no one seems to care about that."

Curtis certainly didn't.

Trumbo turned from the mirror.

He'd tied a perfect Windsor knot.

Curtis handed him *Little Big Man.* "For the plane."

"Well, that's doggone decent of you, Dark. Thank you."

"Let me know what you think. It's like a parallel to Vietnam, in a way."

Intrigued, Trumbo said, "I'll look forward to it. You're not leaving here empty handed, either." Trumbo pointed to the thick catalogue on his desk. "That is your ticket to the big time. *MOS 9913; Special Services liaison.*"

"Oh, man, that's how we do it, brother. Thanks."

"All yours, if you want it," Trumbo said.

"If? You kidding me? I'm on it."

Curtis opened the catalogue and flipped to *35 mm Motion Picture Availability.* "Wow." It was a goddamn treasure trove. Between *Limelight* and *Little Caesar* was *Little Big Man.* "I'm gonna do a movie night, outdoors, like a drive-in and start with *Little Big Man.* Hang a sheet on the wall by the pool. Popcorn under the stars."

"Let me show you," Trumbo said.

Curtis handed him the catalogue. On the inside cover, Trumbo pointed out two sets of numbers that were written there in blue ink. "The top set connects to a diplomatic coaxial cable, so there's no charge. It's a diplomatic line. Dial that as prefix and then dial the second set. It'll connect to Quantico Special Services."

"I just tell 'em what I want?" Curtis said.

"You just tell 'em what you want, yeah," Trumbo said.

"It's a dream come true, requisitioning movies. Thanks, Kent."

"You bet." Trumbo waved Curtis toward the widow's walk. "One last look." Trumbo slid open the balcony door. They stepped outside into the breeze and leaned against the railing. From this angle, Quito went on forever. Curtis saw all three of the volcanoes, not just Cotopaxi but Cayambe and Antisana, too, all looming over different parts of the city. The sky was an endless blue.

"This, I'll miss," Trumbo said. "Hey, here's something." He took out a business card. "When you get back to the States, look me up. Just call my fiancée. This is Amber's card. I'll be an R.A. at American University in D.C. about an hour north of Quantico. Amber always knows where to find me. I'll show you around campus, Dark."

Curtis took the card. "Well thanks, Kent. I will, for sure," he said.

Trumbo turned his face toward the sun and closed his eyes. He looked as if he were praying. Curtis thought about that day in the rain when Trumbo pitched his hat to the two brothers. It was the right thing to do. It never would have crossed Curtis's mind to do that, but now he had an example to follow.

An example of right behavior, you could say.

Curtis had an impulse to tell Trumbo about Paulie and how he had had a great little brother and all, but he decided against it. He couldn't help thinking of the priest at Paulie's funeral and how he'd said, "God answers every prayer. Sometimes his answer is 'No.'" That prick of priest had made his father cry.

Curtis didn't want to burden Trumbo with all of that.

He closed his eyes instead and prayed for Paulie anyway.

CHAPTER
Eleven

Gunny Alfred called the Major in Panama to report in and complain.

Curtis overheard Alfred on the phone. "I will not have these Marines doing whatever they damn well please. They'll benefit from a reality check. I will be that reality check," he said. "They think they're on leave, like this is a goddamn vacation."

The Quito Detachment guarded an embassy that held a zero-threat rating. The peaceful climate afforded the Marines a relaxed camaraderie. Sergeant Baxter recognized that as a good thing, though he expected his Marines to snap in when necessary. Pops had lost a stripe but he'd slowed the booze. Chetbo was by degrees a little less porky. Baxter was good for the Detachment. He wasn't petty, and he led by example.

Baxter arrived for supervision wearing his crisp, pressed Deltas. The local mechanics stopped him in the back lot and asked if he knew anything about Jeeps. Curtis and Duke Sweetzer watched on the security camera as the Sergeant dropped to the deck, crawled under the vehicle, located the problem, and pointed out how to make it right.

In the process, Baxter's inspection ready uniform shirt became saturated with motor oil. He stood up, accepted the thanks of the grateful mechanics, and shook hands all around. He strode into the embassy, went to the Ready Room, retrieved a fresh uniform from his locker and resumed his daily duties without a word.

Curtis knew that the replacement cost of the uniform would come out of Baxter's own pocket. Duke Sweetzer said, "That freaking guy is the real deal. Gunny oughta take lessons." Gunny Alfred was no Butch Baxter.

Curtis enjoyed karate practice at Guard School when Sergeant Baxter was in charge. Whenever Gunny came sniffing around, however, he gave sluggish performances during the Shotokan katas. His kicks were half-hearted, and he pulled his punches. Curtis resented any and all pseudo-military maneuvers under Alfred's dubious direction, as did the rest of the Detachment.

Billy Ray sized up the Gunny Oklahoma style. "All hat and no cattle," he said.

Alfred ordered the Marines to participate in PT as a unit three times a week. Up and out of the rack at zero dark thirty, they were forced to run in boots. Gunny Alfred had the Marines sing cadences at sun up. He had them shout stupid shit like, "Going over to Vietnam! Gonna drop some more Napalm!"

The obnoxious chants infuriated the Marines' sleepy neighbors.

The yelled things like, '¡*Vete a la mierda tu maldita madre, coño!*' from their bedroom windows. A rough translation was, 'Go fuck your mothers, you stupid cunts!' The Marines stomped through the Beverly Hills of Quito for Christ's sake. Curtis refused to so much as mouth the words.

The Gunny yelled, "I don't hear you singing, Dark!"

Curtis benched two-forty on a normal day and didn't break a sweat.

He knew full well he could snap Alfred's pencil neck, if it ever came to that, and Alfred knew it, too. Under the lax conditions of his hedonistic South American lifestyle, Curtis decided he wasn't going to listen to assholes anymore.

The Gunny scheduled a like it or not road race for the entire Detachment that landed on Sunday, the 26th of October, which happened to be Curtis's twentieth birthday. He had planned to lie around in bed while Louise made pancakes. Worse than the time of the race was the birthday card he received from Lila-Ruth. Two squirrels were pictured on the front. It said, "You're 20 today!" Inside it read, "Party like two ten-year-olds!" Under the text, Lila-Ruth had scribbled, "Your birth was a memorable event. I can remember it well. Mother." The card depressed him.

At the road race between the Marine Guards and the Peace Corps volunteers, Curtis tied his running shoes tight and knelt at the start line. He noted the expression of grim determination on the Gunny's face. When Alfred growled another one of his tired-ass Marine Corps' clichés: "Lead, follow, or get the fuck out of the way," Curtis rolled his eyes. Back in Westborough, Coach Doyle had taught all his cross-country runners, "You've got two types of pain; pain of discipline, and pain of regret. When race day comes, you dance with the one you brung."

The road race was a thirteen-mile loop.

Curtis hung at mid-pack and managed to look apathetic for much of the event. He made his move at mile marker seven. He toyed with the Gunny and dogged his heels for two full miles, then stepped it up. He sailed past the Gunny and shouted, "How's that go again, Guns? 'Lead, follow, or get the fuck out of the way?'"

Curtis passed D.L. Sherman and the Peace Corps volunteer who were neck and necking it the entire race. He caught up with Duke Sweetzer and they coasted together for a while. Duke sprinted his finish hard and fast and he left Curtis in the dust. Curtis had to settle for second. Alfred finished fourteenth out of fifteen, just ahead of Chetbo.

A few weeks later, Ronald Reagan won a race of his own.

The Gipper walloped Jimmy Carter in a landslide.

By the end of November, Curtis knew every single one of the dozen lovely prostitutes who worked the midnight alley behind the embassy by their first names. He'd been with six. He learned the exchange rates well enough to calculate prices down to the penny. Most nights he kept the lights on. Curtis thought the ladies' unshaven legs and *au naturel* underarms were quite sexy.

Of South American culture, Curtis was a fan - and not just the hookers.

He liked the mountains, too. Nighttime was his favorite. Curtis loved how the hills encircled the valley where Quito lay so sweetly nestled. Huts and hovels aglow with family fires speckled the dark highlands with dancing rings of red. The nocturnal smoke was tantalizing. The heavy scent was filled with hints of joy to come.

Mornings, too, were a delight. His hookers were happy to teach him Spanish. They sat on the patio for *desayuno en al aire libre,* or for *cócteles,* or for cocktails *with* breakfast. Curtis always brought his notebook. Zoila the cook accommodated every whim. Curtis asked for eggs over easy. The girls ordered whatever they liked.

They sat back and they chatted. They listened to the bells of the neighborhood sheep jingle and ring. Zoila kept the coffee warm. Curtis had not been enamored of high school but he studied hard with each hooker-cum-tutor. The whores were impressed. He was a good student and he paid his teachers well.

His first lesson had started with:

¿Como estas?   How are you?

And had continued with:

¿Quieres tomar algo?	Would you like a drink?
¡Que ojos mas bonitos!	What beautiful eyes you have!
¿Quieres bailar?	Would you like to dance?
Ven a mi casa.	Come to my house.
¿Por qué no?	Why not?
Ya nos vamos.	OK, let's go.
Eres muy amable.	I think you're a nice girl.
¿Puedo darte un beso?	Can I give you a kiss?
¿Solo un besito?	Just a little kiss?
¿Puedo tocarte aya?	Can I touch you there?
Necesitamos un condon.	We need a condom.
¿Quieres fumar?	Do you want a smoke?

As the animals grazed, Curtis sipped black coffee and sighed his bliss.

He carried his Spanish / English dictionary with him whenever he went out. When he had to work, he liked the eve-watch best. The Gunny was a real pain in the ass during the day, but his fellow Marines were usually willing to swap shifts in order to keep their evenings free. As a result, it was a rare day when Curtis had to deal with Gunny Alfred.

Eve-watch had an added benefit.

He liked to watch the sunsets from the embassy roof.

Sometimes Curtis played music as the sun sank behind the mountains.

There were speakers in the Quonset hut on the roof and a giant boom box, too. The selection of cassette tapes stacked in great big cases beside the bullhorns was vast. He could listen to Bruce Springsteen or The Beatles or Pink Floyd or John Lennon or Jethro goddamn Tull. Christ, they had everything a body could want.

Curtis used the Special Services film catalogue left to him by Sgt. Trumbo. He placed orders for movies he believed would have broad appeal. His efforts were a hit. The embassy staff enjoyed the drive-in feel of the movie night Curtis organized. It was held outside by the pool. Butch Baxter put Pops on duty because they had an open bar.

For the inaugural event, Curtis selected *Little Big Man*. He advised Duke and Chetbo to pay attention to General Custer's plans for the Battle of Little Bighorn. "That General Custer was a moron," Curtis said. "Just watch." Then, he winked and said, "Might remind you of someone you know."

The Marines stole glances at the Gunny when Alan Oppenheimer, who played Custer's harried Major, advised General Custer to send a reconnaissance squad into the village of Medicine Tail Coulee.

They shouted, "Listen to him, asshole!" and "Send a damn squad!"

When General Custer informed Oppenheimer that it would cost them the element of surprise, Oppenheimer's character couldn't believe it. He knew that the Indians were lying in wait and that the goddamn element of surprise didn't apply in this case, and when he tried to tell Custer, the son of a bitch wouldn't listen.

The Marines hooted at the screen and threw popcorn at General Custer. Chetbo shouted, "Joke's on you, bitch!"

D.L. hollered, "Rank has its privileges! You get to fuck up everything!"

The Gunny left. The Marines high-fived and chuckled throughout the subsequent massacre. When the movie ended, they were delighted the Gunny had gone home. Had he stuck around, nobody would have gone skinny dipping. Without the Gunny, the pool was full till morning. When the sun came up, Curtis drip-dried naked on a wicker chair.

Christy Keane, who enjoyed the movie, called Curtis a few days later. "Would you be interested in seeing Quito at night?" Keane-oh said.

Their first stop was *Byblos* - a strip club she was quite fond of.

She said, "It'll be a gas. Big Red is headlining."

Inside, the place was cavernous, dank, and dreary.

It felt something like a bus terminal. It had high ceilings and drowsy Ecuadorian men who smoked and drank and looked around, sort of waiting for nothing to happen. A spiral staircase near the stage led to rooms upstairs. Cramped, two-person grottoes lined the walls. Disco bubbles wallowed around the walls and spun across the ceiling. The ludicrous grind of an American porn flick flashed on the scrim above the stage.

Chitty Chitty Gang Bang played with superfluous subtitles.

The star of the spoof was named *Dick Man Dike*.

Curtis might have enjoyed the film a heck of a lot more if he'd been with his fellow Marines, but he was on a date. He felt self-conscious. Even though he'd exposed himself to Keane-oh's thumb, the action on screen seemed inappropriate in the company of a near diplomat. When a topless waitress brought cocktails to the table, Curtis tried to ignore her nipples. He didn't want to come across to Keane-oh as crude. He sipped his beer and studied his glass. Keane-oh shot her tequila and waved for a refill.

The porn flick ended and the lights came up. The announcer on stage said, *"Por favor, un poquito de aplauso para nuestra estrella que nos llega desde Checoslovaquia."*

Keane-oh wagged her eyebrows.

She said, "An Eastern European peeler. Red's a Czech."

A chubby dancer with a massive shock of scarlet hair pranced to center stage.

Curtis cleared his throat. "What color is her bikini, would you say?"

The music blasted. Keane-oh shouted, "Teal!"

Big Red started to swivel to Gloria Gaynor's *I Will Survive*.

"Geez," Curtis said, "I love this song!" Keane-oh whistled sharp.

Big Red was in a distressing squat, with her hands on her hips. Her face was flushed and sweaty. She moved in taxing revolutions like a winded hula-hoopstress. When she finished half-a-dozen inelegant circles, she balled up her fists and began to pump the udders of an invisible cow. The wretched soul remained untouched by spirits of the go-go. She eventually discarded her bikini bottoms. Crimson hair now flamed in *four* places - on her head, under both arms, and at her crotch.

Keane-oh raised her glass to Curtis.

"Here's to real redheads!"

At the merciful end of her clumsy number, *La Roja Grande* blew a kiss, closed her legs, and thumped away in platform clogs. When Big Red returned from behind the curtain, she was no longer nude. She'd put her pathos in a G-string. She dismounted the stage and flounced from table to table. Curtis watched her take in lots of coins and now and then some bills. In response to paper money, Big Red bent forward and braced her hands against her thighs. A slapping bonus was an option for big time tippers.

Christy slid a *Cincuenta Sucre* note to the edge of the table and winked at Curtis to pass it on. He was unwilling to whack ass in mixed company, so Keane-oh gave Red a tender little smack on one cheek and a playful smooch on the other. After that, *La Roja Grande* rose from her provocative *spank me* pose and moved toward the next table.

Curtis watched her ass cheeks recede.

A blushing sense of melancholy covered her behind.

A few shots and several strippers later, Keane-oh said, "I'm a little tipsy."

That was an understatement.

Curtis paid the tab and ended up driving her home. Keane-oh asked if he wanted to come in. "It's pretty late," she said. "Be tough to find a cab." Inside her place, Christy gave him a beer. She said, "Come with me." Curtis followed her into the bedroom.

Keane-oh took all her clothes off and got on the bed – not in the bed, but on it. She reached for her bedside table, opened the drawer, and pulled out a bottle of baby oil. She held it up behind her back, settled her face onto the pillow, and twinkled the bottle.

"You got two choices, Sailor. Take your pick."

Next morning at the Marine House, Curtis found a large envelope on the desk in his room. It was from his father. There was also a letter from Henry. He opened the big envelope first. The November issue of *American Film Magazine* was inside. Robert De Niro was on the cover. He leaned against the ropes of a boxing ring.

There was a card, too - a snow-white owl on a wintery branch.

His father's missive was: *"Curt, let me know that you got this. Sorry to be the barer of bad news. Lila-Ruth seems very confused. I wrote to her sister Phyllis to get her thoughts on the matter. You can write me at Di Pego's Bakery, not at home. I don't have anything more definite to say. When you write, put 'Angela for R.D. at Di Pego's Italian Bakery, 352 Shrewsbury Street, Worcester MA 01604.'*

I'll send more details when I have them.

Shaygro says, 'Semper Fi.'

All best, Dad."

Curtis sighed. His father had a penchant for understatement. That his mother seemed "very confused," could mean a lot of things – none of them good.

He opened Henry's letter.

Henry's lot in life at Twentynine Palms had not improved at all.

Stateside Marines could visit *Movie Mates* and rent a love seat and someone young and leggy to watch porn flicks with on a private screen. It cost sixty bucks for a tandem booth but rumors held that a covert twenty could buy a furtive hand job. Henry'd been hopeful until his "skanky" mate spurned his fistful of cash and told him, *"This is a legitimate establishment, Sir. Sex for money is illegal in the Yucca Valley."*

The letter continued:

"It sounds like you're having a ball. I'll tell you, brother, this ain't Ecuador! There aren't even any hookers around here. Any time I bum a ride to town, its wall-to-wall Marines. If there are any women around, all the Marines swarm all over them, and they fuckin' hate Marines! I fuckin' hate Marines! If you were here, you'd hate Marines, too! You'd be whistling a different tune about loving the Corps, if your ass was stuck in this fucking place, humping hills instead of diplomats. I miss Mass, man.

Write me, soon! Your pal, Henry."

Curtis was sympathetic, but only to a point.

He wrote to Henry that he continued to enjoy South America, but that he was now, *"Kind of on the fence about hookers. Ever since I started dating Diplomats, I'm not so sure about paying for it anymore. Besides, the Dips are really into it, whereas hookers don't get that involved. Don't get me wrong, Baygo. I don't mean I'm above paying for it and I'm not saying I'm totally against it. There are real advantages. A free girl smells like a single flower, whereas a hooker is her own bouquet and I'll be the first to admit, I like ripe..."*

Yet, as Curtis sealed his note to Henry, it was hard to squelch feelings of superiority toward his hard luck chum. He felt that every agreeable interlude with a woman carried him - one embrace at a time - away from his provincial past.

Every affair brought him to a unique place and the rewards were many. He'd recently learned about Georgia O'Keefe from Dominique Castro. She had a beautiful coffee table book in her apartment. She showed him one of Georgia's prettier pictures, *'Iris oscuro,'* before lifting her skirt, so Curtis could compare her female petals to those in the book. The floral metaphor wasn't lost on him even though the book was in Spanish.

Every wondrous female offering gave him the same delicious sense of satisfaction he felt at Penny's Pizzeria whenever Penny brought him and Henry a hot pie, fresh from the oven. Each female flower was like a slice of heaven.

The main perk of Embassy Duty was that the diplomatic community was immune from the social conventions of places like Westborough, Massachusetts. In the good ol' U.S. of A., the goddamn citizenry was divided into *peer groups*, but overseas, you could make love with anyone you wanted, no questions asked.

It was an *anything goes* environment.

His main squeeze was Louise Bennett. For the first month with her it was kind of like being in *The Graduate*. He felt that the Dustin Hoffman character must have been crazy to give up the older Anne Bancroft for the younger Katherine Ross. Katherine Ross was no slouch, he would never say that, but Mrs. Robinson? Holy smokes, maturity was where it's at.

With Louise, Curtis felt his sexual technique improved each time they were together. He was eager to try out everything Louise taught him with other women he met at the T.G.I.F.'s or out in town.

He eventually discovered that maturity *was* important, but it *wasn't* everything. When Curtis asked Louise, "How about if I go down on you for a change?" she suddenly began to cry, which took both by surprise. She covered her face with a handkerchief and sobbed.

"My husband, he wouldn't.... We didn't." Then she said, "God, I feel foolish."

Curtis patted her thigh and told her not to worry. "I'm just trying to return the favor." He said he'd be happy to accommodate her whenever she felt ready.

"My husband traded me in for a newer model," Louise said. She tried to play it off, but Curtis had the impression that she wasn't over the asshole. Not yet, anyway.

Then she needed to know if he thought her skin was *crepey*.

Though it was the first time he'd heard that term, he didn't need to write it down. Louise was quick with the context clues. She continued to put herself down. She insisted that she had "old lady arms," and didn't do either of them any favors when she demanded Curtis examine her flaccid triceps.

"Geez, Louise, you're doing OK." He rubbed her stiff neck, gave her a kiss. He said, "You're fifty, right? Your arms are just fine for fifty. You look really good to me."

She blew her nose and thanked him.

After she ran out of wine, Louise dozed off.

Curtis crossed his hands behind his head and watched the ceiling fan thump against the nighttime heat. He then propped himself up on his elbows and checked out Louise in full slumber. It wasn't fair, but it was true.

Watching her snore depressed him.

CHAPTER
Twelve

Sweetzer came in off the mid-watch. He looked as if he'd been crying.

Duke told the MSG's that some fucking nut had shot John Lennon four times.

"State Department teletype said the guy used a .38 special with hollow points and that the fucking wackadoo dropped the gun on the sidewalk and took out a paperback. He just stood there reading *The Catcher in the Rye* 'til the cops came and put Lennon into the back of a squad car to take him to the hospital to try and save him."

He died, though, John did.

The Marines fell silent at the breakfast table.

Zoila asked what was going on.

Bighorn stammered out a translation. *"El Beatle, uh, John Lennon, uh, esta muerto en Nueva York. Fue asesinado con, uh, una pistola."*

Zoila's jaw dropped. She genuflected and kissed her thumb, then gathered up her bag and jacket. She took little Paulina by the hand and walked out of the Marine House.

The Marines scraped plates on their own and washed dishes by themselves.

Nobody said very much.

Of course, they canceled T.G.I.F. that week. It fell to Curtis to hand out the flyers, but he didn't go office to office. Instead, he slid the flyers into all the cubbies in the mailroom.

In the newspapers, Yoko Ono announced that there would be no funeral. John Lennon had loved and prayed for the human race. She asked people to do the same for him. She signed her message Sean and Yoko.

Sean was John and Yoko's son and he was only five goddamn years old.

Yoko let reporters know that a peace vigil would be held in a matter of days.

If people might like to join, she'd ask for ten minutes of silence on the day in memory of her husband. The vigil was arranged for Sunday, the 14th of December at fourteen hundred New York time, which was thirteen hundred in Quito.

The Marines were on the embassy roof at noon.

Gunny Alfred called for full riot gear, which included flak vests.

Sergeant Baxter suggested it might be a better idea if the Marines were posted on the ground floor in Dress Blues with white gloves - in that it was a peace vigil in lieu of a funeral. The Gunny vetoed his idea. Instead of holding salutes during the ten minutes of silence, the Marines held shotguns.

On the roof, goddamn Bam-Bam racked a round.

Curtis grabbed him at the throat and said, "People are carrying votive candles, motherfucker, and you're out here pretending you're in Saigon."

Butch Baxter told Curtis to let go of Brick.

Baxter then told Brick he was to go below, secure his weapon and to stand by quiet in the Ready Room. After Bam-Bam left the roof, Baxter told Curtis, "I'll deal with you later."

Curtis studied the crowd. It extended well beyond the mermaid fountain and continued in an endless arc through *El Ejido* park. He spotted a few familiar peddlers. One of them was the guy who sold ceviche. All the vendors stood with their hats off and their hands clasped together in front of them. Nobody opened for business.

At thirteen hundred, church bells rang.

Sergeant Baxter called the Marines to attention.

From where he was posted, Curtis saw that all the cars around the traffic circle below him were at a standstill. People stood outside their vehicles, totally hushed, with hands clasped and heads bowed. The city of Quito was a haven for dogs. Not one barked. For ten minutes, not one amazing dog howled. The only sounds Curtis heard were the flapping of flags and the occasional brassy clank of a lanyard against a flagpole.

At thirteen ten, church bells rang again.

Sergeant Baxter called, "At ease."

Duke Sweetzer suggested they give the people what they came for. Baxter gave him the OK to fire up the boombox. He played *Imagine*, of course. Curtis held one of the bullhorns up to a speaker. Bighorn held up a second one.

A sea of Ecuadorian people held "*¡Paz!*" and "*¿Por Qué?*" signs. They rocked back and forth and sang *Imagine* in English in a kind of agonized chorus. Many of them held little kids on their shoulders. After *Imagine*, Duke played more Beatles music.

The Ecuadorians sang the songs they knew.

Curtis had the eve-watch. After the Gunny secured the recall, Curtis stowed the speakers in the Quonset hut and watched the crowd as they departed. Baxter came up and unwrapped a stick of gum and told Curtis that Brick outranked him and it wasn't his place to lip off like that, much less crack on him.

Curtis said, "Aye-aye, Sergeant Baxter."

Sergeant Baxter chewed his gum. He waited.

"You have permission to speak freely," he said.

Curtis took a moment, then said, "I'm not gonna watch some joker hurt people just because he can. I didn't sign up for that. Brick was in the wrong. You wanna ship me back to the Fleet, ship me back."

For some reason that made Sergeant Baxter laugh.

He said, "Relax, Lance Corporal."

Baxter chomped his gum for a good minute.

Then he said, "Let's me and you catch a game."

They set up the chess table but didn't talk very much.

After two games, the sun was lower and it was cooler out.

Baxter said, "Just where did you grow up in the states, Dark?"

"A one-horse town in central Mass. You're from Florida, correct?"

"No, man. Went to high school in Florida, but I'm an Air Force brat." He pinched the bridge of his nose as if he had a headache or something.

Curtis asked Baxter what it was like being a brat and moving all the time.

"For brats," said Baxter, "where you're from isn't a real place at all. You develop a traveling state of mind. You form mental concepts about not belonging. Home is always *elsewhere*. You get me?"

"Sounds like *The Great Santini*."

"It does indeed," said Sergeant Baxter.

"You think that movie was on point about brats?"

"Yeah. Very much so," Baxter said. "Being a brat is a rather noble thing to be when you think about it because brats follow a very real sense of mission from very early on. Granted, it's your father's mission, but you follow it all over the world. It makes for a very dedicated childhood. Very dedicated."

"Where did you follow your dad to?"

"Spain. Haiti. Morocco. A shitload of stateside bases, too."

"Wow. The little town I'm from? It's home, even if I never go back."

Later, Baxter said he'd voted for Ronald Reagan, strictly because Reagan was pro-military, and he, Baxter, was not about to vote against his own self-interests. "I'll do my thirty, man, and then I'll retire *outside* the continental United States."

It had never occurred to Curtis to live outside the U.S. on a permanent basis.

Baxter said, "There is no life in America for a black man out of uniform. Simple."

That set Curtis's teeth on edge. Curtis had a love it or leave it mentality about the U.S.A. *The Star-Spangled Banner* gave him goose bumps for Christ's sake. He thought Baxter's comment was out of line, as if he were condemning the United States.

Then Baxter said something that pulled Curtis up short.

"'I love America more than any other country in the world and exactly for this reason, I insist on the right to criticize her perpetually.' That's James Baldwin. *Notes of a Native Son*. Should read it, Lance Corporal Dark."

Curtis never imagined criticism and love of country could coexist.

He took his notepad out of his pocket and wrote, '*Notes of a Native Son*, by James Baldwin.' Curtis said, "Holy smokes. Can you repeat the quote? I wanna jot it down. I'm guessing Baldwin's black?"

Baxter nodded the affirmative. He repeated the quote and Curtis wrote it down. He was tempted to ask Baxter why didn't he date white women but decided against it. If they were friends, maybe, but they weren't.

Still, Baxter seemed like an intriguing guy.

Curtis said, "*Raging Bull* is out at the *Atahualpa*. Wanna go?"

Butch chewed his gum. He nodded and said, "OK, Dark, I'm down."

It turned out that the embassy library didn't have books by James Baldwin, although Pat Bartok had read Baldwin's stuff and said he was certainly *worth* reading. All Curtis had been exposed to in his student days at Westborough High School had been shit like *The Red Pony* or *The Great Gatsby* or *The Pearl* where everyone was dickless and dull and didn't do anything very exciting. Pat encouraged Curtis to look around the library. He came across *Portnoy's Complaint*.

He remembered the title because it came out as a movie when he was in sixth grade and his mother told him he couldn't go because it was a dirty movie. He was very disappointed. Karen Black starred in the movie with Richard Benjamin. She wasn't as sexy as Sally Kellerman, but she was damn close.

Curtis checked out *Portnoy's Complaint* by Philip Roth.

He admired the horny protagonist - a guy named Alexander Portnoy.

Portnoy's number one interest was sex. Having it. Doing it. Getting laid. He couldn't find any women to have sex with, however, so he ended up jerking off for the first three quarters of book, under very frustrating circumstances. Curtis felt a real kinship toward the character, as if they were cut from the same cloth even though Portnoy was Jewish and Curtis was Catholic.

They shared yearnings that transcended their religious differences.

After *Portnoy's Complaint*, he returned to the embassy library and perused the bookshelves in search of other authors who might grab his attention the way Philip Roth did. Pat stood at the desk. She wore big silver bracelets and large hoop earrings.

"It's nice to see a Marine in the library so often," Pat said.

Curtis appreciated her support. He asked if she liked to read.

"I like it more than just about anything else in the world," Pat said.

"I dig reading. I do," Curtis said, "But I need to cast a bigger net."

"What are you trying to catch?" Pat said.

"I'm looking to expand my horizons."

"Any particular genre?"

"Well, I don't know if Philip Roth qualifies as a genre, but I found *Portnoy's Complaint* hard to put down." Pat smiled, nodded, and disappeared into the stacks. After a few minutes, she returned with *Fear of Flying* and *Tropic of Cancer*. "These, I think, and let me get one more." She went off again and retrieved a third book, something called *The Women's Room*. Pat checked the books out for Curtis.

He watched her use the stamp pad. She was quite sexy.

"Oh. The dive club trip is going to happen mid-January."

Curtis said, "I'm down for that. Absolutely. Let me know."

He thanked Pat and took his trio of books to the Marine House.

Zoila brought coffee and an egg sandwich to him on the patio. He started with *Fear of Flying*. People got laid right off the bat and Erica Jong wrote about something called a *zipless fuck*, which she defined as a spontaneous sexual encounter that took place between two strangers with little or no personal information exchanged.

Curtis fantasized about Pat reading the sexy parts herself. He wondered if there was an implied invitation in her choice of books. Erica Jong's *Fear of Flying*? A little *je ne sais quoi*, perhaps? He conjured a vision of her swimming naked beside a dive boat.

Curtis took that notion back to his room.

In front of his mirror, with Pat in mind, he pulled a *Portnoy*.

Later, he told her how much he enjoyed Erica Jong.

As if on cue, Pat invited him to dinner.

The following Friday night, he found himself seated at the supper table across from Pat and her two incredible daughters. Nicole was nineteen and Lisa was twenty-two. Lisa had a killer laugh and a huge, beautiful smile. Nicole was way more subdued. She had ripped, ropey shoulders and amazing thighs that were cut thick like a guy's in a sinewy way Curtis couldn't help but admire.

Both of Pat's daughters had wonderful skin, too.

Dinner was lamb with mint jelly and something called *couscous*.

There was also a bald guy named Larry, who sat a little too close to Pat.

He talked at length about Nicaragua and how a lot could be learned about economic development if one juxtaposed the culture of that country against the more progressive and far more democratic social structures of Costa Rica.

Or words to that effect.

"What do you mean, 'juxtapose?'" Curtis said.

"To juxtapose is to compare one against another."

Curtis glanced at Nicole and compared her to Lisa.

He imagined juxtaposing them oiled up and in bikinis, lying on hot sand.

The dinner, alas, wasn't enjoyable because throughout the appetizers, the main course and into dessert, Larry could not keep his hands off Pat, which irritated the shit out of Curtis because when Pat invited him to dinner, Curtis began to fantasize about her, and he imagined they would make love and read sexy parts out of books together and maybe eat grapes. He really looked forward to that - only to be met by this fucking Larry.

Who never shut up.

Larry went on and on about the *Sandinistas* - whoever the fuck they were. He griped about how, politically speaking, "their outrageous power grabs" clearly indicated that they couldn't keep their hands to themselves - he was one to talk - and how the new Reagan administration would have no choice but to supply arms to the *Contras*, so they would be able to fight for human rights and freedom.

Or words to that effect.

Curtis didn't follow everything, in part because he missed a lot of the political back-story, and in part because Larry kept a hand under the table to play grab ass with Pat. Curtis was pleased that he wore his shirt rolled up high in a way that showed off his biceps. This Larry guy was a smart S.O.B. - he'd give him that - but no way in hell could he hammer out three sets of twelve with two-twenty.

Juxtapose that, fucker.

Curtis looked at Pat's daughters.

Nicole, a soon to be oceanographer, had spent the last six months recording the mournful sounds of migrating Humpbacks off the coast of Santa Cruz, in California. She claimed that they were the most animated of the Baleen whales. Curtis couldn't think of anything to ask about whales, so he said he'd always admired them and asked what did she think of sharks? Nicole said she liked sharks, and he said he loved *Jaws*.

That did not seem to impress Nicole.

Lisa was almost finished with her degree in political science at Temple University. Curtis was excited to learn that Temple was in Philadelphia and that Lisa had, in fact, visited the *Rocky* steps. Curtis said he'd love to run them.

"Would you like to explore the museum?" Lisa said.

"What museum?"

Lisa explained that the *Rocky* steps led to the Philadelphia Art Museum.

Curtis always figured they led *somewhere*...

Still, he felt like a real rube.

He thought the sisters were well informed. Their opinions were thoughtful. He was interested in what they had to say, and he was positive they'd look nice naked. But he had a sinking feeling they were out of his league, though he wasn't sure why. At one-point, smart guy Larry asked Curtis if he had any plans to attend college after his discharge from the service.

Curtis gave a truculent shrug and said, "I'd rather work in a gym."

When Pat and her girls looked down at their empty pie plates and said nothing, Curtis felt embarrassed by his own comment and by his biceps. He mumbled hopelessly, "I mean, like, as a trainer…" At the end of the evening he said, "Thanks for inviting me."

Pat juggled her wine glass and gave him a firm handshake. "I'm so glad you were able to join us." Larry was in the bathroom so Curtis seized the opportunity to lean in and kiss his thanks. He went for Pat's lips. His nose smacked into her jaw.

The way she turned her head and avoided the awkward overture was graceful and unequivocal. It was an elegant move that was both painful and instructive for him. When she patted his shoulder and gave him a warm smile, it became clear that sex was not only out of the question, but totally beside the point.

Pat, too, was out of his league. Curtis made a quick exit.

As he wandered down the hill in search of a cab, he thought about his dad.

After Korea, Ronald Dark was sent to Germany.

He told Curtis, "I liked Europe. They had the better broads."

In Stuttgart, Ronald picked up his first German prostitute. She didn't have a room, and the city streets were crowded so they ended up in a deserted churchyard. "She flat out wouldn't go for it. I tried to tell her the place wasn't sacred anymore since it was bombed out and vacant. I didn't speak German worth a shit, so I'm in this churchyard with a hard-on going, 'Boom, boom, boom! No holy! No holy!' and trying like a bastard to get up her skirt. I musta looked like an asshole."

"Well, what made the German broads better, Dad?"

His father told him, "There was this one girl one time up in Bremen, near the North Sea. She brought me to a dinky little apartment, and she had this little blondie girl, about four, five years old. We went at it, you know, while her daughter was asleep. Nice, but awkward. In the morning, it being Sunday, I asked her, 'You wanna go to the beach?' and she says, 'You'd be seen with me?' and I says, 'Sure, why the hell not?'"

"That sounds pretty nice, Dad."

"Oh, she got all excited, and then she says she had to get a babysitter, and I tell her, 'Let's take the kid,' and she got teary-eyed over that. So off we go to the beach, and Christ we musta played five, six hours out there, body surfing, sand castles, ho, we had a ball and we kept going back to the *Kartoffelpuffer* stand. It's a type of potato pancakes. Jews call 'em *latkes*. Well, this girl, she wouldn't take a dime for the food. She bought everything all day long. The weather and the two of them, together. Quite the lovely."

"But why were they better? What quality? Why did you like them best?"

"Well, Europeans, they're more… Christ. What's the word? *Demonstrative*, I could say. They were much more demonstrative with their affections. Not just with me, but with each other, see? Koreans are much less so. Your Asian hooker is quite reserved. To this day, I wonder what happened to those two in Bremen. You could tell she loved her kid. I think that's what was better. You could feel the love."

Curtis waited for the cab under a mango tree.

A piece of fruit dropped close to his shoe and landed with an ugly splat. It didn't fall far from the tree. He'd felt a wave of humiliation when Pat rebuffed his advances, but now he began to wonder if it might be possible to become friends with Pat, and instead of sex, they could talk books, period. Maybe that could be its own reward. He climbed into a taxi and on the ride across town, he decided it was worth a try. If he played his cards right and tried to keep everything on an intellectual level with Pat, who knew? He might get lucky with one of her daughters. Or, Christ, maybe both.

In South America, *Raging Bull* was called *El Toro Salvaje*.

Before they went, Curtis told Sergeant Baxter that he had the latest *American Film Magazine* and that Baxter could borrow it if he wanted to because the issue was all about *Raging Bull*. He said Martin Scorsese saw Jake LaMotta's life as one of personal redemption where a guy attains something really big and ends up losing everything and then redeems himself, but Baxter passed on the magazine. He said, "I like surprises."

They went early that Sunday.

Raging Bull did not disappoint.

Cathy Moriarty was off the charts beautiful.

Robert De Niro was totally convincing as the world's biggest asshole.

A brand-new actor named Joe Pesci damn near stole the goddamn show.

According to *American Film*, Martin Scorsese had a lot riding on the movie. His last film had been an epic piece of shit called *New York, New York*, which was a complete flop. Robert De Niro had also starred in that one too, but with Liza Minnelli and Liza Minnelli was no Cathy Moriarty, boy.

Curtis thought *Raging Bull* was a goddamn masterpiece.

After the matinee, he and Baxter stepped out of *The Atahualpa* into brilliant sunshine and Curtis told Baxter, "Guy named Mardik Martin took *two years* to write the screenplay and Scorsese didn't like it because there was too much boxing in it, so he and De Niro brought in Paul Schrader, who'd written the screenplay for *Taxi Driver*, and Paul took a crack at it, but Scorsese and De Niro still weren't happy so they flew to Saint Martin in the Caribbean and hammered it out until it became what we just saw."

Curtis wanted to know if Baxter had liked it, and Baxter nodded yes.

"You know what else?" Curtis said, "A guy named Peter Savage helped Jake LaMotta write his true-life story as a book, but Savage wasn't only a writer, he was an actor, too. He played the seedy john in Travis Bickle's back seat in *Taxi Driver*, who rides around groping the black hooker wearing the blonde wig."

Baxter unwrapped a piece of gum and said, "That so?"

"Yeah. Absolutely true. He gave De Niro his copy of the LaMotta book back during the shooting of *Taxi Driver*. If he hadn't, who knows? Maybe no *Raging Bull*."

"You certainly know your movie trivia, Dark."

Curtis waved away the gum Baxter offered and said, "Man, to me it's not trivia. The writer's contribution is the opposite of trivial. How do you figure *knowing* a lot about a subject is trivia? It's *important* knowing details, is what it is. It's not trivia. Think about it, man. No writer, no movie. 'It if ain't on the page it ain't on the stage,' as they say."

Baxter said, "That's a point," and they hailed a taxi.

Back at the Marine House, Baxter asked Curtis if he wanted to do a deck.

Curtis said, "Sure," so they went out to the pull-up bar near the deep end of the swimming pool. Baxter grabbed a deck of cards out of a blue bin which was stowed at the bottom of the towel cabinet. He snapped off the rubber band, shuffled them quick, then held out the deck. Curtis pulled an eight of diamonds.

He hopped up on the bar, did eight chins and jumped down.

Baxter pulled the five of hearts and did his five.

"So, what's your favorite *black* movie?" Baxter said.

That stumped Curtis for a minute. He had to think about it.

He pulled a seven of clubs, leapt up again, did the seven and dropped.

"*A Raisin in the Sun,* with Sidney Poitier," Curtis said.

"Well, that comes as absolutely no surprise." Baxter looked disappointed.

Curtis said, "What? Why? Poitier is great. That's Louis Gossett's first movie."

Baxter unwrapped another piece of gum for himself and deliberately crammed that into his mouth before he said, "White people love Sidney Poitier."

"That's crazy talk," Curtis said.

"No. No, it's not. He's safe. He's *'civilized.'*"

"Sidney or no Sidney, it's my favorite black movie. So what?"

"Your favorite? OK, I'll bite. Who wrote *A Raisin in the Sun,* Dark?"

Curtis felt his face flush. What kind of a question was that? Who *wrote* it?

He had to confess he had no idea, so Baxter started asking about the goddamn stars. Curtis didn't know who played Sidney Poitier's mother, so then Baxter asked about Sidney's wife. Then about his sister. Then about his son. Curtis didn't know any of those actors by name and he didn't know the name of the actor who played the Nigerian Prince who falls in love with Sidney Poitier's sister, whoever the hell she was, although he was pretty sure he'd seen the Prince on *Hogan's Heroes*.

Baxter pulled the six of hearts. He did the six easily.

He jumped down and chewed his gum.

"What about Linder? Who played Mr. Linder?"

"Look, man, I don't have every single role down."

"The little guy with the high squeaky voice?" Sergeant Baxter said.

"Oh, yeah. OK. He was in *Twelve Angry Men*. He does lots of T.V., too, man. *B.J. and the Bear* and *Fantasy Island*. Shit like that." He snapped his fingers. "Ho! That's John Fiedler! That's John goddamn Fiedler. Sure. He did the voice of Piglet in *Winnie the Pooh*. John Fiedler. John fucking Fiedler."

Baxter kept right on chewing his gum.

Then he said, "You realize he's the only white man in the movie? One little scene at the end? Look, Brother, Lorraine Hansberry wrote *A Raisin in the Sun*. First successful Broadway play ever written by a black woman. Her screenplay, too, but you don't know thing one about Lorraine Hansberry, and you're the movie man, right?"

"Well, when you put it like that…"

"You don't see my point?"

"Like how?"

"Like how black people don't even exist in your movies or in your mind."

"They exist. What are you talking about?" Curtis thought about all the movies he'd seen with Pam Grier and Jim Brown and Fred Williamson. They were cheap as shit in terms of production values, but he liked them well enough. They showed black action movies every Tuesday at the Marlboro Twin. In fact, Tuesday was called "nigger night" in his town. There was no way in hell he was gonna say that out loud.

Baxter held out the deck.

He said, "Pick a card."

Curtis pulled the queen of clubs.

He leapt up, did a dozen and hopped down.

"I get your point, Sergeant Baxter. What am I supposed to do about it?"

CHAPTER
Thirteen

Tie a Yellow Ribbon Round the Ole Oak Tree was rededicated and brand-new lyrics were added to celebrate the release of the fifty-two American hostages who'd been on their asses in Tehran for four-hundred and forty-four days. Reagan's U.S. Ambassador to Ecuador played the latest version over the embassy loudspeakers.

"*It feels so good to have you home, though you were gone, you never were alone. Our country pulled together, like one big family, with a simple song of freedom – about a ribbon and a tree – a song for liberty! Tie a yellow ribbon round the ole oak tree! What a wondrous sight for our eyes to see! While one of us is hostage, none of us are free, cause it's one for all and all for one, for all the world to see! A simple yellow ribbon – round the ole oak tree...*"

The Ambassador killed the music and announced he would host a colossal, made-in-America style costume party at his residence. The full embassy staff, locals included, were invited to celebrate the release of all fifty-two hometown heroes and to "whoop it up a little bit over our nation's newfound freedom."

Curtis saw Gunny Alfred pump his fist at the loudspeaker.

He glanced over at Butch Baxter. Baxter had a more stone-faced reaction.

The Ambassador agreed wholeheartedly with Ronald Reagan's recent inaugural address. He cribbed a quote from the new President's speech and declared, *"Those who say we're in a time when there are no heroes - they just don't know where to look!"* He gave a chuckle and hooted, "God bless America!"

The Gunny called Curtis over the squawk-box.

Curtis responded, "Post One. Go ahead, Gunny."

The Gunny squawked, "You're the Special Services Liaison for the Detachment, are you not, Lance Corporal Dark?" Curtis acknowledged that he was and the Gunny told him, "Get costumes on order for the *entire* Detachment. Requisition whatever you need through Battalion and use the diplomatic pouch. All Marines not on duty will be in attendance and in costume. We will represent."

"Need me to order any kind of a getup for you, Gunny?" Curtis said.

There was a pause. "I already have something, so, no. Have Sergeant Baxter assign Dillard and Boseovski to the watch. Is that clear?" It was plenty clear that Pops and Chetbo would be assed out of the Ambassador's shindig because the Gunny didn't trust them not to drink. It was less clear how anyone could get Bam-Bam Brick to attend a costume party. That guy didn't go to anything.

Duke Sweetzer arrived to relieve Curtis of the watch. They switched over the walkie-talkie, and Duke checked the chamber on the duty pistol. Curtis told Sweetzer he was gonna do a mail check and head out. He asked Sweetzer for costume ideas and Duke suggested they could all dress like crew members of *The U.S.S. Enterprise*, adding, "You could probably get Spock ears from Quantico. That way half of us could go as Vulcans."

Curtis thanked him, and said he'd think about it.

That was a lie, of course. Curtis was no *Trekkie*.

He was, however, intrigued by the idea of a costume party at the Ambassador's residence. For Curtis, the goddamn T.G.I.F.'s at the Marine House had grown stale. He'd pick up a date, ask her to his room, offer her a cigarette, and invite her to undress. He kept a large bowl of condoms on his headboard and there were three types of smokes to choose from. He had a variety of body oils, too, and a jar of honey his mother had sent. Most of his companions spoke English poorly, if at all, and his Spanish lacked subtlety, so there was never much in the way of scintillating conversation.

On top of that, some uber religious Ecuadorian women were reluctant to disclose what felt most stimulating, sexually. That forced Curtis to guess. He learned to pay close attention to a woman's breathing. How it either sped up or slowed down. He used rates of respiration to gauge levels of pleasure. It was a reasonably effective system.

Still, panting and puffing were open to interpretation.

And moans could be misread.

Verbal approbation in the form of the occasional *attaboy* went a long way in his book, but it wasn't really about that. Curtis wanted someone to talk to. Conversation with Louise had been great. After her initial reluctance to let him go down on her, she became a huge fan of cunnilingus. She'd sometimes greet him at the back door wearing nothing but earrings. He learned a whole bunch of sexy things from Louise, boy.

But they talked about life, too. Louise was *interesting*.

She told him what it was like to grow up on a farm. She used to ride horses and knew tons about them. Plus, she had been all over the world with the foreign service. She had a nice laugh, Louise did, and she was goddamn kind. He taught her to play chess, and she taught him to play pinochle. Sometimes they cuddled and Louise would fall asleep with her head on his chest. That was a joy. More than anything else Curtis enjoyed their heart-to-heart conversations. And then he'd completely fucked things.

One day, he and D.L. Sherman had been standing Post One. Louise came by to pick up her office key. Curtis handed it to her, and she signed for it. They acted like they always did when other people were around – very cordial – while keeping their intimacy under wraps. Louise gave him a pleasant nod and then stepped over to the elevator. Curtis heard the elevator ding and assumed she'd left the lobby.

D.L. sang, *"Every little breeze seems to whisper Louise..."*

They chuckled and did an idiotic high-five. As D.L. lowered his right hand, his smile disappeared. He jerked his chin. Curtis turned. Louise stood right behind him. Her eyes were moist and her chin quivered. She'd forgotten her goddamn key. She snatched it up quick and spun on her heel. Her heels clacked. The elevator doors slid open, then closed behind her.

That afternoon, the Gunny received a security memo from the PSO. Louise Bennett was granted permission to keep her office keys with her. She would no longer need to sign for them. Curtis hadn't seen her in weeks.

He missed the chitchat more than he thought he would and to say *sayonara* to all those exquisite Sally Kellerman fantasies was incredibly painful, too. Curtis wasn't going to get that lucky again, any time soon. Movie star doppelgangers were as scarce as hen's teeth. Curtis considered leaving a note in Louise's mail slot but decided against it.

He picked up the Detachment's bundled mail and left.

Curtis waved to Duke Sweetzer on his way out the door.

In the parking lot, Shorty sat on a padded stool in the shade of a leafy tree. The tree's lower limbs were festooned with yellow ribbons. Curtis tapped a thick branch that loomed above Shorty's head and extended out over the embassy fence. He traced its path for Shorty's edification and explained, "¿*Unos enemigos* could climb this, no? Jump right in, easy as pie, see?"

Shorty shrugged and then put a toothpick in his mouth. Either he didn't fully comprehend that somebody could shimmy up from outside and hop the fence, or else he did get it, but couldn't give two shits. Neither the Gunny nor the PSO were impressed by Curtis's security concerns. Low branches still dangled outside the fence like wiseass invitations even though Curtis had complained about the risks weeks ago. He was tempted to saw the fuckers off himself.

As Curtis continued to frown at the tree, Louise walked out of the embassy. She spotted Curtis and hurried back inside. Curtis sighed and climbed into the Marine van. He asked Shorty to drive him home. He kept his eyes on the Angel of the Apocalypse for as long as he could, right up until it made him teary-eyed.

He blinked and shuffled through the mail.

There was a letter from Henry. Curtis tore it open.

> *"Sorry I haven't wrote in a while but, I met this awesome girl. Her name is Brandy and she has a little kid named Tiff and she's a hairdresser. She stays over at one of the trailer parks, around about two miles off base. Which is where she does all the officer's wife's hair-dos. Brandy has cooked dinner for us two times. You'd really dig her. Because of the kid, we haven't got naked, which blows. Tiff is almost five. But it sounds like you're doing great, you bastard!"*

He folded Henry's letter and closed his eyes.

He didn't feel great at all. Seeing Louise bummed him out. He dozed off.

Shorty slammed the brakes and Curtis's eyes flew open. The van fishtailed and tires screeched before it came to a full stop. They'd stalled out in front of the goddamn *Conocoto* guard shack inches from the boom barrier at the base of the hill. Curtis glared at Shorty. "What the fuck? You couldn't see this coming?"

The guard came out of the kiosk to raise the railing.

As they rode past, the woman waved, and Curtis scowled at her.

Halfway up the hill, Shorty pointed to a pile of gore near the sidewalk.

He said, *"Un animal desafortunado."* Shorty always pointed out disgusting shit. Curtis ignored the roadkill. He scanned the hills and chose to focus on the sheep that roamed the slope behind the Marine House.

Shorty tooted the horn. Guillermo opened the gate.

Curtis returned to Henry's letter and read.

> *"Curt, they have cocaine out the ass down there, right? The reason I ask is because Bud (who is Brandy's ex) says that people who work for the State Department can ship shit on the sly. I'll get more details as things develop, only because there may be money to be made. Big money. Bran has turned me on a couple*

of times, man. Her ex is a pusher, more or less, you could say. So, whenever he comes around, she acts all happy to see him. Bud's a real douche, but it's complicated. Bran's car crapped out, so Bud drove my ass back to base, and he outlined some plans. I can't wait to get back to Westborough, and I wouldn't mind having a little nest egg, you know? In the meantime, we should maybe consider Bud's 'supply potential.' Could be sweet.

Keep livin' large and keep the letters coming.

Your pal, Henry Brewster Stabinowitz, the third. Ha!

P.S. I looked up 'sodomizing bastard.' You take a nice picture..."

As Shorty backed the van in beside the fountain, he bashed the rear bumper. Curtis accused him of parking by braille, then shouldered open the door. He walked past the garage. Brick was in there. He shuffled around with a tool box, naked from the waist up. Goddamn Bam-Bam never wore a shirt. He and Brick walked right past one another - neither said a word.

In his room, Curtis dropped the mail onto his bedside table, kicked off his shoes and lay on the bed. He put his hands behind his head and studied *The Poseidon Adventure* poster. He examined the row of star photos that lined the bottom of the poster. He moved his eyes from Gene Hackman to Ernest Borgnine to Stella Stevens.

Henry was a lot of things. *Smart* wasn't one of them.

He was a goddamn gullible bastard, too.

Curtis rubbed his eyes and ran his fingers through his hair. He shook the DCM's new *Playboy* out of its brown bag. Barbara Bach was on the cover. Curtis hoped Barbara would appear as Miss January, but Miss January wasn't Barbara Bach. Miss January had great tits but terrible taste in movies. Her favorite films were *Heaven Can Wait, The Blue Lagoon, Starting Over,* and *Airplane!* Four fucking dogs.

Henry dug *The Three* fucking *Stooges*.

The idiot even laughed at the ones with Shemp.

Miss January was just gorgeous in her centerfold. In the tri-fold she looked like a dream come true. On the next page she sat with her head canted to the side. She was kind of fondling one of her large breasts. She looked like she didn't know what to make of it. Curtis had to admit she looked ridiculous just sitting there holding herself.

He wondered who'd put her up to it.

The Barbara Bach pictorial was even worse.

First, they didn't show much. They had her lying around fully clothed in a blue shirt and red tie. Next picture, she sat in an empty bathtub. She wore a black fedora and held an oversized magazine. Barbara Bach was naked alright, but only from the waist up and only in profile. She looked chilly. In the photo that followed, she was on her feet in the same bathtub. She wore the same fedora and still held the same magazine.

But somebody had turned on the shower.

So, Barbara was under the nozzle. Water cascaded all over the goddamn fedora. She held the water-logged magazine plastered against her body and only the teeny tiniest hints of her can be seen because everything was obscured by the deluge. Curtis wondered what whiz kid photographer came up with that scenario.

He pitched the magazine aside.

Curtis flexed his right bicep and felt it with his left hand.

This *French Connection* jerk-off named Bud was bad news. Henry was just enough of a dunce to fall for some trailer park junkie and find himself pussy-whipped into a drug deal. Curtis would instruct Henry to tell that fucker, "No deal. Back the fuck off." He thought of James Remar in *The Warriors* when he told some douche bag in face paint he was gonna shove a bat up his ass. The idea of cracking off on Bud with a baseball bat gave Curtis something to think about.

It also gave him a vision for the Ambassador's costume party.

The Marines would go as *The Baseball Furies*.

Curtis would do the makeup. He hopped off his bed and grabbed his supply book. From the phone in the hallway, Curtis dialed Sergeant Ken Shipley, the Quantico Supply Sergeant, and requisitioned a dozen baseball uniforms, six bats, and a rainbow of theatrical face paint. He told Shipley about his *Warriors* plan and Shipley promised the delivery within a week.

On Friday, after another rum soaked T.G.I.F., Curtis and a guest were in his room. He reached for his tape deck and pulled the plug on *My Sharona*. That left his bedmate bewildered. He invited his nameless consort to stay the night if she were so inclined, but he himself was gonna get some shut-eye. The woman gathered her shoes in the dark and left unsatisfied. Curtis felt guilty, so he got out of bed and went downstairs to apologize, but the woman was nowhere to be seen. The Marine House was quiet except for Chetbo.

He danced by candlelight to Michael Jackson's *Rock with You* with his arms wrapped around someone very pretty. Curtis waved at them both, climbed the stairs and went back to bed. In the morning, he went for a run with D. L. Sherman.

They passed the *Plaza Monumental De Toros* sign a second time and began another loop around the bullring. They dodged between street vendors. One sold roasted corn and the other lemon drinks. D.L. kicked at a skinny garbage dog that snapped at his ankle. He shouted, "Get the fuck outta here!" He connected with the mongrel's ribs. It yelped and ran away.

"Did you see Chetbo's whore last night?"

"Yeah," Curtis said, "Guy's drinking heavy again. So's Pops."

"Well, this morning, I came in off mid-watch and get this..."

Curtis leapt over what was left of an animal carcass.

A swarm of flies shot up from the remains.

"Fucking disgusting. I'm headin' home."

They jogged away from the bullring.

D.L. panted out more of the story. "So, when I came in, I see Chetbo out on the patio swaying with this girl to that Michael Jackson *canción* he's always playing..."

"*Rock with You*."

"Yeah. All the time with that noise."

"Late last night, too, at like three in the morning," said Curtis.

"I go up and grab a beer and go out on the patio and I'm like, 'What the fuck, Chetbo?' because now he's *crying* like a bitch. This pretty little *Rock with You* chick is sitting way over in the corner and looking like a whipped whelp. Naturally, I inquire as to what's up with these two, secretly wondering if maybe this girl is gonna come available any time soon, as she's quite a good-looking prostie. So, Chetbo tells me he's just tryin' to work things out with her. *'Work things out with her!'* Fuckin' A."

"Chetbo gets misty over everything. He's kind of a crybaby," Curtis said.

"I leave 'em alone, go grab another beer, and ask Zoila for breakfast. Well, ten minutes later Chetbo wanders into the kitchen blowing his nose and I ask, 'Where'd the girl go?' and he says he sent her home with Shorty. I express heartfelt disappointment at that news and Chetbo tells me, 'I'm not so sure you would have dug her.' I'm thinking he's nuts. She was hot. Then he tells me that last night, when he got with the *Rock with You* chick he reached down betwixt her legs and encountered a startling beige penis. Right there! Instead of the anticipated vagina. Imagine that?"

"For real?"

"A male member at half-staff."

"What did he do with that information?" Curtis said.

They jogged past the *Conococto* shack. Curtis and the guard waved.

"He said they worked things out," said D.L.

Curtis said, "Wow."

"Yeah. I got a real good look at her, man. I gotta admit he was a good-looking girl." They continued up the hill. D.L. panted. "That fucking Chetbo is something else."

Guillermo opened the gate.

Curtis and D.L. sprinted up the driveway.

They went straight into the gym and slid big plates onto the Olympic bar.

Curtis grabbed a towel, spread it on the bench, then pulled his shirt off and lowered himself under the bar. D.L. took off his shirt, too, and came around to spot him.

Curtis grabbed the bar.

D.L. said, "You got it?"

"I got it."

Curtis brought the weight to his chest and pressed it up hard and fast. He did seven more reps and racked the bar. D.L. switched out towels and lay on the bench. He gripped the bar and licked his lips. Curtis stood at the ready to spot him.

Dan heaved the weight off the rack, did his set, and racked the bar.

He grabbed his sweaty towel off the bench and mopped his face with it, then stood before the mirror flexing his triceps. Curtis came up beside him and fanned out his lats, then flexed his triceps, too. "Looking good, Dark. How's my back?"

D.L. turned and flexed slowly. He said, "Go ahead. Feel that shit."

Curtis traced Dan's traps with his fingertips. "Impressive," Curtis said. "I like it."

D.L. turned. They stared at one another's muscular reflections in the mirror.

"Couple of real heroes," Curtis said.

"It's in all the papers, Yardbird," D.L. said.

He started to ask a question, then stopped himself.

Curtis said, "What, man? What were you gonna say?"

"Well, the *Rock with You* chick. She's as pretty as Teresa."

Teresa was D.L.'s latest girlfriend. Curtis thought she was nice.

Curtis said, "Indeed." They both hit a double biceps pose and said, "Urah!"

After they put their shirts on, D.L. offered Curtis a smoke. Curtis declined. Now dressed, they continued looking in the mirror. Curtis said, "That jar of honey you have on your night stand? Where'd that come from, man?" D.L. shrugged. Curtis said, "That's the jar my mom sent me, isn't it?" Lila-Ruth sent random care packages on occasion. Her last one had contained a jar of Kalamata olives and a book by Thomas Harris called, *I'm OK, You're OK*. D.L. didn't answer directly. He just chuckled.

"You been dippin' your dick in my mother's honey," Curtis said.

"Sweets to the sweet," D.L. said, "And don't blame me. It was Teresa's idea."

CHAPTER Fourteen

Curtis was meticulous in recreating *The Baseball Furies* makeup.

When he finished, the Marines looked exactly like the mindless thugs in the movie. Bam-Bam Brick said, "You got it right." He grabbed a bat and said, "Do me." Duke Sweetzer asked Zoila to take a group photo after Curtis had finished with Brick, but Zoila couldn't get the camera to work, so Guillermo took the last two shots that were left on Duke's roll of thirty-six. Curtis hoped they'd come out.

Pops and Chetbo weren't in the picture.

They stood outside the frame and looked miserable.

Curtis called shotgun. He hopped in the van and checked his makeup in the rearview mirror. He bared his teeth. He'd made himself up as the lead *Fury* who takes on James Remar. In the movie, the guy got his ass kicked, but he had the best makeup.

Billy Ray, Bighorn, Duke and D.L. slid into the van dressed as *Furies*, too.

Brick marched over to the garage, swinging his bat. He yanked open the door and from what Curtis could see, Brick's Harley-Davidson looked pristine. Apparently, Bam-Bam wasn't just an asshole.

He was a *talented* asshole. The sidecar was hidden under a tarp - but the bike itself looked as if it came straight out of *The Dirty Dozen*.

Brick kickstarted the motorcycle and revved the rig.

His Harley made an awful racket - a profoundly ugly sound.

D.L. raised his finger and in a mocking tone said, "Yes, Virginia, there is a Harley. Please note the deep-throated, syncopated vibration. Lo, the phrase of *potato-potato-potato-potato*."

Curtis took out his notepad, wrote down *syncopated*, then listened to the motorcycle's throbbing engine. It *did* sound like *potato-potato-potato-potato*. Goddamn Harleys were always a helluva lot louder than they needed to be.

The excessive noise gave Curtis another reason to loathe Brick.

Pops climbed into the van and Chetbo followed, both in uniform.

Brick rumbled out of the garage.

Bighorn Custer said, "Jesus Christ, would you, uh, look at this idiot?" Brick squealed forward and his tires spat gravel. You could tell he was proud, boy. Bighorn's face was painted orange. He said, "That ain't cool..."

Brick shouted, "Anybody want a ride?" He pointed at the sidecar.

Billy Ray said, "That might be fun. Hell, I never rode in nothin' like that!"

Bighorn said, "Stick to horses, Billy Ray," and he didn't stutter. "Hey, Brick," called Bighorn, "Uh, shut that shit down a minute!" but Brick revved the Harley all the louder. Bighorn pointed at the *swastika* adorning Bam-Bam's sidecar and shouted, "This ain't Alabama, Brick!"

Brick placed his bat in the sidecar.

He put on a pair of goggles and looked at Bighorn.

Bam-Bam raised his fist and then he raised his middle finger.

He revved his Harley one more time and roared off down the driveway.

The Ambassador's palatial two-story residence was decorated to look like Frankenstein's Castle. Curtis thought it was a bit of a cheat. It wasn't Halloween. The Residence staff even put out Styrofoam tombstones on the front lawn with silly ass names like "Ima Goner," and "Izzy Dead." The effect was cheesy.

Inside, papier-mâché ghouls and fake cobwebs hung from a crystal chandelier.

The Marines thumped across the dance floor as Diana Ross sang *I'm Coming Out!* The *Kiss*-like face paint worn by Curtis and his gang looked even better under the flashing strobe lights. The Detachment raised their bats over their heads and twirled them. Guests applauded the group. Curtis took a bow.

Diplomats, Peace Corps volunteers and American ex-pats in from the oil fields bopped around the dance floor. There was a guy dressed as a cop and a pair of zombies, and there was a priest and a hobo and a pregnant nun, who was asked to leave by the Ambassador. The poor woman was actually pregnant.

She told the host she didn't mean to be offensive, but claimed the nun's habit was the only costume she found that fit. The Ambassador's aide loaned her a yellow poncho and handed her a sombrero. He told her to lose the habit, which she did.

Dominique arrived done up as a dinner table. She had a groaning board of plenty balanced atop her shoulders. A checkered tablecloth was draped in such a way as to make her head appear to be the severed centerpiece of a table set for four.

A Japanese geisha seemed to walk on air as she entered.

Her robes floated in behind her.

Curtis saw Pat Bartok dressed as one of *The Blues Brothers*.

Beside her stood a rotund fellow garbed as John Belushi to Pat's Dan Ackroyd.

Curtis didn't recognize the man, though he was sure it wasn't Larry.

Curtis said, "Hiya Pat."

"Hi, Curtis. You guys look fantastic."

Curtis twirled his bat. "We do look good," he said. "How are your girls?"

"Back at their universities, studying hard and doing fine. Thanks for asking. I'd like you to meet my Uncle Ben. He's in from Boston. A very good sport to attend as my brother in blue." Curtis shook hands with Uncle Ben and then asked after Larry.

"He's in Tegucigalpa. TDY," Pat said.

Curtis hoped he was gone for good.

The Ambassador stepped onto the DJ's elevated platform, waved for a spotlight, and tapped the microphone. He adjusted its height and cleared his throat. He said, "Is this on? Is this on?" Then he growled, "I'm paying for this microphone, Mr. Green!"

About half the guests laughed at what sounded like an inside joke.

Curtis could tell Pat didn't find the Ambassador amusing.

Pat was a Democrat, and the Ambassador was a Republican.

Or else it was the other way around. Different parties for sure.

The Ambassador said, "Welcome everyone! And welcome home fifty-two!" People whistled and cheered. The Ambassador gave thanks for the Iran hostages' safe return and for a new dawn in America. A couple of the knucklehead ex-pats in from the oilfields chanted, "U.S.A.! U.S.A.!" The Ambassador put the kibosh on that and asked for quiet. He said, "You all look wonderful. Later this evening, we'll do a parade of costumes and award prizes for the top three. Enjoy, enjoy, enjoy!"

Curtis figured the Marines were a shoo-in. Pat shot him a thumbs up.

The Ambassador yammered on but Curtis didn't pay any attention.

He elbowed D.L. Sherman and said, "Holy smokes. Look what's coming in." Curtis pointed toward the foyer, where Christy Keane had entered. She wore pigtails and a leather coat. Beside her was a much taller woman in a snazzy purple suit. It looked like it was made of velvet and it was topped off by a matching turban.

"They're doing Liz Taylor and Mia Farrow," Curtis said. The movie was *Secret Ceremony*. Mia Farrow was even creepier in *Secret Ceremony* than in *Rosemary's Baby*.

Elizabeth Taylor was at her sexiest in that movie.

"Hold my bat, will you?" Curtis said. He handed his bat to D.L. and started across the dance floor. He was eager to meet the woman dressed as Liz Taylor. She looked sexy as hell. Really fabulous. Strobe lights flashed and Diana Ross wafted over the dance floor with *Baby Love*. The party people dug the music and looked all herky-jerky as they danced. Then somebody screamed for help.

It was Dominique Castro. She was frantic. She threw off the table-top part of her costume and pointed at the buffet table and shouted a second time, "Her! Help her!"

Curtis looked to where Dominique pointed.

It was flashy under the strobe lights. Peoples' movements looked like Ray Harryhausen's stop-motion in a black and white movie. The woman in the Ambassador's poncho thrust her head back. Her sombrero appeared to take flight in segments. She clawed at her throat and appeared to choke, one freeze-frame at a time.

People danced. Diana sang.

Curtis moved toward the distressed woman.

Two strides and he was behind her chair. "I'm gonna help you. I need to stand you up." He was set to apply the life-saving skills he'd learned at Quantico. He put his hands under her armpits "Can you breathe?" he said. She shook her head violently from side to side, which meant, *'Fuck no, I can't breathe,'* and came as no surprise. "I'm not gonna hurt you. I'm going to help you," Curtis said. The woman didn't have the strength to stand. Curtis pulled her to her feet.

The former nun was profoundly pregnant.

With his arms secured around her torso, Curtis placed his right fist into his left palm and hooked his fingers into a tight ball. He braced the top knot of his clamped fists below her breasts, above the baby, and then heaved *up and in* as best he could against the hopeful spot on her sternum. Curtis asked again, "Can you breathe?"

She shook her head and flailed her arms.

Heimlich maneuver strike one.

Curtis felt sweat. Fucking flop sweat.

You can't get a good thrust if you have to avoid crushing a baby.

He adjusted his arms and tightened his grip. He thought if he fucked this up it would be in front of the entire goddamn embassy. He delivered a second Heimlich thrust.

Which is to say, Heimlich strike two.

Diana Ross seemed to disappear.

Curtis heard himself inhale and exhale, inhale and exhale...

The woman felt heavier and slouchier. He could smell her hair - a little like shampoo but mostly rank like fear. He decided he'd better give the dying woman a *Hail Mary* compression to end all *Hail Mary* compressions and do it quick.

Curtis drove his fists up and inward with all his might and lifted the woman six inches off the floor. He was beyond bearish and almost mean. He grunted with effort and much to his surprise, a perfectly round ball of bread flew from her mouth and skipped across the buffet table in stop-motion stages. The pregnant lady gulped air.

It sounded as if she'd been underwater and finally broke the surface.
Curtis said, "Fuckin' A."
He could hear Diana Ross again.
It was one of his favorites – *Upside Down*.
Curtis eased the pregnant lady onto a folding chair.
Dominique Castro sat down beside her and held her hand.
Curtis kissed the top of the pregnant lady's head. "You'll be OK," he said.

He looked around the ballroom and realized a bunch of fuckwits continued to dance, right through the rescue. The goddamn DJ took a bow. Their applause was for the music, not for Curtis. The roomful of happy-go-lucky Diana fucking Ross fans were totally unaware that he had saved a life. He spotted a *second bunch* of fuckwits at the opposite end of the buffet table. They continued to stuff their faces like nobody's business, all la-dee-fucking-dah.

From the looks of things, nine tenths of the attendees had no clue that a pregnant lady had almost choked to death, or that Curtis had swung into action. The guests stood in groups. They swapped stories, sipped wine, and scratched their asses. The heroic DJ put on another record. This time Barry Manilow garnered rabid applause for *Copacabana*.

On top of everything else, with all the goddamn sweating Curtis had done, his makeup was ruined. And nobody said boo. He felt so incredibly unappreciated that he considered grabbing his goddamn bat and going home but he couldn't bring himself to do it. Not yet. Not before he identified at least a few friggin' witnesses, for Christ's sake.

Dominique asked him to help her put her table-top parts back on, which he did.

She thanked him for the help with her the costume.

She did not, however, make mention of his Heimlich. What a fucking gyp.

Behind Dominique were several more guests who lingered at the buffet table. They loaded up their plates with Swedish meatballs. Curtis moved over to them, eager to receive some sort of acclaim. The guy dressed as a cop said, "Not only that, but they had mock executions and the guards made them play Russian roulette." The cop's date was a chubby little ballerina who said, "They didn't bathe for months at a time. Ugh. Can you imagine?" The third guy, dressed as Abraham Lincoln announced, "The psychological abuse was very real and it was relentless. It was an absolute horror show."

Curtis said, "Can I get a few of those?" He reached for the meatballs.

The trio politely stepped aside. Curtis realized that all three of the oblivious clucks had been so absorbed in their conversation about the hostages, they had no clue that a flesh and blood hero stood right next to them, dripping sweat, *after he'd saved not one life - but two - lest anyone forget about the unborn babe!*

Curtis looked at the folding chair.

The pregnant damsel had flown the coop.

It felt like he'd dreamt the whole friggin' thing.

He chomped a meatball. The *hors d'oeuvre* was cold.

He ate another and scanned the room. Curtis heard a wolf whistle and looked up. It was Christy/Mia. She stood on the balcony and waved. Elizabeth Taylor - whom he'd forgotten about - stood right beside her. Curtis waved to Keane-oh while looking at Liz.

Liz winked.

Curtis bounded up the steps and at the top, Keane-oh high-fived him. She said, "Great Heimliching!" and then gave him a drunken pinch on the ass and threw her arms around his neck. That was more like it. With Mia Farrow's arms around him, he turned to Liz Taylor and waited for her verdict. *"Bien hecho, Señor,"* said Liz, *"Eres un hombre de acción.*" Curtis blushed under his melty makeup. She'd called him a man of action.

"My name is Curtis," he said. "What's yours?"

With a thick accent, the lovely Liz said, "*Soy Maria de las Mercedes Parea Aragon.* Call me *Mercy.*"

"Mercy. Holy smokes. That's a nice name."

He found it more than a little ironic that the tough chick character Deborah Van Valkenberg played in *The Warriors* was also named Mercy. He didn't want to get ahead of himself, but he wondered if maybe he and this Mercy were *meant* to meet each other, in a karmic sort of way. Mercy wasn't the sole witness to the rescue of mother and child but she was the only one so far who'd deemed him *un hombre de acción.*

"Care for a drink, Mercy?"

"*Si, por favor.*" She switched to English, "Perhaps the vodka and tonic."

Curtis trotted over to the bar. He ordered Mercy's cocktail and asked for *dos cervezas, tambien.* A beer for himself and one for Keane-oh. Curtis brought the drinks to the women. There was one free table but it only had two chairs. Curtis lied to Keane-oh and said, "Dan Sherman is looking for you downstairs."

Keane-oh gave Curtis a thumbs up and hurried to the main floor.

Curtis sat with Mercy and asked where she had learned English.

"Teaching skiing," Mercy said.

Curtis asked if she was Ecuadorian and she was but only half. Her father was Chilean. She was from a mountain town down there called *La Parva* which was fifty kilometers northeast of Chile's capital city of Santiago. Mercy's family owned and operated a ski resort there. She'd started skiing when she was three.

Mercy took out a cigarette. Curtis used one of her matches, held it out and Mercy cupped his hand. He saw a tiny white scar on Mercy's lip, a very thin, almost invisible vestige, no more than a quarter inch, on the left side.

He wondered how it got there.

Curtis knew, of course, that some men hit women.

That was something he'd never do. Not in a million years.

"Would you like to go downstairs and get some air?" he said.

They went downstairs and stepped out on the terrace. They were alone. Mercy rose up on her toes and just like that, said, "A kiss for the hero." She leaned in.

Curtis kissed her slightly damaged mouth. Mercy moaned. Nothing over the top. It was just a hint but the sound came in spite of itself. She had one honey of a mouth, boy. After the kiss, Curtis looked into her eyes.

"Wise eyes," he thought. Like she knew what she wanted out of life. He touched Mercy's face and said, "I got some of my makeup on you."

Mercy said, "I don't worry." They went inside after the one kiss.

From outside, Curtis heard *potato-potato-potato-potato*. What an ugly sound.

The noise died and Brick entered the party, bat in hand. Beside him was Butch Baxter. Baxter was dressed up in his karate uniform, black belt and all. You could tell he was pissed off. He leaned over Square Head Brick. Brick backed up. Baxter jerked the bat out of Brick's hand and held it tight at his side. For about one second, Curtis thought Baxter was gonna use the fucking thing on Brick.

"Testing! Testing!" The Ambassador stood on the DJ platform. "Hey, everybody. Gather round. It's time to announce winners for best costumes." People shuffled towards the DJ.

"I'll be back in a bit," Curtis said to Mercy.

He squeezed her hand and then joined the other Marines.

"Third-place prize," the Ambassador said, "goes to Greg Brenner." He was an oil rig worker who'd come as The Tin Man. When he accepted his prize - a handmade serape - he made a creaking sound and gave a thumbs up.

Dominique let out a whoop when her table costume took second place. She was awarded a double album of Ecuadorian flute music. Curtis smiled at Pat Bartok and mouthed, "Number one." He'd joined Billy Ray, Bighorn, Duke, D.L. and Brick.

The Marines did a drum roll by stamping their feet.

The Ambassador tapped the microphone. "Tough call," he said. "In first place, ladies and gentlemen... *our lady of the geisha!*" The stunned geisha gave an obnoxious screech before stumbling forward. The Marines' jaws dropped as the geisha wrenched the magnum of champagne from the hands of the Ambassador's aide.

"I've never won anything," the geisha said. The bun atop the geisha's head sat at tilt. She turned to the crowd and held the epic bottle overhead with both hands. "None of you know how much this means to me! You simply *can't* know!"

The party guests reacted with disdain to the saccharine delivery.

The overwrought geisha shouted, *"Arigatō Gozaimasu!"*

The geisha plunked down the champagne and tossed the *Shimada-styled* wig high into the air. It sailed above the gaggle of spectators who milled around like so many eager bridesmaids.

It was goddamn Chetbo who shouted, "Get the fuck back! That bun belongs to me!" He wore a rubber Jimmy Carter mask which didn't fool anybody. The leprechaun's big dick gave him away. The moron was drunk and shirtless. Chetbo made a spectacular diving catch, then leapt up and did a jig with the wig before running it back to the geisha.

Chetbo bellowed, "I caught your hair, Missy!"

The geisha tore the ebony *katsura* from Chetbo's hands.

It slowly dawned on Chetbo and on everyone else; the geisha was the Gunny.

Gunny Alfred yanked the Jimmy Carter mask off Chetbo's head and stood stock still in his kimono. His eyes blinked with contempt. Sergeant Baxter told Chetbo he better go wait outside. Gunny Alfred ordered the Marines to leave the party immediately. Curtis didn't have a chance to get Mercy's number or to even say goodbye. In the Ambassador's driveway, the Gunny called Chetbo a fucking disgrace.

He ordered Sergeant Baxter to have the entire Detachment in his office at zero seven. Baxter asked the Gunny what he wanted to do about Corporal Brick's Harley. Baxter showed him the *swastika*. "That fat-assed leprechaun is my primary concern right now," Gunny

Alfred said. "Have Corporal Brick pilot the bike back to the Marine House and stow it in the garage. I'll deal with him in the morning."

Baxter said, "Aye-aye, Gunny."

The Gunny stormed off toward his Jeep.

To Curtis, the Gunny's priorities didn't make any sense. Chetbo did stupid shit when he was drunk, which was nothing to be proud of, but Brick's *Neo-Nazi homage* was the result of a sustained effort, done while stone cold sober. U.S. Marines swore an oath to protect and defend the Constitution of the United States, for Christ's sake.

A goddamn *swastika* did not jibe with that oath.

The Marines piled into the van. Curtis looked at Chetbo who was already passed out in the back seat. "Sergeant Baxter, mind if I catch a cab? I don't feel like associating with that clown right now," Curtis said.

Baxter glanced at Brick, who kick-started his Harley.

"Which clown do you mean?" Baxter said.

"Either one. I'd rather walk."

"Go."

Curtis turned and looked at the Ambassador's residence from the base of the driveway. He shrugged his shoulders against the cold and wondered if he'd been a bit hasty when he opted for a cab at such a late hour. He touched his face and examined the paint on his fingers.

He thought of Mercy and their single kiss.

As he walked, it dawned on him he'd forgotten his bat at the Ambassador's residence. Too late to go back. He also needed to take a leak. Bad. Near *La Avenida Amazonas,* Curtis found a row of rose bushes. He peed on the roots. He buttoned up his baseball trousers, then plucked a red rose. It smelled nice. He closed his eyes and spent a moment enjoying the scent. That was spoiled by the dark rumble of *potato-potato-potato-potato*. Brick was no more than two blocks away. The sound of his Harley was obnoxious this late at night. Curtis turned the corner, his pretty red rose in hand.

Amazonas was bright and busy.

Street lights and neon lit the action.

Huddled gangs drank booze from bottles.

There was dog shit and vomit all over the place.

Plenty of hookers strutted their stuff, but not a single taxi.

Curtis heard someone shout; *"¡Qué pasa contigo, maldito maricón!"*

The question came from someone in a group of six Ecuadorian men who staggered across the street headed his way. Curtis translated what he'd heard: *"Hey! What's up with you, you fucking faggot!"*

It hit him that he stood solo in the middle of a red-light district well after midnight, amidst a gaggle of whores. On top of that, he, himself, was slathered in garish face paint, wore a flashy major league baseball uniform, and held tight to a delicate flower. Various members of the gang of six called to him again.

Curtis heard, *"¡Oye coño!"* which meant, *"Hey pussy!"*

Someone added, *"¿Quieres jugar béisbol, puta pequeña?"*

That meant, *"You wanna play baseball with us, you little bitch?"*

Then he heard *"¡Ven aca, concha!"* which meant *"Come here, cunt!"*

Curtis had no interest in playing *béisbol* or anything else for that matter.

He turned back the way he'd come. As soon as he rounded the corner, he took off at a sprint and charged toward the hedgerow of rose bushes. Thorns tore a big hole in his left sleeve, along with a large chunk of flesh. After he cleared the rose bushes, Curtis tripped and fell on all fours. He scrambled to his feet and continued to sprint.

Mercy had called him *"un hombre de acción."*

He thought of the five or six Teddy Boys who chased him.

They'd called him a little bitch. One of the pricks had called him a faggot. This was one awful fucking pickle to be in. Curtis knew he was in serious trouble and he was goddamn well afraid. Jesus Christ. He figured honest to God gay guys must be scared shitless all the time. Gay ladies, too, probably. He ran harder.

Curtis heard the rumble of *potato-potato-potato-potato*.

He jetted up an alley and came out at the top of a hill.

Below was Corporal Brick. He slowed for a yellow light.

Curtis hurdled two sets of shrubs as he raced down the embankment.

"Brick! Hold up, Brick! I need a lift!"

He reached the bottom of the hill and was thrilled beyond measure as he leapt right into Brick's goddamn sidecar. "Go, man, go!! We gotta haul ass! Motherfuckers chasing me!" Curtis looked at his arm. It bled from the thorns. He turned to Brick and lied. "Fuckers pulled a knife. Got me pretty good."

As the Teddy Boys crested the hill, Brick ran the red.

The irony of his rescue by a Neo-Nazi dickhead was not lost on Curtis.

He examined his wound. If it left a scar - and from the looks of things it was going to - Curtis knew he would tell a precise lie for the rest of his life. "Knife fight in Ecuador," would become a perpetual fabrication.

Brick coasted back to the Marine House. Guillermo swung open the gate.

Once inside the garage, Brick let the Harley idle. He leaned back in the saddle and methodically cracked his knuckles. "You're so full of shit," Brick said. Then he killed the Harley. "You ever hear this one?" He offered up a ditty for Curtis's benefit.

"Daniel Boone was a man, a big man, but the bear was bigger..."

"Shut your fuckin' mouth," Curtis said.

He knew the jingle. He'd heard it plenty as a kid.

"Whatever, man. Whatever," Brick said, "You should thank me."

Curtis pulled himself out of the sidecar and stepped around to Brick's side. He punched Brick in the face, hard. Landed his jab across the bridge of his nose. Brick's head snapped back. He brought his hands to his face and rocked his shoulders.

Brick moaned and said, "You motherfucker."

Billy Ray's practice pony stared mute and stupid from the corner.

Curtis said, "You wanna finish this, fucko, you know where to find me."

CHAPTER
Fifteen

Gunny Alfred cancelled T.G.I.F.'s.
The suspension of Friday festivities was indefinite.

Pops Dillard said he tried to convince Chetbo not to abandon his Post and to forget about the Ambassador's party. Chetbo backed him up. No one believed them, but the Gunny couldn't prove otherwise, so Pops dodged a bullet.

Chetbo wasn't so lucky.

He was relieved of duty and ordered back to the Fleet.

The Gunny escorted Chetbo's ass to the airport himself.

He put the entire Detachment on restriction for three months.

The Marines were allowed to go on walks or take runs but they had to carry beepers whenever they left the Marine House. As bad as that was, Henry had it worse.

He wrote:

> *"Dear Curt –*
>
> *I got some good news and some bad news. First the good news.*
> *I know this might seem sudden, but me and Brandy are getting married. You'd be the best man, if we weren't gonna end up at a Justice of the Peace. With Bran and me, it feels like we've been around each other forever. Brandy likes <u>not</u> having sex,*

because she was married to such an asshole. Most nights I go over, and we don't do anything much sex wise, maybe some Doritos and the boob tube and we fall asleep. Maybe things will pick up over time. She is hot as hell when she makes the effort, so don't get me wrong. Basically, Bran is very comforting as a person.

Also, Bud kept lookin' to get a deal going, but I told him to just back the fuck off like you said and it seemed to work. Oh, I got one for ya! We went to see Insatiable and when John Holmes started boning Marilyn Chambers, Brandy leaned over and said he must've taken a lesson from Curtis! I told her you're way more handsome than that ugly fucking guy, but not to get her hopes up too high because Johnny Wad's got you beat by five miles in the dick department! Ha! I'll keep you posted about the wedding or about the J.P., which is more likely since Marine Corps Privates don't make shit.

So that's the good news. The bad news is I'm in some hot water over here. I flunked a piss test. My case is pending. It's for using, not for selling. I'll keep you posted but I'm letting you know now because it doesn't look too great because the Marine Corps is cracking down. See you in Mass. Enjoy the ass!

Henratus Fortatus Jones."

"Goddamn Henry," said Curtis.

He decided to take a walk and discovered a flock of sheep hemmed in by cinder blocks about a mile from the Marine House. He asked the shepherd who tended the flock if he could sit and watch them for a while. He was a nice old guy and he said, "*Siéntete libre,*" so Curtis sat on the wall.

The sheep were playful. The lambs acted like dogs. They nosed all around for attention. He scratched a few behind the ears. Paulie would have gotten a kick out of them. Curtis rolled up his sleeves to get sun on his injured arm. He wondered about Henry and what he expected to find back in Westborough with a wife and a kid.

What was he gonna do? Take 'em to the Shrewsbury Drive-in?

He picked a few stalks of tall grass and held them out for the lambs. The bigger sheep butted the little ones out of the way and nibbled the grass themselves. Curtis asked the shepherd, whose name was Jose De La Cruz, if he could bring any special treat just for the lambs. Señor De La Cruz suggested apples so Curtis decided to return to the Marine House and pick up a bunch from the kitchen.

He bagged a dozen and took them back to the corral.

Señor De La Cruz said, "*Debes cortarlas en trozos pequeños de antemano.*"

They sliced the apples into little cubes so the lambs wouldn't eat too much. Jose said that sheep were too greedy for their own good. He said they were like people.

Curtis asked what else did lambs enjoy and he learned sheep ate peanuts and bananas and goddamn daisies when they could get them. Jose placed the apple cubes in two pails and they fed little handfuls to the lambs. The way they ate tickled the palm.

"*Gracias por las manzanas,*" Jose said.

"*Mi placer. Vendré de nuevo otro día,*" Curtis said.

He strolled back to the Marine House gate. He heard a car door slam.

Mercy wore the same purple jacket she'd had on at the party but with a black skirt and no turban. Curtis smiled. Mercy laughed. Curtis jogged over to her. He traced the tiny scar on her lip, looked into her eyes, and said, "*¿Cómo me encontraste?*"

"Christy told me where you live," said Mercy. "Get in my car, Gringo mio."

Curtis hopped in on the passenger side.

Mercy slid behind the wheel.

He took her hand.

"We go. I drive," she said.

Curtis waved his beeper. "I'm on restriction. It's like a house arrest. We all are." Curtis looked toward the Marine House, then back at Mercy. She said, "*Vamos hombre. La vida es muy corta.*" He hadn't come to South America to feed sheep, so Curtis said, "OK, sister. Let's go."

They arrived at a part of the city where the streets were narrow and paved with cobblestones. She parked the car. They got out and walked and Curtis ducked his head against strung up turkeys and pieces of butchered livestock that buzzed with flies.

They held hands in the crowded marketplace and Mercy spoke *Quechua* to the native people who wore felt fedoras and colorful serapes. She pointed out various plants and told Curtis the Indian names for them and extolled the curative properties of the leaves. They ate shrimp ceviche, which was pretty damn good, and there was rice and empanadas, and they drank warm beer from bottles.

Curtis and Mercy sat on a stone fence and savored dessert.

It was a sweet custard flan with one spoon.

Mercy then led him up a hill that overlooked the city.

At the top, Curtis wrapped his arms around her waist and hugged her from behind. Mercy told him that she was headed back to Chile. He asked her how much time they had together and she said, "Just enough, I think."

The hotel had a bellhop stationed at the front entrance but they didn't have bags. Curtis was concerned how Mercy might feel. He said, "We don't have to go in, if you're worried how it looks."

"You are a polite man," she said. "I never trust the polite man." Mercy waited a beat, then laughed. "I don't worry how it looks, Gringo. I know how it looks." She took a hold of his chin, pulled his face straight, and kissed his mouth. "I did not find you to tease you. The *chismosas* here at this hotel mean nothing to me. I know a better place."

About an hour outside the city, Mercy pulled her car onto a dirt road.

They entered a forest and drove on a path. "*Ya estamos,*" she said and stopped. They stepped out of her car and walked hand in hand. The moon shined a blue cast over rocks and roots. A layer of mist made the path shimmer and a slight breeze made the leaves on the trees rustle. Everything was touched by the moonlight.

There was a slope. He could see a hot spring.

They climbed carefully down a stony drop.

The air was misty, private, and warm.

"A secret place," she said.

They kissed.

Mercy stepped out of her shoes, then out of her skirt. Curtis stripped off his clothes. They walked together to the water's edge. Curtis placed his hands on her hips and turned her toward him. They kissed again. Then Curtis knelt.

Mercy stepped wider and lower. Curtis looked up and leaned in. His mouth warmed with her. He wondered why some women were cool, even there, and why some were awkward in how they moved and others were not. He marveled at Mercy, at how she was formed and how she flowed, so irresistible and so warm.

Curtis felt he had Louise Bennett to thank for any pleasure he might provide. She had become frisky in sex and had given him nifty lessons in what felt good and why. Out of respect for both women, he kept those thoughts to himself.

Mercy held him at his shoulders, her fingers tight, and he held his mouth on her. She pushed hard against him, cradled the back of his neck, and made circular motions.

She rode up on her toes and then down, in round circles.

He wanted to be inside her but he waited.

Curtis took her wrists and pulled her down until she knelt with him. They faced each other. She tasted his mouth and his cheeks and his chin. He stood and lifted Mercy so that her legs came up over his hips. She moved higher and put him inside her and they coupled like that for a time. Curtis felt strong. He moved them to the shallow water of the hot springs. He lay Mercy in the soft clay.

He held her wrists over her head and pushed the backs of her hands into the soft mud. They touched where he gripped her wrists and where his quads rubbed at her inner thighs. He positioned himself close against her. He pushed forward slowly and she was warm, and then warmer, deeper.

He held himself still inside her.

They started to move together. And they did this. And they did this.

He slowed. Time passed. Her arms bucked. Curtis let her wrists go free and Mercy moved her hands to his face. He looked into her eyes and as they moved together, he heard a deep and almost forlorn sound, that was low and animal. It came from them both. Their breathing slowed. They kissed. Curtis lay in the warmth beside Mercy.

They dozed in the shallow water.

Soon the moon was gone.

Morning light came up.

She traced his silver chain.

Mercy said, "Catholic boy."

Curtis said, "It's from my mother."

They rinsed in the hot water and then dressed as the sun rose. He asked if he might see her again before she left. Mercy explained that she had family obligations in *La Parva*. There was always more to do in the off-season than the on-season when you ran a family-owned resort. She promised to call when she came back to Quito, perhaps in March or maybe April. Curtis didn't want to leave it like that.

Mercy said, "*Es todo lo que podemos tener por ahora.*"

Curtis translated her words. "That's all we can have for now."

On the drive to the Marine House, they were quiet. When Mercy parked outside the gate, Curtis said, "Mother of Mercy, is this the end of Rico?" He took off his Saint Christopher medal and hung it on her rearview mirror. He tapped it.

"Present. From me to you."

He squeezed her hand, kissed her, and stepped out of the car.

Curtis entered the Marine House alone but with a smile on his face.

He figured any guy who had a night like that with a girl like Mercy should count his goddamn blessings. She was something, boy. He was so happy to have been with her.

He was also damn happy that no one discovered he'd broken curfew.

Chetbo's replacement arrived later that week.

The new Marine was named Gil Parker.

Morale wasn't at an all-time high so the Marines didn't bother to give Corporal Parker a nickname. He was just Parker. Curtis ran him through the paces in the Ready Room, snapped him in on burn, and taught him to play chess.

To pass the time at the Marine House, Curtis smoked cigars.

He read *Princess Daisy*, by Judith Krantz, and read *Playboy* by the pool.

Miss February had great taste in movies. Her favorites were *Midnight Cowboy* and *One Flew Over the Cuckoo's Nest*. There was an interesting article by a journalist who'd hung out in Malibu with David Carradine. He said Carradine never wore shoes, seldom changed his clothes, drove his Ferrari very fast, and didn't believe in seatbelts. Carradine had just directed a film called *Americana*.

In the movie, he fought with a real live wolf in a pit.

To make the fight authentic, he starved the wolf for a couple days. Carradine smeared dog food under his costume and dove head-first into the pit. The black belt skills he developed when he played Caine in *Kung Fu* were the real deal, so Carradine went *mano a mano* with the wolf. He had the scars to prove it.

In Twentynine Palms, things went from bad to worse for Henry.

He'd failed a second urine test and was given a "Big Chicken Dinner." A Big Chicken Dinner was Marine Corps slang for *Bad Conduct Discharge*. BCD discharges were reserved for Marines whose offenses were non-felonious, but serious enough to deem the Marine ineligible for continued military service. Whether it was from tough luck or bad choices, Henry had fucked himself but good.

On the 30th of March there was some excitement, but it was not the kind of excitement the Marines hoped for. In Washington, D.C., some lunatic named John Hinckley shot President Reagan. This wackadoo said he wanted to kill Ronald Reagan in order to impress Jodie Foster, Travis Bickle style. Gunny sounded the recall and Curtis ended up on the roof with Sergeant Baxter.

The assassination attempt on Ronald Reagan didn't attract the same size or type of crowds that John Lennon's death had. In fact, it didn't attract any crowds at all. You never knew how people would react, but Butch Baxter seemed quite agitated by it. The shotgun Baxter had brought to the roof was in its green nylon case. It looked more like a cue stick than a weapon, like something Fast Eddie Felson might carry.

Curtis said, "You a big fan of Ronald Reagan?"

Baxter exhaled, "No. Not particularly."

"So, what's the matter with you?"

Butch rubbed his hand over his face.

"There's nothing the matter with me, man." Baxter kept his eyes locked on the archway at *El Ejido* Park across the street. "That was the President of the United States." They brought their campaign chairs to the edge of the roof. The streets were quiet. Baxter unzipped the shotgun case. He snapped together the cleaning rod and he took out solvent and a rag. He glanced at the empty streets again. "Nothing's gonna happen today." He sat down and squeezed gun oil on the shotgun. Curtis took a seat, too. He fished out a pack of gum and offered the Sergeant a stick. Baxter said no.

"Wanna play chess, Sergeant Baxter?"

"It's not time for that." Baxter ran the rag over the shotgun.

Curtis unwrapped a stick of gum. He crammed it in his mouth.

"Dark, what do you know about Arthur McDuffie?"

Curtis said he didn't know anything about Arthur McDuffie.

Baxter continued to pay close attention to the shotgun.

"You are aware of the Miami riots, are you not?" Baxter said.

"Yeah. I heard about 'em," Curtis said. "I don't know the details."

"You know what the *ouroboros* symbol is?" Baxter said.

Curtis shook his head.

"No clue."

"It's a snake eating its own tail," Baxter said, "It's coiled in a figure eight. And just so you know, Arthur McDuffie was a Lance Corporal in the United States Marine Corps. Before he was beaten to death."

Baxter knew how to get your attention. Curtis had to give him that.

"Oh, that McDuffie," Curtis said. "The speeder the cops killed in Miami."

"Yeah. Right. That McDuffie." You could tell Baxter was pissed off. He put the shotgun back in its case and continued to stare straight ahead for a while. He broke the spell when he looked at the city below and said, "Like the man says, *'You Can't Go Home Again.'*"

"Who says that?" Curtis said. He was thinking of Henry.

"Thomas Wolfe says that," said Baxter. "In the case of Arthur McDuffie, the brother did try going home again. See, Arthur went back to Liberty City after he got out of the Marine Corps. He borrowed a buddy's bright orange Kawasaki. Arthur was gonna ride it from North Dade County to South Dade. Go see a friend. At midnight, story goes, McDuffie ran a red light. Sitting beside that light was one Ira Diggs. Officer Diggs later testified that McDuffie flipped him off, popped a wheelie, and sped off into the night."

Baxter chuckled.

"A high-speed pursuit ensued. Pretty soon, a caravan of cops is chasing Evel Knievel McDuffie all over Miami. At the on ramp of the one-twelve expressway, Arthur pulled over, threw his hands up and yelled, 'I quit, man! I surrender!' It's too late. The cops yank him off the bike, cuff his hands behind his back, drag him to the curb. Then they start taking turns..."

"Taking turns what?" Curtis said.

"Beating the life out of Arthur McDuffie. What the fuck you think?"

Curtis nodded but didn't say anything. It was the first time he'd heard Butch Baxter use a curse word. The guy never swore.

"A massive investigation follows," Baxter said. "The Miami Herald puts out drawings of what these cops did. No pictures. Just drawings of what they had done to the man's skull and how they'd rode up over his Kawasaki with a squad car, trying to make it look like an accident. Trial lasted seven weeks..."

"We heard something on base. Like about dirty cops," Curtis said.

"I was in Miami, and my sister Janice called me. She said, 'They acquitted every damn one of 'em.' My father pulled out a bottle of Jack Daniels. He just started drinking. He knew it was gonna be bad. Janice asked me if I was aware of what was happening over on 62nd street, so I said no, and I went out to take a look."

"You were there?" Curtis said.

"That's what I'm telling you, Dark. I was on leave when the verdicts came down." Butch looked at Curtis, but just for a second. "Took my dad's car and drove 'til it got too crazy. I parked at a store and started walking. People were out, man. Everywhere, elbow to elbow. On the median I saw what looked like rumpled up old clothes. That was a dead white boy, and then I turned and saw a group of black youngsters pulling a driver out of a car. They yanked him out, maybe eight, nine guys. They knocked him down and dragged him off, and then they started using a Miami Herald dispenser, a newspaper dispenser, to bash his head in. Repeatedly bash his head in."

"What did anybody do?" Curtis said.

"A hundred people watched the killing. This is in broad daylight, maybe five o'clock in the afternoon. There was a girl, a white girl, still in the car. These two ladies from the projects, they pulled her out and they sort of tucked her back behind them. They moved her back in the crowd and got her inside some kind of way and hid her, and they saved her. Then someone said, I'll never forget it, someone said, 'We gonna go get the Uncle Toms next.' After all that, I got back to my car. I just sat there and that image struck me; the *ouroboros*. A snake eating its own tail."

Baxter looked Curtis in the eye.

Butch nodded his head, then turned away again.

"I thought, 'America. That's America. The *ouroboros*.'"

Curtis thought of Ronald Reagan. Then of Jimmy Carter.

"Is there anyone who can unfuck America?" Curtis said.

Sergeant Baxter heard the question, but he didn't respond.

A few minutes later, the Gunny secured the recall and they left the roof.

Curtis asked Pat Bartok if the library had a copy of *You Can't Go Home Again* by Thomas Wolfe, and it happened that they did, which was perfect. Less perfect was the news that Pat would rotate back to the states in a few weeks in order to live with Larry in Olde Towne, Alexandria. Pat gave Curtis their new address in Virginia. She wrote it on the back of the business card Kent Trumbo had given him.

Pat said it was too bad Curtis had had to miss the dive trip.

"Yeah," said Curtis. "Couldn't be helped. We were all on restriction. I really hated to miss it." But he didn't. Not really. He was pretty sure Louise Bennett would be on the boat and that would have been awkward as hell. "Maybe next time," he said, even though he knew there wasn't gonna be any next time. He thanked Pat for the book. He said he'd be sure to visit as soon as he got stateside. Pat offered her right hand, and they shook on it.

He joined Shorty in the Marine van.

They passed the Angel of the Apocalypse on their way home.

CHAPTER Sixteen

Ed Asner was interviewed in the April *Playboy*.

Curtis was bored to death with *Playboy Interviews*.

He thought *You Can't Go Home Again* was pretty damn good, though.

It featured a guy named George Webber who wrote a book about his hometown. He drew back the curtains and revealed the dirty laundry of the thinly disguised residents. Everyone in the town read the book and *hated* it. George became *persona non grata*.

Curtis thought Thomas Wolfe was clever.

He told D.L. about the book, but Dan wasn't interested. He was a short-timer. Thirty days and a wake-up. He was anxious to leave Ecuador, return to the States, grab his honorable discharge and hustle back to Quito to open *Sherma-Clean*.

The only thing that interested D.L. was his goddamn carwash.

Duke Sweetzer was even shorter. He was booked on the same flight as Pat Bartok, so Curtis took Duke to the airport. He was surprised to see Christy Keane in the departure lounge. Keane-oh was headed back to D.C., after which she'd be posted to Islamabad.

Curtis would miss all three of them to some degree, but Pat most of all.

In a moment of candor, Curtis wrote to his father and told him that more than anything, he wished he could see this one great girl named Mercy again before it was his turn to leave Ecuador. They'd had such a beautiful night together.

His father wrote back, "Wishing? You should wish in one hand and shit in the other and see which one fills up faster. You said you had a nice night, right? Be happy with that." His father also told Curtis that his mother was "becoming increasingly fragile." Whatever the fuck that meant.

Sweetzer's replacement, Lance Corporal Halstead, was a bit of a smack-ass. He always sniffed around the Gunny and bellowed "Urah!" every time the Gunny ran the Marines at P.T. He loved to go bowling, of all things. Halstead was mopey as hell his first week on Post because there were no bowling alleys in Ecuador.

It was Heath Halstead who found Mercy's card in the mail box outside the Marine House gate. The Marines seldom checked that box because mail typically arrived via the diplomatic pouch. The note from Mercy had been in there for two weeks.

> *My Dear Gringo;*
>
> *I will be in Ecuador in the month of May, for my girlfriend's wedding. Perhaps we could meet me at the Lord Byron's on Monday, the 25 of May, 1981. Would you say 6:00 PM? That would be wonderful to see you then.*
>
> *Maria De Las Mercedes Parea Aragon.*

There was no phone number.

He'd grown used to the idea of not seeing Mercy again but he was delighted to have the chance to be with her. It was fabulous news. It gave him a goal. Curtis decided he'd hit the gym twice a day and hammer out *beaucoup* pull-ups and push-ups so he'd look buff as hell when he got another chance to flex for her.

Exercise helped pass the time.

Curtis enjoyed the routine.

D.L. Sherman told Curtis he had scheduled a spectacular send-off for himself on his final Saturday night in Quito and to hurry home after shift. When Sergeant Baxter came in for the mid-watch and swapped out the duty pistol with Curtis, he said, "Tell Sherman I said, 'Semper Fi,' and to have a few rounds on me."

Baxter stuffed a thick wad of *sucres* into Curtis's shirt pocket.

In the van, Shorty said the Marines had spent the afternoon at the Marine House bar. *"Todos se emborracharon y luego fueron a buscar putas,"* which meant, "After they got drunk, they went out shopping for prostitutes."

Driving up to the Marine House, Shorty wagged his eyebrows. He licked his lips. In English, he said, *"Fucky-fucky tonight!"*

Shorty parked the van, and Curtis took the keys.

"You got a definite knack for saying stupid shit, Shorty."

Curtis climbed the front steps and pushed open the front door.

The Marines sat in folding chairs. They smoked cigars and drank.

A gaggle of semi-nude women were at the base of the living room stairs. They scrambled around on all fours. One was in her bra and panties, but the rest wore combat boots. That's all. Just boots. Curtis guessed the boots were borrowed from the Marines themselves. There were ones, fives, and ten-dollar bills scattered on the floor.

There were also *sucres* of various denominations underfoot.

The girls scooped up the dough.

They stuffed what they grabbed into the purses they dragged around.

At first blush, the near naked ensemble seemed kind of sexy. Upon further scrutiny, the girls looked quite vulnerable. Evidently, the world's oldest profession was a hazardous one. The poor women were in dire need of softer lighting to cover up their startling collection of welts and bruises.

D.L. must have come to the same conclusion. He placed votive candles in strategic spots on the stairs. When he finished, D.L. said, "Now we're cooking." He clapped his hands and called, "OK Chicas, places if you please." The girls ditched their purses and shuffled into a raggedy-assed line.

They mounted the steps with little enthusiasm. "Come on, ladies," D.L. said. "Singing for supper is not required, but you gotta dance for your dollars." At the top of the stairs, the assembled hookers turned to face the Marines.

Some of the women were pale. Others were cold. All were bruised.

The nine sets of kneecaps on display were dirty from the crawls for cash. The stupid boots looked big and clumsy. D.L. killed the overhead lights, but his awful candles didn't help. The mandatory nudity and godawful boots stripped the hookers of their dignity. Every single one of the girls looked like somebody's dejected daughter.

It wasn't sexy.

It was sad.

D.L. eyeballed the girls. "Do proud your pimps. Let's see some pink!" he said. D.L. pressed play on the boom box and Pat Benatar's *Hit Me With Your Best Shot* filled the Marine House. The most modest hooker, the one still dressed in bra and panties, kept her arms in tight and covered up as best she could. The other girls began to swivel their hips, but they were lethargic and self-conscious, and it wasn't just because of the goddamn boots. The girls were embarrassed.

Heath Halstead bellowed, "Urah!"

Curtis looked toward his fellow Marines.

Candlelight flickered against their horny faces.

Gil Parker hoisted his gin glass, spilled booze, and said, "Semper Fi! Do or die!"

Billy Ray wore his dimwit goddamn Stetson so low that he had to squint up from under the brim to see. He slugged whiskey out of a bottle.

Pops slurred his appraisal, "They look just like bare-assed ballerinas!"

Curtis pulled out the wad of *sucres* that Baxter had stuffed in his pocket.

He laid the money on the coffee table, turned his back on the spectacle, and left the room. On his way to the kitchen, Curtis made the sign of the cross. Sometimes when he genuflected, he'd whisper, "Bless me, Father, for I have sinned." That's exactly what Curtis said as he entered the kitchen. He was startled to see Corporal Brick by the refrigerator. He wore a burgundy bathrobe with matching slippers.

Goddamn Square Head had heard Curtis's confession.

He was holding a bag of *Chips Ahoy!*

Brick took a cookie from the bag and dipped it into his glass of milk that sat on the counter. "And how have you sinned, my son?" he said. Brick popped the wet cookie into his mouth and chewed it slowly. He then turned, gathered up his milk and cookies and shuffled out of the kitchen without another word.

Curtis poured himself a glass of water.

He guzzled it down and put the glass in the sink.

Curtis held his arms out straight and examined the backs of his hands. He rotated them and studied his palms. His hands were clean. They just *felt* dirty. He turned off the kitchen light and wandered to his room.

He took off his uniform, hung everything in his closet, and hit the rack without brushing his teeth. In bed, he folded his arms behind his head and closed his eyes.

No doubt the men who bruised those girls had done that shit on purpose.

He wondered about the black and blue contusions on the hookers' arms and legs.

Curtis was so disgusted with himself and his fellow Marines that he didn't get a single goddamn wink of sleep. By first light, when the cocks finally crowed, he'd arrived at two definitive conclusions. He vowed he would never again touch a drop of alcohol. Nor would he buy another whore. With that, he dozed off.

An hour later there was a knock at his door.

D.L. swung it open before Curtis said come in.

"I lit up eight chicks in one night, Yardbird!" D.L. said. "Eight, man! Felt like Hanukkah!" He whistled forward a hooker and said, "Got a nice lil' parting gift for my fellow Masshole. For all you do, this one's for you."

A girl poked her head in under D.L.'s arm.

"Wanna bounce her on your knee?" he said.

"No. No thank you," Curtis said.

"She's clean as a whistle," D.L. said. "Better be. But wear a condom just in case. Wear two." Curtis declined. D.L. threw up his hands in mock surrender. "Hey, you gonna drop me at the airport?" He tapped his watch and said, "T-minus one hour." D.L. slung his arm over the girl's shoulders. "Methinks I got time enough for one final how-do-you-do. Then I gotta pack my shit!"

Curtis looked out the window.

Rain poured down in sheets.

He could see snowcaps on Mount Cotopaxi.

The phone rang in the hall and Curtis heard D.L. answer, "Marine House. Corporal Sherman speaking. How may I help you?" There was a moment of quiet. "What about me, though?" Curtis turned from the window. D.L. said, "Christ, Gunny, I'll miss my flight!" Then he said, "Aye-aye." He slammed the phone down. "That red-headed rat bastard." D.L. reached above the phone and hit the recall switch. He shouted, "All hands fucking recall! Let's move, motherfuckers!"

Baxter radioed a message to the Marines in the van.

He told them the recall was real. It sounded chaotic as hell on his end.

By the time the Marines arrived, a hostile crowd had formed in front of the embassy. The Marine van was pelted with bricks and bottles. The windshield and side windows splintered and cracked and D.L. plowed straight through the boom barrier.

The local guards needed the Marines to help secure the front gates.

In the embassy lobby, Sergeant Baxter gathered the Marines and told them the reason for the recall. The President of Ecuador, Señor Jamie Roldós, the John F. Kennedy of South America, had been killed in a plane crash.

Baxter read one line from the official communiqué.

"The President's airplane fell to the earth causing a fire."

A rumor had spread like wildfire that President Roldós' death had not been an accident at all, but was a political assassination that was engineered by the United States government.

In the Ready Room, the Gunny ordered the Marines to grab shotguns, pistols, flak vests, helmets, and gas masks. Curtis was posted on the roof with D.L., and they hunkered down at the front facing bunkers. The protestors were chucking all sorts of shit at the embassy now. Everything from eggs to iron spikes.

Billy Ray Poore and Pops Dillard were posted on the roof, too, at the rear facing sandbag nests on the far side of the Quonset hut.

Curtis's poncho felt thin against the spitting rain.

He watched as the Ecuadorian militia prepared to deploy mini-tanks. Three squads, maybe thirty soldiers in all, lined up behind the tiny two-man vehicles. Curtis counted a dozen of the small tanks. He told Sherman to put his helmet on. D.L. wrapped a towel around his neck and stuffed it in under his poncho, then peered over the parapet.

"Fucking morons," D.L. said. He bellowed, *"¡Oye! Nosotros no matamos a tu presidente, pendejos!"* Pissed-off people looked up from the streets below.

Curtis grabbed D.L. by the elbow and told him to cut the shit.

The rain had slowed enough for D.L. to light a smoke.

Curtis watched the melee in the street below.

He saw a woman cradle a man in her arms.

The guy's face was a bloody pulp.

They looked like Michelangelo's goddamn *Pieta*.

Curtis thought of Montgomery Clift and Liz Taylor after Monty had had a horrible car accident. The car was wrapped around a tree and he was pinned under the steering wheel. Elizabeth Taylor climbed through the back window and managed to get to Monty. She brushed broken glass off his face and saw he couldn't breathe. She jammed two fingers between his ruined lips, then down his throat. She plucked out his two front teeth that had been lodged in his airway. Liz saved Monty's life.

Clift had the teeth mounted into a necklace for her.

Liz Taylor wore Monty's incisors to the *Raintree County* wrap party.

Curtis heard the unique pop-pop-pop noise that signaled the launch of projectiles. He was pretty sure he'd heard it. He judged it came from Billy Ray's side but it was still windy and rainy so it was hard to tell. The sound was distorted.

Curtis waited for confirmation from Billy Ray but none came.

He heard it twice more. Somebody had fired something for sure.

"I'm gonna check with Billy Ray," Curtis said to D.L. He was soaked under his poncho. Most of it sweat. He jogged low past the Quonset hut, looked left and saw that Billy had already donned his gas mask and was ensconced in his own comfortable little world enjoying the show.

Curtis peered over the eaves.

Mini-tanks fired teargas canisters into the crowd.

Protestors fled en masse and thick clouds of teargas wafted skyward in toxic waves. Curtis shouted, "Okie, what the fuck?" He leapt up from the bunker and bolted toward D.L.'s blindside position. He called, "Gas! Gas! Gas! Don and clear!"

The roiling cloud of acrid white smoke reached the roof. Influenced by the fluctuating wind, it dropped quick and engulfed both Marines as they attempted to pull their gas masks from their utility belts. Curtis managed to secure his mask and breathe. No gas leaked in. D.L. couldn't see. He had trouble making a seal. Curtis snapped the clasps under Dan's chin, pumped his shoulder and shouted, "Breathe!"

They crossed the roof to Pops, who had puked into his gas mask.

Curtis tugged the seal loose and removed the mask. D.L. tossed him the towel from around his neck and Curtis doused it from Pops's canteen. He splashed water over Pops's face, rinsed the mask and strapped the stinking rubber in place.

He lifted Pops in a fireman's carry and moved clear of the gas.

Curtis lay Pops down against the sandbags. Pops shot him a weak thumbs up.

Baxter was on the roof now having checked status with the Ecuadorian militia.

His radio crackled and he made a loop the loop motion. Baxter shook off his flak jacket, removed his helmet and mopped sweat from his brow. "Pretty much a wrap," he said. He focused on Billy Ray. "Are you totally unaware of proper protocol, Okie, concerning call signal and use in a gas attack?" It was a rhetorical question.

Curtis and D.L. left Billy Ray to the ass chewing they knew he was about to receive. They walked to the front-facing bunker and looked down. The street was littered with rocks and bricks and shattered glass. The cops chased after a few stragglers, but the gas had done the trick. The show was over.

D.L. pulled off his gas mask and spit.

Curtis peered down at the trash in the embassy courtyard.

He heard a kind of rustling toward the top of the tallest tree.

D.L. glanced at his watch and said, "I'm supposed to be on a plane right now." Without warning his head snapped back. Then his knees buckled and he landed flat on his ass. D.L. sat still with his legs splayed. His hands covered both of his eyes like a corny-assed kid playing peek-a-boo. Blood leaked through his fingers and streamed heavily down the side of his face.

It took Curtis a minute to figure it out.

The poor fucking guy had been shot in the head.

CHAPTER Seventeen

AMERICA SMELLED LIKE coffee and doughnuts, and it wasn't very crowded.

Curtis hoisted his olive green duffle bag. He passed a sleepy janitor who buffed linoleum side-to-side, clicking like a metronome. The cashier at the Quantico Greyhound terminal wore a baseball cap with the flag of Puerto Rico on it. His radio played *Another One Bites the Dust*. Curtis told his itinerary to the clerk and asked for his ticket in Spanish. The man was sullen when he hit the change button.

"I speak English," he said.

The trip was a straight shot. 95 North to the 495.

He got off the bus at the King Street station in Alexandria and bought a map of Olde Towne. Pat's house wasn't hard to find. It was a two-story brick number at the corner of North Columbus and Queen. Curtis knocked at the door of #308.

He heard a dog yip.

Christy Keane opened the door, the very same Keane-oh who'd taken him to see *Big Red's* show at the sad-assed strip joint back in Quito. Christy leapt into Curtis's arms and wrapped her legs around his waist. She was a tiny woman with a zealous tongue.

The kiss was deep and unexpected. Curtis thought it insincere.

Pat said, "You made it!"

A tiny Tibetan spaniel whimpered while turning circles at Pat's feet.

Out of the corner of his mouth, Curtis stammered, "I did do." Christy turned her face to Pat and said "Yum!" She jumped off and grabbed hold of Curtis's arm in a way that suggested he had come to visit her and not Pat. She whispered, *"So fucking good to see you."* Curtis didn't understand why she would make such a claim. After *Big Red's* pathetic performance in Quito, they'd gone back to Keane-oh's apartment.

They'd fucked without focus, then taken a shower.

In the morning they'd had pineapple juice. A week later, they'd done it again. Same juice. They hadn't liked each other that much. In Ecuador he really hadn't known how to react to Christy, and he really didn't know how to react to her now.

So, he asked, "What are you doing here?"

And she said, "Studying Urdu."

As if that were obvious.

Keane-oh turned to Pat and said, "Thanks for these." She hefted her book bag and said, "I'll be back tomorrow." Christy smiled at Curtis, punched him playfully on the arm and disappeared out the front door.

Larry called from upstairs, asking, "Is he here?"

Pat called back, "He is here, Larry, come on down."

The house was furnished with elegant artifacts from Pat's career in the Foreign Service. Pat and her late husband Jake had purchased the house sight unseen. They had a ton of incredibly pretty artwork. There were ornate Persian rugs everywhere and a half-dozen exotic footstools made of leather that you could sit on.

It was like a cozy museum, where you could park your ass on the art.

Curtis asked about the pumpkin-colored walls in the dining room.

Pat had done them with her girls and Jake, and they'd used sponges to get the mottled effect. She looked a little wistful as she told him. Curtis guessed she missed Jake. Pat showed him a black and white photo where Jake stood on the deck of a great big sailboat. He looked like a more handsome version of Sterling Hayden.

Larry took forever to show. It made the conversation awkward between Curtis and Pat, because Curtis expected to be interrupted by Larry at any moment, so he looked over his shoulder at the staircase every other word.

The yip-yappy dog didn't help much either.

When Larry finally showed, he yawned and announced, "I'm bushed." Then he slung a proprietary arm over Pat's shoulders and tugged her to his side of the couch. He gave her a kiss.

Pat said, "How is the Marine who was wounded doing?"

"It was a .22, so it wasn't as bad as it could have been. A small caliber," Curtis said. It was the same caliber as Henry's piece of crap rifle that Curtis had used to shoot the crow. "D.L. lost his left eye for sure, but they don't know about his right eye yet, because the bullet cut through sideways. He's in Bethesda Naval Hospital."

"I'm so sorry," Pat said. Curtis could tell she meant it.

"He'll get great care," Larry said.

"We took off in an evac helicopter but we couldn't get the right help in Quito," Curtis said. "Panama sent a C-130, and we flew to Quantico. I'm gonna let the Shermans know that it was Sergeant Baxter who knew to bandage up both eyes and to keep 'em both shut. The medics said that was a good move. So, we'll see. Hopefully..."

"How long will you be stateside?" Larry said.

"The Supply Sergeant at Quantico, he's a good guy named Shipley. He pushed through ten days leave, so I still have a week." Curtis indicated the seabag by the door. "Shipley got it all squared away. New uniform issue, dough for civvies and TDY pay. I cashed out at S-1, so..."

Pat said, "You can stay here."

Curtis looked to Larry, wondering what he had to say.

"Come and go as you please," Larry said. "Call this home base."

That surprised Curtis. Maybe this goddamn Larry wasn't so bad after all.

"Any plans to visit your parents?" Pat said.

"Yeah. I'm gonna head up to Mass and see 'em. I'd also like to visit Sergeant Trumbo." He pulled Amber's card out of his wallet. "I called his girl. His dormitory is Leonard Hall at American University." Pat said that American was a forty-five-minute drive, and he'd be welcome to borrow Nicole's car.

Larry yawned again and said, "That's settled. Shall we?"

Before he knew it, they showed him the guest room and said goodnight. Curtis had to admit that Pat seemed happy. She held hands with Larry, and they'd headed for bed. From the looks of things, they were quite compatible.

He wondered how Mercy was doing.

Because of the riot and how everything had gone down, Curtis missed their date at Lord Byron's in Quito. He'd been hooked in a web seat, his back against the fuselage of a C-130, as he escorted D.L. Sherman on his medevac to the states.

It looked like seeing Mercy again just wasn't meant to be.

Curtis hit the guest room light and turned toward sleep.

In the morning, he had coffee with Pat.

She gave him the keys to Nicole's Toyota.

His first stop was the Chamber of Commerce on King Street. Curtis bought a street guide for the D.C. metropolitan area, and a very kind woman behind the counter helped him map out directions with a highlighter.

At American University, there were people strolling around the campus in international attire - students and professors in flowing robes and turbans and beaded hats with wild patterns. The buildings weren't numbered, they were named; *The Graydon Center, The Bender Library, The School of International Service*. The granite pillars reminded Curtis of Faber College in *Animal House*.

People tossed frisbees and played guitars.

Inside Leonard Hall, the student clerk at the front desk bent her head to the resident check list. "Trumbo, Trumbo, Trumbo..." she said, "Kent Trumbo. Sixth floor, room 614." Curtis thanked her. He wondered how smart a person had to be to get into a college like this. Inside the elevator, Curtis pumped his biceps in front of the mirror. His muscles might not help on a test, but they had to count for something.

At the sixth floor, he stepped out and read the sign.

"Welcome to Leonard! Kent Trumbo, R.A. Room 614. Come rap!"

He assumed an R.A. would be like the Senior Sergeant on a fire team.

There were horns and people shouted outside, but the hall itself was quiet.

A pencil sketch was taped to the Men's room door. It said, "The Sixth Floor Coalition," and showed the cartoon faces of a half dozen rats, all smoking cigars. Curtis took out Shipley's new notepad and wrote down "Coalition."

Then he knocked at Trumbo's door.

No one answered. He left a note.

Outside, Curtis climbed a hill that led back to the main quad.

Someone in boots shouted, "Professor Bawa!" and jogged up to a black man who wore a swirly purple caftan. They headed into *The School of International Service*. Curtis followed. Coffee and candy bars were on sale inside. Beside the coffee pot were paper cups. Beside the cups was a Chock-Full O' Nuts can with a slit in its yellow lid.

Curtis poured coffee and picked up a Snickers.

He didn't put any money in the can - he just jiggled it - and then waltzed off with the stolen goods. He wandered over to the outdoor amphitheater. He sipped at his coffee and scanned the crowd. He unwrapped the Snickers, bit and chewed. Curtis didn't catch the bearded speaker's name, but he heard him ask the assembled students, "What type of thinkers do you consider yourselves to be?"

The speaker wanted to know how they reacted to rain.

Did they watch rivulets trickle down fogged panes of glass only to become disenchanted or did they find poetry in each drop and feel inspiration pouring from the clouds? It seemed like a silly question. Curtis tossed the coffee and moved on.

Inside the bookstore, a woman with a *Dotty* name tag asked if he needed help.

She reminded Curtis of Louise Bennett.

"Just browsing," said Curtis. He picked up an econ textbook and opened it to the middle. There was a complex looking equation with a delta symbol. He read, "Expression translates to change in quantity demanded."

He continued to page through and spotted several more preposterous looking formulas that he couldn't make heads or tails of. The equations made him nervous.

Curtis asked Dotty, "You got anything by Thomas Wolfe?"

He returned to Trumbo's room, carrying *Look Homeward, Angel*.

Lugging the big book helped him feel a little less out of place. Curtis rapped on Trumbo's door. Kent opened it and said, "Curtis B. Dark, as I live and breathe. I got your note. Get on in here!" His hair was longer. Not long, but longer. The goddamn guy was as friendly as ever. He invited Curtis to sit on the couch and offered a cup of Sanka.

Trumbo sat down and asked about what had gone down on the embassy roof. Curtis told him how it had been Billy Ray Poore who'd killed the sniper - firing quick draw, no less - and from the hip. The fucking guy turned out to be a real cowboy. The sniper had climbed over the fence using the low hanging branches and shimmied to the top and then taken his single goddamn potshot.

"I told Gunny about those fucking trees," Curtis said.

"Gotta let that go, Dark. The genie's out of the bottle," Trumbo said.

"It was so strange, man. I watched Billy Ray shoot him. I watched the body fall out of the tree. Bodies don't bounce and roll like they do in the movies. They land, cripes, like a bag of trash with an awful splat. Seams split or leak but there's no bounce. The guy landed smack outside the fence. This Ecuadorian soldier who was wearing a snow-white helmet walked over and kicked him in the head."

It had sounded hollow, like the soldier had kicked a cantaloupe.

"I tell you, Kent, it was all so fucking unnecessary. So damn ridiculous."

Curtis had heard more scuttlebutt from Shipley later in Quantico. Bighorn, Brick, Parker and Halstead's ranks would remain the same because they hadn't been on the roof. All the topside Marines were credited for *repelling an armed attack*, for Christ's sake. "Every swinging dick on the roof received a meritorious promotion!" he said.

Curtis shrugged in disbelief.

He was now a Corporal for the fireman's carry.

Billy Ray was now a Corporal for shooting the sniper.

D.L. Sherman was now a Sergeant for losing his left eye.

Butch Baxter was now a Staff Sergeant for performing first aid.

Even Pops got promoted - he was a Sergeant again – for doing nothing.

"A bumper crop of bootleg heroes," Curtis said. "What a load of horseshit."

Trumbo sipped his Sanka like he'd been there and done that. He chewed at his bottom lip, then said, "Let's eat." On the way to the chow hall, Trumbo waved to lots of students and gave plenty of high fives. Curtis kept his hands in his pockets. Trumbo said, "Look, Dark, you can consider the Marine Corps as a chapter in your life. It's not the whole story." That sounded like a good way to think about things.

Curtis told Trumbo how he'd been mystified by the econ text in the bookstore.

"The objective," Trumbo said, "is to understand the course content *after* you've taken the class, not *before*, and sometimes not even then!" He clapped Curtis on the back. He said, "Don't sweat it, Dark."

Curtis crooked his chin toward a group of students.

"But how smart are these people? They gotta be pretty bright."

"Unless you're pre-med, it ain't brain surgery," Trumbo said.

Curtis had no real concept of how college worked, but it seemed like Kent Trumbo fit in just fine. He had a goddamn fiancée. He was a resident advisor. He had plenty of friends and the guy was enrolled in actual college courses. Kent lived a life beyond the Marine Corps, and he hadn't done it by moving backasswards like Henry had done. That sap was back in Westborough doing nothing.

You can't go home again, for Christ's sake.

The cafeteria in *The Graydon Center* was about as large as the chow hall at Quantico. It was crowded. Trumbo was popular. He introduced Curtis to Rudolph Habesch, who said, "Please be taking a chair and joining with me."

Trumbo said, "Nice fruit salad, Dark. You good with that?"

"Sure, Kent," said Curtis. Trumbo went off to stand in line.

Curtis spun a chair around and faced Rudolph Habesch.

"I hail from the Jordan. Nice to meet you."

Curtis knew Amman was the capital.

He asked Rudy if he liked American movies.

"I do. Yes. Very much so. Do you enjoy being American soldier?"

Curtis said, "I'm a Marine, man. There's a big fucking difference."

As soon as he said it, he felt foolish, but he also felt it gave him a leg up. Trumbo returned with the fruit salads and two club sodas. Curtis said, "Thank you, Kent," and he ate his grapes.

Rudy said to Trumbo, "What does this word, *'Malapropism,'* signify?"

"A malapropism?" Kent said. "OK, a malapropism is a word that sounds very close to the correct word, but it isn't right. Like if I were to say, *'I danced a flamingo.'*"

"What's wrong with that?" Curtis said.

"It's *flamenco,*" Trumbo said, "not *flamingo*. Dance versus bird." He sprinkled salt onto a chunk of watermelon. "Malapropisms can be amusing. I kind of like them," he said and laughed. "What I don't like are expressions that obscure the meaning of a thing. Labels that are imprecise or misleading. *'The Final Solution,'* for example. Exactly the wrong connotation. Of course, that was by design."

What charmed Curtis most about Trumbo was that he didn't lord it over you. Sure, he knew his way around college and he knew what a word meant and where it came from, too, but his energy and over-all demeanor made going to college seem doable, if you had guts enough to give it a try.

Trumbo looked at his watch.

"Finish your fruit, Dark. We've got somewhere to be. You'll appreciate this."

They sat in the front row of the University theatre.

The movie was called, *Démanty noci,* which meant *Diamonds of the Night*.

It was the first movie Curtis ever saw with subtitles. It started off with a bang. Two boys leapt from a prison train and bolted into the woods. They were shot at. They wore lousy prison shoes in ice and snow, and you could tell they were starving.

The more they ran, the more it felt like the whole goddamn world was on the hunt for them. They had to duck and hide and try to climb icy hills. They were all cut up. Their hands and feet bled and later, when they scrounged a loaf of bread, they couldn't chew it because their teeth and gums were too weak from hunger.

Then, when you think they're about to catch a break, they're betrayed by the villagers and turned over to a group of toothless old bastards from a hunting party. The old geezers force the boys to put up their hands and tell them to turn around and face a blood-stained wall. All the boys can do is wince and wait.

They know they're going to die.

One old bastard raises his arm and commands, "Ready! Aim! Fire!"

The first boy slumps against the wall and the other one pees his pants.

But the hunting party didn't fire. The fuckers lower their rifles and start to chuckle and then they start to sing and they clap each other on the back like they've had their fun and they're done for the day. The two boys begin to back away, one step at a time. They can't believe it. They're not full of holes. They're not dying. They're not dead. Finally, they turn and run for the woods.

It plays out like a goddamn miracle - because they live.

When the house lights came up, the audience was hushed and quiet.

A muscular guy in glasses, who was maybe fifty-five stepped onto the stage.

Trumbo said, "That's Arnošt Lustig, man. He lived that. He wrote the movie." Lustig waved in a way that looked humble and the students let loose with whistles and cheers. Curtis joined the applause. It was clear that the audience not only dug the movie, but that the whistles and cheers were for Arnošt himself.

"Lustig is *everybody's* favorite professor," Trumbo said.

Students asked about everything during the Q & A.

Curtis was amazed. It was like there were no taboos.

One girl asked if the two boys in the movie were virgins.

It seemed as if everyone in the auditorium had a question for Arnošt, and he answered each one with a story. Curtis learned of creeps named Streicher and Heydrich and Himmler and about places like Babi Yar and Sobibor. Arnošt told of Auschwitz and Eichmann. He was the single most interesting person Curtis had ever listened to.

After his last story, Arnošt looked at his watch. In his thick Czechoslovakian accent, he said, "Sank you. Sis was marvelous. Now we must go home to sleep in our beds." He came off the stage. Students milled around to say goodnight.

"I gotta meet that guy," Curtis said.

"Of course, Dark. That's why we're here," Trumbo said.

When it was his turn, Curtis said, "I admired your picture very much."

Arnošt said, "Tell me what was in sis picture to admire?"

Curtis thought for a minute.

"Did you ever see *Die! Die! My Darling!*, Mr. Lustig?"

"Oh yes. Vis Tallulah Bankhead."

"Well, Sir," Curtis said, "There are hundreds of movies where a person gets abducted, and then they spend the entire movie doing foolish things. But when Stephanie Powers gets kidnapped by Tallulah Bankhead, she keeps on hatching plans to escape no matter what. She does what a person would actually do. She tries really hard to get out of it. In your movie, everything those boys did looked like what boys would *actually do* in a situation like that. Your movie looked like the truth, Sir. Authentic, like."

"Sis commentary, I appreciate," Arnošt said. "You see, sis is what the artist must endeavor to do - create a world and remain true to sis conception. If sis film accomplishes it, I am happy." Arnošt slapped Curtis on his bicep. He said, "I see strength." He touched Curtis on his temple, "And a second strength." He raised his right index finger and said, "In life, to live with dignity, we must have both. So, I salute you."

It was the most inspiring thing anybody had ever said to Curtis.

Curtis told Arnošt it was very great to meet him, and then he took his leave. He wanted to give Kent some time alone with his favorite professor. Outside, Curtis thought about Arnošt's movie and how the guy had outfoxed the Nazis and lived to write about it. Curtis liked *Démanty noci* even better than *The Sand Pebbles*, and better than *The Devil at Four O'Clock*, and, Christ, maybe even as much as *The Poseidon Adventure*. In all his favorite movies, the hero died at the end, but they'd survived in *Diamonds of the Night*.

Maybe the hero didn't have to die at the end.

Just look at Arnošt Lustig.

That goddamn guy was full of life.

When Trumbo came outside, Curtis pumped his hand.

"I'll tell you this, Kent. If guys like Arnošt Lustig teach college, count me in."

CHAPTER
Eighteen

P AT SAID HE could take Nicole's car home to Westborough. Curtis thanked her but took the bus instead.

That was better. It gave him a chance to think about college.

When Arnošt was asked by that girl whether the boys in *Démanty noci* were virgins, he had said, "At fourteen going on fifteen my father asked me, 'Have you been vis a woman?' and I said, 'No father, leave me alone.' One week later, I went to see a prostitute and she asked, 'Have you been vis a woman, boy?' and I told her, 'No, but I know everything.' I didn't like it. I did it for my father. So, in sis movie, yes, one was a virgin. The other was not."

Curtis had asked Paulie about his babysitter once, a long time ago. His brother said, "Oh, Gabby is really nice. We sat together on the couch and read. That was fun. I really liked her. Something about Gabby smells naughty." Paulie was eight at the time. Curtis wasn't sorry his brother had missed out on prostitutes, but it would have been terrific if he could have had one night to make love to a special girl.

A night like he'd had with Mercy.

Paulie would have loved girls. He'd have treated them great, boy.

The bus dropped Curtis off at West Meadow Plaza near the junction of Routes Nine and One-Thirty-Five. The hometown sun felt good on his face. Instead of hitching, Curtis hoofed it from there. He turned up King's Grant Road and reached his parents' house. Ronald Dark was in the driveway washing his Ford pick-up truck.

Ronald turned and saw Curtis, then smiled around his cigarette. "Jesus H. Christ. The prodigal returns." Ronald shut off the hose and grabbed a towel. "Christ kid, you got big," he said, and he slapped Curtis on both shoulders. "Those are some arms, boy. You look good, Sam." Curtis smiled. He liked that his dad called him Sam sometimes.

He said, "Thanks, Dad," and they hugged.

"What'd you do, walk from Ecuador?"

"Just the last mile."

"Well, Christ."

"Yeah…"

Ronald pulled out his pack of Chesterfields, and said, "You're old enough. You want one of these bastards?" Curtis said no, so Ronald put the cigarettes away. He said, "I got one for you. We had a chance to see Kenny Rogers in Boston with the Stepanians, but your mother says to Cowie, 'No, no, no, we gotta stay home.' I told Lila-Ruth, 'Come on, we got nothing planned.' She's been refusing to do very much lately, so I encourage her, but tonight she insisted we stay in and next thing you know, here you are."

Ronald shrugged his shoulders, then frowned.

"She'll make something mystical out of it. 'Everything happens for a reason,' or some damn thing." Ronald then put his fist against Curtis's chin in a chip off the old block gesture. "You really got big."

"How 'bout you, Dad?"

"How 'bout me, what?"

"Do you believe everything happens for a reason?"

"For a reason? Nah. But I believe everythin' happens."

Inside the house, Curtis felt awkward around his mother. He hoped she wouldn't ask after the Saint Christopher he'd given to Mercy. As it turned out, Lila-Ruth didn't ask after very much at all. She was boney as hell when Curtis hugged her, and she just sort of wrung her hands and didn't look him in the eye. She asked if Curtis was hungry.

Lila-Ruth looked like she was worried about the answer.

Curtis said, "I'm fine, Ma."

He went upstairs to his old room.

His *Death Wish* poster was still on the wall.

Curtis took only a few things out of his seabag.

He knew already he wasn't going to stay very long.

Later that night, Curtis watched his parents watch television.

During a repeat of *Quincy,* Lila-Ruth said that the actor playing the ambulance driver was inept at performing C.P.R. "By bending his elbows during the compressions, the victim's heart would fail to receive adequate stimulation," she said.

"I seen this one," Ronald said. "The guy dies. Maybe that's why."

During the commercial breaks, his parents' heads swiveled in his direction. Lila-Ruth told Curtis that he seemed more worldly. Ronald said that Curtis had gotten to be a big bastard. Ronald asked Curtis how much he was bench pressing, but the commercials ended and their heads swiveled back. After the show, Ronald stood and waved Curtis into the dining room. Ronald sat at the head of the table. He rolled up his cuff and crooked his arm. "Let's see about this, boy."

Curtis sat in the chair to Ronald's right.

He placed his elbow on the table.

He met his father's hand.

Palm to palm.

"Call it, kid."

Curtis nodded.

They adjusted their fingers.

Curtis said, "Ready... set... go!"

In one conclusive pull - non-stop and straight down - Curtis pinned his father's knuckles to the butter-colored tablecloth. It was over in an instant, which surprised them both. It was that definitive. Ronald pulled his hand free – offered a sad smile - then stood.

He turned and left the room.

Later, Curtis lay awake in his boyhood bed. He listened to the trains pass under the Milk Street Bridge. He wished he'd thought to let his father win, like how Ronald used to let him win, when Curtis was a kid.

In the morning, he put on his new set of Dress Blues, with the Corporal chevrons now on his sleeves and the new blood stripe that marked his trousers. Ronald let him use his truck. Lila-Ruth was still in bed when Curtis left the house. He turned right on Milk Street and passed Frankie Ferrandino's house. Frankie could draw like a madman.

Kids used to pay Frankie a quarter for superhero sketches at school. Curtis passed Village Hardware and then the Fire Department. VFW Post 9013 stood right beside The Dairy Queen, like always.

Through the window at Penny's Pizzeria, Curtis saw Penny serve a grinder.

Near Henry's house, Curtis spotted Roger Green and his golden retriever, Big Goldie. The dog was on its back enjoying a belly scratch. Old Lady Bostwick rounded the corner on Cottage Street. She was carrying a CVS bag and walked with her head down, like she'd done since Curtis was a child.

Curtis parked Ronald's truck and switched off the ignition.

Sergeant Mickey Voutas rolled up Cottage Street in his police cruiser from the opposite direction. He drove at a children-at-play pace. Voutas pulled to the curb and waved at Roger who ambled over to the cop car and leaned in at the window.

Roger threw his head back and laughed. Mickey Voutas was a funny guy.

Curtis stepped from the truck, just as Big Goldie gave Roger the slip.

The dog bounded across Henry's lawn and made a beeline for Old Lady Bostwick. Goldie startled the old lady, and she swatted at him with her plastic bag. Goldie got excited and grabbed her red and white sack in his mouth.

Old Lady Bostwick said, "Gimme that, you son of a bitch," and yanked the bag free. She placed it on top of her head, attempting to protect her pharmaceuticals from the dog. Big Goldie wagged his tail, then launched forward.

He planted his front paws on the old woman's shoulders and began to lick her forehead and gnaw at the bottom of the bag that now rested atop Mrs. Bostwick's head. Bostwick managed to shrug the dog's paws off her tiny shoulders and get them down to her waist. From there, Big Goldie started a full hump assault against the old woman.

His awkward paws grabbed her from the front.

Goldie's missionary thrusts were backwards for a dog.

Roger remained oblivious as Mickey Voutas remained hilarious.

Old Lady Bostwick started to pinwheel her arms and tilt backwards.

As she reached her tipping point, the plastic bag flew from her hand. It bounced off the lowest branch of the big bark elm in Henry's front yard, just a few feet above her head. Silver stars, the kind a grade school teacher might stick to a good pupil's forehead, sprang from a plastic box and rained down upon the stupefied woman, who was now slumped at the base of Henry's tree.

Goldie woofed and whined at the glittery display.

Roger remained absorbed in his good-time guffaws beside the patrol car.

When Old Lady Bostwick screamed, "I'm eighty-four! I'm gonna shoot your stupid dog in his bright red pecker! I'll shoot him! I'll shoot!" Sergeant Voutas tapped Roger's elbow and pointed at Big Goldie.

Roger gasped, then shuffled over and grabbed hold of Big Goldie's leash.

Curtis got to Old Lady Bostwick and helped the angry woman to her feet. She turned to Curtis and complained bitterly. "That dog humps on everything," she said, "I've seen it go after a pumpkin."

Roger tugged at Big Goldie's leash.

"I can't do everything," he said and bolted.

"Are you alright, Mrs. Bostwick?" Curtis said.

Arms akimbo now, Old Lady Bostwick glared after Roger.

She watched as he and Goldie took the nearest corner at Pine Street.

"Even as a kid, Roger was a turd. God-awful paperboy, always dirty and all the time tugging at his repugnant dogs with their cheeky hard-ons." Mrs. Bostwick looked up at Curtis and asked, "Are you Jimmy Day?"

"Curtis Dark."
"Juniper Circle?"
"King's Grant Road."
Mickey Voutas backed up slowly.
He pulled a quiet U-turn before duplicating Roger's Pine Street escape.
"Voutas," spat Old Lady Bostwick.
Curtis asked if there was anything he could do.
Mrs. Bostwick said, "Your father climbs telephone poles, and you used to play around here with the Fonda kid. You're in the Army now, I see. The Fonda kid was, too. Got skinny for a while. Not anymore."
"We joined the Marines together, Mrs. Bostwick."
"He brought back a girl with big hair."
"I haven't met her, yet."
"Big hair for a small town."
Mrs. Bostwick put up her right hand as if she were about to give testimony. Then she touched Curtis on his forearm and tapped twice. "I remember. You lost your brother." She licked her lips and said, "Welcome home, honey bunch." She gave his arm a final squeeze, then put her head down and went the way of Mickey Voutas.
Curtis walked around to the back of the Fonda house.
He checked out his reflection in the window. He'd worn his Blues for dramatic effect. He thought of Bruce Dern in *Coming Home*. Curtis loved Bruce Dern. He rapped on the door and adjusted his cover. He knocked again and Henry appeared behind the screen door. His hairline had receded and he wore an alarming moustache.
He'd gained, at a guess, some thirty pounds.
Henry flung open the door.
He said, "Baygo!"
"How the heck are you, Fondue?"
"Married! Got fucking fat!" Henry said.
"I can't even believe it. How's that going?" Curtis said.
"Bowl of fucking cherries, Baygo." They both laughed to the point of tears. One said, "Holy smokes," and the other said, "Jesus

Christ." They both said, "Westborough." Henry wiped his eyes and said, "Come on in, Darkie, and meet the lovely…"

Henry's mother was surprised they spoke Spanish in Ecuador.

Brandy said, "Good God, Anna, of course they do. South America? They speak Spanish in all of those places down there. Columbia, Venezuela, Brazil." Brandy gave Curtis a *rubes will be rubes* look that hinted at a cosmopolitan solidarity.

It was strange to watch Henry cut up food for a five-year-old. He wondered how Henry felt about adopting this pretty little girl, having been adopted himself. Henry and Tiffany seemed to like each other. It was harder to tell with Henry and Brandy.

They were not what you'd call patient with one another.

Brandy's hair *was* big. It was dyed an adamant red. She reminded Curtis of someone, but he couldn't put his finger on who. He puzzled over that until it hit him halfway through his second helping of Mrs. Fonda's outstanding lasagna. Brandy's doppelganger was Keane-oh's favorite stripper – Big Red.

Brandy and *La Roja Grande* looked a helluva lot alike.

Slurred speech brought Curtis back from his daydream. Leland Fonda said, "I'd always wished you boys woulda come over to Bay State together in your blue uniforms." He jerked his thumb at Curtis. "And that you woulda said to my foreman, 'We want to see our father.'" Mr. Fonda slugged his beer.

Henry rolled his eyes and leaned over to Curtis.

He whispered, "Brandy found the Polaroids you sent. We got to talkin'."

Curtis cut his eyes to Brandy, who stopped wiping her daughter's fingers. She looked over at Henry and then briefly locked eyes with Curtis. He wasn't sure what to make of her. For Henry's sake, he wanted to like her. The Polaroids in question (which Curtis had sent to Henry a few weeks after his arrival in Ecuador) had close-ups of him *in flagrante delicto,* that had been snapped by D.L. Sherman on the sly. D.L. had taped the pix to the refrigerator in the Marine House after a raucous T.G.I.F.

Anna Fonda said, "Careful with dessert," as she set down two hot pies.

Brandy put a dollop of Cool Whip on Curtis's piece. Henry wolfed a forkful. A second later he grabbed some more. "Leave that alone," Brandy frowned, "and don't eat so fast." She turned to Curtis and asked, "Why does he eat so fast?" Curtis shrugged and said, "He always ate kind of quick." Then Henry stole another chunk of pie.

"That's his!" Brandy said.

"Who are you, the pie police?" Henry said.

Anna Fonda let Brandy know that Henry liked pie.

"Liking pie is one thing," Brandy said. "Being a pig about it is another."

Anna Fonda went upstairs.

Little Tiffany wanted to play on the porch.

When they got there, Curtis stepped over the kid's scattered toys and then sat where he always sat. He waited for Henry in the love seat. Brandy sat Tiffany on the floor and handed her a Barbie.

Henry sat beside Curtis.

Brandy continued to stand. It was awkward.

Curtis said, "Oh, you know what?" He moved to Leland Fonda's easy chair. Brandy sat in his place, and she took a bite off of Henry's pie plate. Henry said, "Man, get your own. There's more."

Diff'rent Strokes was on the television. Conrad Bain tried to help Arnold accept the fact that he would never grow tall. He introduced Arnold to a friend's daughter. She acted very cheerful about being stuck in a wheelchair. Curtis glanced at Brandy, who sat beside Henry in the loveseat. He didn't like her there.

Brandy flew to her feet and said, "Depressing!"

She walked over to the T.V. and changed the channel.

"Can't you ever ask me?" Henry said.

"I will when I have a question," she said.

Brandy stopped channel surfing at the knife fight scene between Montgomery Clift and Fatso Judson in *From Here to Eternity*. Curtis loved that movie. It made him feel better about Brandy until she said, "I adore Sal Mineo." Henry laughed at her and he said, "That's Ernest Borgnine, for Christ's sake."

"I know that! Not the fat one, the skinny one."

When Henry said, "Oh," as if the skinny one was, in fact, Sal Mineo and was not, in fact, Montgomery Clift, Curtis couldn't believe it. He didn't feel Henry's marriage to Brandy was of benefit to anyone.

Curtis picked up Henry's Rubik's Cube and fiddled with it.

Apropos of nothing, Henry said to Brandy, "You looked better blonde." Brandy wanted to know what the hell that was supposed to mean. "It means what it means, Bran. I thought I married a blonde. I'm just sayin'."

Brandy said, "If you thought you married a blonde, you must have had your eyes closed every time we did the dirty." She punctuated her remark with a snort of laughter. Her retort struck Curtis as perhaps inappropriate but not unfunny, and he gave a spontaneous, if regrettable, Judas chuckle.

"It ain't funny, Curt," Henry said. "At Saint Luke's everybody keeps on lookin' over like Lucille Ball's in town. I'm friggin' Ricky Ricardo over here." This time Curtis laughed in Henry's favor. Their buddy-buddy giggles annoyed Brandy.

On a merciless roll, Henry pressed his advantage with a well-timed, "Babalu!"

"I don't think you're funny at all," Brandy said. She rose to leave the room.

"Come on, Branny. I'm just messin' with you. I'm kidding," Henry said. "Your hair looks great." Brandy paused and crossed her arms. Henry belched. Then he added in pitch perfect Desi, *"Lucy, you got some 'splainin' to do!"* Curtis wept.

"You guys think you're so damn cute," Brandy said.

Then she offered three more observations.

That it was time for Curtis to go home.

That it was time for lil' Tiffany to go to bed.

And that it was time for Henry to go fuck himself.

The Fondas' fights had a redundant two-person rhythm.

Curtis felt like the proverbial third wheel. Henry walked him out to Ronald's truck. He glanced back at the house and said, "Brandy can be a gigantic pain in the ass - but look," and he lowered his voice, "Bran can get playful as hell if she gets properly lubricated. She's hot, right? Don't you think she is, Darkie? Super hot? Sort of?"

"Sure, I do," Curtis lied. "But I'm not lookin', man. She's your wife."

Henry scratched the back of his head and exhaled. "She is that," he said.

It was after midnight when Curtis drove past the post and rail fence that ran between his parents' home and the Dickerson's property. The neighborhood kids used to play a version of lava tag on that fence and when they did, they'd all gang up on Brucey Dickerson. Tagging Brucey was easy because he was small and moved like a goddamn snail. Eric Preusse would tag Brucey, followed by his brother Dave, then Keith Fasold would slap him on the head and, of course, Curtis tagged Brucey's ass, too.

During one game, Ronald Dark showed up at the fence.

Curtis had looked to the lawn mower he'd left idling and then looked back at his father who was all of a sudden piggy-backing Brucey Dickerson and jogging him over to the Dickerson's picnic table. Ronald plunked Brucey down smack dab in the center of the table. "This here is the winner's circle!" Ronald said.

Keith Fasold said, "That's not fair."

"Bullshit," Ronald said, "it's my fence. Brucey wins."

He congratulated Brucey and raised his arm in the air like he was some kind of heavyweight champ. "Here's your winner, boys. Game over. Grab your jackets." Ronald slipped Brucey his handkerchief.

Curtis heard Brucey say, "Geez, thanks, Mr. Dark."

He gave Ronald a reach around hug.

Ronald said - and not unkindly - "You gotta start using hankies, Brucey. Don't put fingers up your nose no more." He let Brucey keep his handkerchief, and he ruffled the boy's hair. Ronald had then walked over to Curtis who still stood on the fence.

He leaned in. "When you see something ain't right, it's bad enough just standing there with your thumb up your ass doin' nothing, but by

Christ, it's worse when you join right in and participate in someone else's sufferin'."

"What suffering, Dad?"

"Don't gimme that shit. You know exactly what. I saw you tagged him, too. It's not hard enough bein' that kid without you guys doggin' him all the time? In fact, get off that friggin' fence and get in the house. I don't wanna see you."

His father was in the kitchen when Curtis got home.

"How did you like the truck?" Ronald said.

"Good, Dad, thank you," Curtis said.

"How's Henry?"

"He seems fine," Curtis said. "I met Brandy. I saw Mrs. Bostwick, too."

"I saw the wife in church. She seems a little worldly for Henry. Hey, come outside," Ronald said. "Your mother don't like me smoking in the house. I gotta smoke outside like a friggin' hobo." They used the side door and stood under the apple tree. Ronald said, "Look, Sam, I'm gonna cut to the chase. I'm puttin' the house on the market. I already talked to Mike Mathieu."

"Yeah?" Curtis said. "Geez. Really, Dad?"

Ronald stepped beneath the porch light and took out his wallet. "This you saw," he said, as he unfolded a 5 x 7 of his Bell System buddies alongside two waitresses. The group was at *Di Pego's Italian Bakery*, hoisting coffee cups near the counter.

Curtis knew the picture. He said, "Mr. Charbonneau's retirement party."

"Yeah. Now this one here, that's Angela. She held on to your letters for me over at Di Pego's." One waitress was white and one was black. Ronald tapped the one that was black. Curtis had sent several letters from Quito addressed to *'Angela for R.D.'* at Di Pego's Italian Bakery, telling his father about his wild life at the Marine House.

"So, that's Angela? *'Angela for R.D.'*?" Curtis said.

"I been with Angela a long time. Since *before* your mother, even."

"You got a girlfriend, Dad? Holy smokes, how the hell does that work?"

"Hey! You ain't a kid no more and I don't need you judgin' me. That ain't your role. Grown men have secrets. I'm tellin' you what's what. I'm not askin' for opinions."

Curtis shoved his hands in his pockets and sighed.

Any tone of voice that his father found even slightly off-kilter would send him around the bend. He'd go from zero to sixty in two seconds. There were never gray areas with the fuckin' guy. He'd even been a hard-ass with Paulie. *Paulie!* A kid who every time he rolled the dice, landed on *nice*.

"I'm just a little surprised, Dad. That's all. You gettin' a divorce? Is that it?"

"Your mother's a Catholic, Curtis. We'll stay married. Technically married. She's gonna go live with Phyllis. We got it all worked out. She ain't gonna be on the street. I'll continue springing for the bills, and Lila-Ruth gets my pension when I finally kick. After the house sells, she'll start livin' with your Auntie Phyllis in Phoenix."

"Phoenix?" Curtis said.

Ronald crushed out his cigarette.

"Correct. I hear it's nice, all year-round."

CHAPTER
Nineteen

It was supposed to be just Curtis and Henry.

They were gonna grab Chinese at The Honolulu.

Curtis nursed his club soda and looked at his watch.

The bartender answered the phone, then put his hand over the mouthpiece and said, "Someone calling for Curtis Dark?" Curtis waved the phone over.

"Hello?"

"Baygo," Henry said. "Listen, we're at the 9-20. Just pick up chow to go, will ya? Come over here. I'll spot you back. We can eat in the room and catch up. Brandy wants you to come, too. You can't say no, Darkie. Room one eleven."

He could have said no, but he didn't.

Curtis ordered the *hun su yuk*, because it was Henry's favorite. He got egg rolls and spring rolls both, plus beef with oyster sauce and chicken lo mien and a couple orders of the pork fried rice. He asked for plastic plates and chopsticks, too. The last time he'd been in The Honolulu was with George Weir. They were sophomores.

They'd ordered a bundle - feasted like mad - and pulled a chew and screw.

Curtis parked Ronald's truck at the 9-20 and found room one eleven.

There was a broken Schlitz bottle in the gutter outside.
He stepped over it and rapped on the door.
"Baggintin?" Henry said from inside.
"Well, yeah," Curtis said and he shifted the bags of food.
The door opened a crack before Henry pulled it wide. "You can't ever be too careful," and then he stuck his tongue out and lolled it around at the corners of his mouth.
Curtis heard The Pointer Sisters singing *Slow Hand*.
"What's with your tongue, man?"
He stepped into the room.
Henry closed the door.
Curtis watched him do a kind of a yawning motion with his jaw. Not like he was tired – more like he was stretching it.
He snorted loud and swallowed in a lumpy way.
Brandy came out of the bathroom holding a small mirror.
"You didn't change! I told you to change, Branny!" Henry said.
Brandy said, "I will," and she wiped at her nose with her thumb. She snorted and swallowed the same way Henry did, all loud and lumpy, then ran her tongue up under her front lip. "Hey, Darkie," she said, "so glad you could make it." Brandy sat on the yellow sofa and picked up a rolled bill. She twisted that, took a little red case from her purse, and poured white powder onto the mirror. She carved out lines and divided them with her library card.
Curtis knew nothing about drugs except that they terrified him.
He said, "I gotta hit the head." As he put the bags of Chinese food on the coffee table, his sleeves rode up. It was a new shirt, Hawaiian style, like Montgomery Clift's in *From Here to Eternity*. Brandy pointed at the scar on Curtis's bicep.
She said, "Ouch. How'd you get that?"
"Knife fight in Ecuador," he said and rubbed the scar. Curtis went into the bathroom and splashed water on his face. He looked in the mirror and whispered, "Fuck me. What are you doing, Baygo? What are you doing?" Water dripped from his face.
He heard cars pass. Perhaps on Nine. It might have been Twenty.

When Curtis emerged from the bathroom, Henry was now only wearing socks, which were black. Henry said, "Bare-assed wild, Curt!" He shuffled over to the bed as if he were on ice skates, then raised his arms in the air like he'd won something.

He put his arms down and waited for Brandy to do another line.

He tugged on his penis while he waited.

It wasn't a sexual thing. It was just what Henry did. Curtis had seen him do it after gym class in the showers. Whenever they went skinny dipping at Lake Chauncey, Henry fumbled around with his dick.

Brandy took a hit and then pulled her face away from the mirror and tilted her head back like a person might do if they had a bloody nose. She shook her head side to side and said, "Woo-hoo-hoo!" and then pretended to beat an imaginary drum.

"*Yuh - heesssss,*" she said.

Brandy sniffled loud and pinched her nostrils.

"Stop pulling your pud and make sure he gets some."

She passed the rolled-up bill to Henry and Henry turned to Curtis.

Brandy made noises like she could use some Kleenex or something.

Henry indicated the lines.

Curtis turned them down.

"You're up, Darkie."

Curtis didn't budge.

Henry leapt up and sock-skated across the room.

He turned up the radio and he flashed his fists open and closed like the music was now fueling a finger dance. The bulldog that was tattooed on Henry's shoulder had dull red eyes. The dog was pudgy as hell. So was Henry.

Both struck Curtis as brainless animals.

He wanted to tell Henry to blow his fucking nose already.

Brandy said, "I'll be right back." She grabbed her bag and walked to the bathroom. She pointed at the lines of coke that remained on the mirror and said, "Save me some." As she passed Curtis, she ran a hand over his shoulder and said, "You don't know what you're missing." Brandy closed the door to the bathroom.

Henry skated to the lines of coke.
He put his finger to his lips and made a shush signal.
Henry knelt before the table, winked at Curtis, and snorted.
Between lines, Curtis heard Brandy pee.
Henry fingered the mirror.
Brandy left the bathroom.
She shrieked, "God! Fuck! Pig!"
She had changed into a nightie.
Henry rubbed his finger on his gums.
"There was hardly any left, Bran-doot."
Brandy threw her palms skyward and said, "Fuck a goddamn!"
Her satiny silver teddy had a big bow cinched underneath her breasts. Spaghetti straps held the garment up. She was big and strong. The teddy was little. It looked like she'd pulled it off someone half her size. She stomped across the room, called Henry a complete prick and threw herself onto the upper corner of the bed. Henry went to the opposite side and said, "Calm down, Branny-fanny," and he reached for her. There were pen marks on the comforter in the shape of a Christmas tree near Brandy's ankle. She shifted away from him and exposed more of herself.

It was true. She was no blonde. Nor was she a redhead.
Brandy said, "I don't feel like fucking anybody anymore."
"Christ, come on. Let's don't be rash." Henry passed her a pillow.
Curtis sat atop the low dresser beside the TV at the foot end of the bed. He watched Henry crawl over to Brandy and bury his face in her neck. Then he stuck his head up. Henry had a fat ass. From behind, with his head poked up, he looked like a turtle. He climbed onto Brandy, reached down, and shifted something.

Then he purred, "Bran-Bran be nice." Henry lowered his head.
"I'm plenty nice, blockhead. You're the thoughtless greedy pig."
Henry said, "I know I am, Branny-fanny. I can score more."
Henry whispered something in Brandy's ear.
The bed squeaked a little.
Brandy's nose twitched. She fiddled relief with her thumb.

Keys jangled in the room next door. As the neighbor's door opened, Curtis looked toward the far wall. After the door closed, he heard a man's voice say, "Somebody had a dog in here." A woman's voice asked, "Can you get some ice?" Then there was TV.

Curtis glanced outside through a gap in the curtains.

A car pulled into the lot.

A blue Datsun.

Curtis looked back at the bed where Henry was quietly humping Brandy.

Beads of sweat had formed on the small of Henry's back. Brandy held her hand palm down. Her fingers strummed against the mattress. Curtis glanced up at the headlight patterns cast against the ceiling by the Datsun which cruised the parking lot. There was a groan. Then another. Curtis looked toward the noise.

Henry's ass clenched, then clenched again.

He brought his head up and groaned, "Babe, Jesus."

Henry buried his face in close against Brandy's neck.

His commentary was hard to hear. Mostly it sounded like, "Muff-muff."

Brandy said, "Ouch, fucker," as Henry's butt clenched in harmony with his muff-muffing. A shave and a haircut rhythm underscored his final strokes. A double clunk from the ice machine marked his two-bits finish. It was quiet.

Henry peeked his head up.

He sighed and said, "Sweet."

The low-watt bulb cast shadows. Henry's tattoo looked like a scab.

Brandy said, "You're pinching my arm." Henry moved. The teddy was stained. The ice machine clunked again. Henry turned to Curtis and said, "I bet Branny you'd get us the *hun su yuk*. Did you?" Curtis gave a weak smile. He said, "I did," and he folded his arms. Brandy's hands were behind her head now. Her breasts had slid, one east, one west, both yearned to touch the mattress. "Let me at it," Henry said. He went to the bags and dug at the Chinese food. He pulled free an eggroll and took a big bite. Henry said, "That's a good egger." He farted and said, "So fresh!" He laughed and then he said, "I still got it, Rich!"

Brandy said, "You're disgusting."

"Maybe. Hey, you know what's really true?" Henry waved what was left of his eggroll. "Being back ain't half bad. Good food. Good friends. See what I mean? It's a dream come true being in Westborough again, when you stop and think about it."

Curtis stopped and thought about it.

It didn't seem like a dream come true at all.

"You dig livin' with your parents, man?" Curtis said.

Henry said, "You can't have everything," and then he jammed the rest of the eggroll in his mouth, grabbed another and chewed as he closed the bathroom door. Henry opened the door again and said, "Don't be shy on my account." He closed the door. The shower hissed. Brandy sighed, then strummed an invitation next to the wet spot. Curtis moved to a chair. "No, sit here," she said, "Tell me about *Machu Picchu*."

"I was in Ecuador. Machu Picchu is in Peru."

"OK, Mr. Geography. It's still down there. Why so defensive?"

Curtis stared at their dark reflection in the void of the television set.

Brandy sat up a little, adjusted the sheets over her breasts and pushed back her hair. "I'm guessing," Brandy said, "that you can be a nasty boy." She used her top teeth to pull at her bottom lip, then left her mouth kind of open. "Come over here for a sec."

Curtis moved to the bed.

She said, "Try me," and they kissed.

They kissed again. She bit his lip. Hard.

"You gonna let me watch, Sweetie?" Brandy said.

Curtis breathed hard. He said, "Watch what?"

"Watch you and Henry get it on," Brandy said. The bathroom door opened.

Henry stepped out, wrapped in a towel. He was wet and the bathroom was steamy. "While I was scrubbing up, I remembered a little something." He rushed over to the hook on the closet and plucked up his jacket. Henry reached into the inside pocket and quickly produced a shiny black vial.

"Voilà!" Henry said and he galloped over to the bed and lost his towel along the way. "I got a very bright idea." He crossed the bed on his knees and pulled his pud. Now it *was* a sexual thing. Henry turned to Brandy and brandished the vial of coke.

"I can spike my schlong in a jiffy!" he said.

Brandy looked at Curtis.

Her lips curled into a grin. She said, "Go for it."

Curtis looked from Brandy to Henry and back to Brandy.

"This doesn't jibe with my plans," he said. "We were gonna have Chinese." Henry thrust his hips forward making himself more prominent. Curtis said, "I don't do drugs, Baygo. You know that." Henry sat back and pulled a pillow over his lap.

"I got coke on my wang. You guys gonna waste it?"

"Let me be perfectly clear," Curtis said. "You're barking up the wrong tree." He stood. "You guys can keep the lo mein. To tell you the truth, I'm not hungry."

With that, Curtis left the motel.

It was a short drive to the Shrewsbury Drive-in.

It was a double feature. *The Hand* with Michael Caine and *Friday the Thirteenth, Part 2*. Curtis bought a ticket and rolled in. He passed skid row where Eddie Belder had parked the night that Henry had pulled a rabbit out of his ass.

Curtis stayed fifteen minutes.

The Hand was pretty fucking stupid but that wasn't why he left. Curtis was eager to get back to his folks' house so he could pack his bags and go. It was true what Thomas Wolfe said. You can't go home again.

CHAPTER
Twenty

HENRY JAMMED AN orange drumstick into a ramekin of bleu cheese dressing. He was seated with Curtis in a horseshoe shaped booth at Bullwinkle's Pub. Spread out in a semi-circle in front of him was a greasy selection of sliders, fries, and Buffalo wings.

Curtis watched him stuff his face.

Henry looked flabby and forsaken.

He'd been eager to offer Curtis future employment at the Indian Meadows Country Club, where they'd be able to spend their time, "fucking around in golf carts," when Curtis got out of the Corps. As far as Henry was concerned, it would be like old times. Curtis rejected the "sweet-ass" job offer. "Look, Henry, I'm just tryin' to do the right thing. I'm goin' to college when I get out. My old man is splittin' with my mom. He's selling the house. There'd be nothing here for me when I get out."

"Sorry you feel that way," Henry said. "I'd be here."

They were silent. They stared at the wretched food.

Henry munched a miserable fry and scarfed a lukewarm slider. He wanted to know why in the hell his best friend had to opt for college all the way down in friggin' Washington, when Lake Quinsigamond Community College was right up the street.

"Cause Quinsig sucks," Curtis said.

Henry tapped a drumstick against his bread plate. Then pitched it back in the basket. "When you get down there," Henry said, "you should find some wingnut in the science department and see if he can figure out a colossal mystery for me."

"Like what?"

"Like how a person's *best friend* can claim his wife is smokin' hot on the one hand and then fucking run out on him when he has the chance to get a little something special going. Ask about that colossal mystery."

"Give me a fuckin' break," Curtis said.

"*You* want a fuckin' break?"

"A fuckin' break. Yeah."

When Brandy came in, Curtis watched her cross in front of the bar.

She brushed back her brand-new flaxen hair as she made her way to the booth. Curtis had taken Brandy to the hairdresser that morning, which Henry didn't know. "I wanted to find out," Brandy chirped, "if gentlemen prefer blondes."

The comment fizzled. Minds were elsewhere.

Henry paid exactly no attention to Brandy's new hair.

"Did you bring something? Gimme your bag," Henry said.

"Nice to see you, too. Can I have a seat at least?" Brandy said.

She slid to the middle of the horseshoe. Henry took her bag but kept it on the seat as he rifled through it. He removed her red case and shoved it in his jacket pocket, then disappeared into the Men's room. Curtis and Brandy were alone.

"Is it me, or is the energy in here totally toxic?" she said.

"That's the colossal mystery," Curtis said.

Brandy gave him a quick squeeze above the knee.

"Don't," he said and looked toward the Men's room.

"If you start worrying about Henry, it becomes a full-time job," Brandy said.

"I don't know what I'm still doing in Westborough. I mean, Christ," Curtis said.

"We're having a bon voyage drink, Curtis." She looked around for a server and said, "If I can get one." Brandy waved at the waitress, then focused on Curtis. "Are you sulking? My god. That takes the cake. You're the one who called me."

Which was true.

After the 9-20 fiasco, Curtis phoned Henry to explain his non-participation at the motel. Henry wasn't in, and Brandy didn't hang up. So, Curtis and Brandy met in the Stop & Shop parking lot and drove Ronald Dark's truck to Lake Chauncey where they parked beside the semi-secluded boat ramp. They pitched stones in the water, and commiserated over what a bummer the 9-20 had been. Curtis suggested that at least some solace, of benefit to them both, might be had in the grass.

"Not out here if someone comes," Brandy said.

"How about in the truck?" Curtis said.

"You're a real romantic."

They climbed into the cab.

From there, as he glanced through the windshield, Curtis saw the rope swing that dangled over the lake. That caused his mind to drift to memories of his boyhood summers and of Henry doing cannon balls. His guilt began to overwhelm his desires. He shut his eyes tight and pretended that Brandy was Sally Kellerman. Their kisses grew heated.

Brandy climbed over and straddled his lap.

All of a sudden, along came Gary Haskins in his friggin' motor boat as he hauled Donny Trudeau on water skis. They started to wave with yuck-it-up familiarity at Ronald Dark's small-town truck. Haskins pulled right up to the boat ramp. Brandy ducked below the dash and Curtis drove off with deliberate speed.

"Lake Chauncey was a mistake," Curtis said. "That was a goof."

Brandy shot him a disgusted grimace and stubbed out her Parliament.

"Let me guess. Now, I get to watch you wallow and not just Henry?"

"What's your problem, Brandy? The guy's been my best friend forever."

"You wanna know my problem? I've got a gorgeous little girl, who talks like a tiny trucker. 'Ma, I guttah go down-ah Mary's.' 'I guttah go ovah-dah Jeannie's.' Guttah? Ovah-dah? Down-ah? Ma?" She nodded to herself, confirming something unpleasant that was fixed in her mind. "'Down-ah.' This whole state is a *'down-ah.'*"

The waitress stopped at their booth.

"Looks like you could use a *bee-ah.*"

"Get lost," Brandy said.

The girl left in a hurry.

"I've been drinking the Mass-a-freakin'-chusetts Kool-Aid long enough. I knew from day one I should have turned around and gone back to Encino. The day I pulled into his parents' driveway, I knew. The day my brand-new husband whispered, 'It would be *bettah* if you kept the Jewish *paht* quiet.'"

"He said that?" Curtis said.

"You find that surprising?"

"Well, it seems kinda..."

"Typical," Brandy said. She sat up straight and enunciated each syllable. "It seems typical, Curtis. All the friendly folks I've met in Westborough, Massachusetts are absolutely committed to remaining as dumb as a box of rocks. I can't understand their provincial pride in such endless ignorance. Or haven't you noticed?"

As she dug through her purse, Curtis studied her face.

She *was* prettier blonde. Either way, she was done.

Brandy's keys jangled and then she looked up.

"You know what people in Maine call you all? *'Massholes.'* They're right. You can tell Henry for me, I'm sick of his bullshit, and I'm sick of his entire backwater clan."

But Curtis didn't have to tell Henry.

He stood right there. His pupils were dilated. His nostrils flared.

His eyes clicked back and forth between Curtis and Brandy and Brandy and Curtis like a tubby bull, trying to decide which way to charge. "You're sick of my clan?" Henry seethed. "You are? You know what? You're a fuckin' bitch! You know that?"

"Hey, Henry, whoa," Curtis said.

"You stay outta this, Curt."

"Nah, man. I'm in it already."

"You think this friggin' concerns you?"

A response to his own rhetorical question formed in Henry's clouded brain.

"You two have been fuckin' behind my back!" The bar got quiet. To no one in particular, Henry bellowed, "Well, ain't this about a bitch?" He stood there, stupefied. Then he screamed, "You're a backstabbing pair of cunts!"

The manager hurried over to the table.

"You need to calm down, pal."

Henry said, "Fuck you," and grabbed the chicken basket.

He flung its contents across the table. Wings splattered Brandy's sweater and bounced off Curtis's shirt. Henry snatched the car keys from Brandy's hand and stormed out the front door.

Curtis and Brandy waited awhile before Curtis asked the waitress for the check.

They paid out and then left by the rear door because it was the closest exit.

Henry didn't see it that way. He'd been waiting in the parking lot. Henry sneered and said, "Where are you sneakin' fucks off to?"

Curtis stepped down the three wooden stairs. "Listen, Henry..."

"You rat ass bastard," Henry growled.

He pushed past Curtis and grabbed Brandy's wrist.

Brandy said, "You're hurting me." That got the attention of the parking lot bouncers. Henry twisted her arm and jerked her forward. Brandy did a shoe slide down two steps and teetered on the third. Henry yanked again. Brandy sprawled face down on the pavement. It might have been an accident. Henry said, "Get the fuck up."

He reached down and wrenched her arm.

Brandy screeched, "Stop it, Henry! I'm hurt!"

When Curtis said, "Let her go," he said it to a stranger.

Predictably, time slowed down, just like Sergeant Baxter said it would.

"When things get ugly, you're gonna fall back. You're gonna be prepared. You'll step outside that adrenaline rush. When that ignorant S.O.B. comes

at you swinging wild, you'll step back, you'll think, and then you'll end it with just one punch."

The ignorant S.O.B. was Henry. He telegraphed his intentions with knucklehead clarity. He balled his fist, reared back, and swung like a little leaguer going for the fence.

Curtis simply turned his body and let the swing whistle past.

That left Henry off balance.

Curtis slid in low at a tight crouch and planted his left leg forward. His right leg stayed anchored solid and back. He turned his body sideways and hitched his upturned fist in tight against his hip and then leveled his left arm forward, still, and ready.

In the seconds before Henry's predictable second swing, Curtis heard Sergeant Baxter bark his counsel. *"Torque is the measure of the turning force on an object, like on a flywheel. You get me? With that force you get a full hundred and ninety pounds or what have you, behind the strike. When you drive with full body torque, you'll ring some bells."* Curtis chewed his lip. Their friendship was already over.

Henry started his wind-up. Curtis countered first. He began low at the hip. He cranked his entire body into a three-quarter turn, then snapped his left arm back to sling shot his right fist forward. He followed the targeted through-line and adhered to Butch Baxter's end-in-one advice: *"Focus just beyond the point of impact. Punch through."*

His fist slammed into the middle of Henry's face. Both groaned.

Henry crumbled and landed on his ass.

Brandy screamed.

Curtis danced backward and looked down at Henry.

The parking lot bouncers whistled. One shouted, "That's how we do it, baby!"

On the ground, Henry shook his head and snorted. His cheeks puffed and waffled.

His upper lip was split. His nose gushed blood from a jagged black gash.

Brandy ran toward Henry, arms outstretched, breasts bouncing.

She stumbled and fell forward. "Ouch! Fuck! Ouch," she said as she hit the pavement and crawled over beside Henry. She touched his face and said, "Honey grams." She craned her face toward Curtis and spat, "You stupid fucking ape!" Brandy sobbed once and tried to cradle Henry's head.

Curtis felt wired and efficient.

A little bit, he liked it.

Henry pushed Brandy's arm away.

She had chicken grease and blood on her sweater.

Henry spit once and then he spit again.

Twice into his hand.

A tooth and a half lay in his palm. Henry tried to stand.

He thought better of it, sat back down, slumped, and bled.

Blue lights flashed and there was the urgent blip of a siren.

Two cops walked over to Curtis. One wore golden Sergeant stripes. The Sergeant jerked his chin toward the parking lot bouncers. "They said he was beating on the woman and you stepped in." Curtis didn't say a word.

The second cop got Henry to his feet, spun him around and cuffed him.

As Henry and that cop walked past, Henry made a half-assed attempt to kick Curtis. The cop said, "Put your foot down, dummy. You're in enough trouble." He leaned Henry face forward against the back panel of the police cruiser and opened the rear door.

Through tears, Brandy said, "It wasn't his fault."

The cop tucked Henry into the back seat of the squad car.

He said to Brandy, "You wanna join him?" He signaled his partner.

The Sergeant turned to Curtis.

"You military?"

"Yes, Sir."

"Army?"

"Marine Corps."

"I was in the Marines, too."

The two men looked at each other.

The Sergeant said, "Go home before you hurt somebody."

Brandy looked terrible in her blonde hair and bloody sweater.

"What about her, Sergeant?" Curtis said. "She didn't do anything."

The Sergeant shrugged. "Up to you two," he said. "She's free to go."

Curtis approached Brandy. She shivered. "I'll give you a ride if you need me to," he said. Brandy turned without a word and walked toward Bullwinkle's. She walked funny because the heel of one shoe had cracked off.

After Brandy went inside, Curtis glanced at the bouncers.

They gave him two thumbs up.

CHAPTER
Twenty One

Curtis pulled his father's truck into the garage. He worked his thumb over his knuckles. Two were torn and raggedy. He wedged free an off-white sliver of something and examined it under the dashboard light. He played it between his thumb and forefinger and realized it was a piece of Henry's tooth. Curtis put the chip in his pocket and shut off the ignition. He crossed the garage and entered the basement. A circle of red burned bright in the dark. He heard, "That garage door is stickin' like a bastard."

Ronald yanked the lightbulb cord.

He exhaled smoke from his covert cigarette.

"What happened to you?" Ronald said. "Whaddya got on ya shirt?"

"My shirt?" Curtis looked down. "I don't know. A little blood maybe..."

"A little what? Come here to me." Curtis walked under the bulb and Ronald put on his glasses. He examined the spots on the Montgomery Clift shirt. "That ain't blood. You got orange on ya. Your hand's cut, too. You been fightin'?"

"I don't want to talk about it," Curtis said.

"No dice, Sam," Ronald said. "You're under my roof. Spill."

Curtis told Ronald his version of being at the 9-20 and Lake Chauncey.

He didn't mention any drugs and he implied that mutually satisfying sex had taken place between Brandy and himself in Ronald's truck. It was important to Curtis to present himself as both sober and masculine to his father.

When he'd finished his embellishments, Curtis cleared his throat. He plucked absently at the stains the Buffalo wings had left on his chest. "Damn it, this was a brand-new shirt," he said.

"New shirt?" Ronald chuckled. "What'd he do? Ruin ya shirt? I can see it all now." He offered an impromptu ditty. "'Rip my shirt, I'll fuck your wife. Rip my pants, and I'll fuck her twice.'" He laughed long and loud and finished with a snort. "Oh, Christ, you're a piss-ah. You bang his wife? You break his teeth? And now you're worried about ya friggin' shirt? Some friend you are. Ha. Ha. Ha."

Ronald opened the clothes dryer and dug around.

He pulled out a *Ma Bell* sweatshirt and tossed it.

Curtis caught the shirt.

His shoulders slumped. "I ... feel... really... really... bad..."

That gave Ronald pause. He said, "Whoa, take it easy, huh?"

"I hurt him, Dad. The cops arrested Henry and now he's fucked."

Ronald ground out his Chesterfield on the cement floor and said, "Look, Sam, there's a basic rule of thumb in play here. If you go out and you hump somebody's wife - even your best friend's wife – *guaran-goddamn-teed* it'll bring nothin' but *heartache.*"

In true Mass-hole fashion, *'heartache'* came out *'haht-ache.'*

The next morning, as Curtis hugged his mother goodbye, she started to cry. She said, "I hope I do well in Arizona." Curtis said he thought she'd do just fine. It had been almost six years since Paulie died. Lila-Ruth said, "I miss him. I always miss him."

"I know, Ma. I know how much you do."

He'd heard his mother sob a lot.

This was the first time they cried together.

Curtis promised he'd visit Phoenix as soon as he got back from Ecuador.

At the Greyhound station, Curtis bought his ticket to Quantico from Mr. Garvey. He asked for a first stop in Bethesda. His father came right on the bus with him and said, "You're still my boy." He kissed Curtis on his forehead. "Proud of you, Sam." Ronald squeezed Curtis at his shoulders. He said, "So long, ya big bastard."

Ronald left the bus and stood outside in the parking lot, all alone.

When Curtis graduated from boot camp, Ronald drove sixteen hours to Parris Island all by himself, so he could watch Curtis become a Marine. His Dad shook his hand after the ceremony and said, "You're a man now." That was the thing that Curtis cherished the most about being a Marine.

It didn't end up having anything to do with Travis Bickle.

Curtis lowered the bus window. He called, "Hey, Dad."

His father turned.

Curtis said, "I love you."

Ronald called, "Joe College!" and he tipped a salute.

Curtis fought an impulse to go chase his dad and hug him hard, but Ronald had already said, "I'm proud of you, Sam," so he decided it was best to let him go at that.

He met with D.L. Sherman's parents at the Bethesda Naval Hospital.

Curtis told Mr. Sherman that it was Butch Baxter who had performed the initial first aid on the roof. D.L. had been deemed legally blind, although he'd still be able to see a little bit out of his right eye, if objects were close enough to his face.

That D.L. retained any vision at all was thanks to Sergeant Baxter.

Mrs. Sherman said it was a blessing.

D.L. was sedated and asleep.

His eyes were taped shut with butterfly strips.

When the black Navy Doctor came in, Mr. Sherman acted pretty stiff. You could tell he was uncomfortable. The Doctor finished up and left.

Mr. Sherman said, "Will wonders never cease?"

Mrs. Sherman said, "Stanley, please."

"Please, nothin.' *He's got a doctor for a coon!*"

Curtis stayed for an hour. When D.L. came to, he was groggy.

There wasn't much to say. Curtis wished him all the best and D.L. nodded. He groped for Curtis's hand and they shook. Mrs. Sherman offered to take Curtis to Virginia.

Quantico was only forty-five minutes south of the hospital.

"It's the least I can do, considering all you've done for Daniel."

On the way to Pat's house, Mrs. Sherman told Curtis that Dan's father had been able to arrange a job for D.L. at *EPI Plastics*. She said Daniel wouldn't need 20-20 vision to be a press and stacker because Daniel could count the rings with his fingers. "They're planning to station a chair directly in front of the machine he'll be assigned to." She felt her son's future was secure. Mrs. Sherman said that was a blessing, too.

At Pat's house, Curtis asked Keane-oh about Mercy.

Keane-oh had contact information for Mercy's family's resort in *La Parva* filed on her rolodex. Christy also told him she was thirty days sober. "And I've been attending group therapy sessions for sex addicts." She blushed and looked sheepish. "I no longer fuck everything that walks," Christy said.

Curtis drove Nicole's car to American University to see to Kent Trumbo.

At Leonard Hall, he knocked on Trumbo's door. No one answered. Curtis was about to leave a note, but an Italian kid walked out of the shower room with a shaving kit and said, "Kent's in Arkansas helping his sister. He's not back for a couple days." The kid's name was Pete Carboni. "Call me Sky," he said. Sky wanted to know if Curtis knew Kent from the Marines.

"Yeah, I do."

"I figured that with the haircut, man."

"You got any idea how I can find Arnošt Lustig, Sky?"

Sky Carboni said he could walk Curtis over to Lustig's office in the Fine Arts Building. He grabbed a sweater and his guitar. Curtis asked where he was going with the guitar and Sky said, "There's a vigil for Bob Marley." He said Marley had died of some kind of skin cancer. Bob Marley was only thirty-six. Curtis didn't even know he was sick.

Sky dropped Curtis at Lustig's office, then spilt.

Arnošt was in the middle of office hours. His door was wide open. "So, then sis is a deal?" he said with his heavy accent. Lustig was talking to a nice-looking girl.

The girl said, "It's a deal."

Arnošt gave her a bear hug.

She said, "Saturday, then, at *The Source!*" She smiled at Curtis as she left. Her eyes were yellowish green and very pretty. Arnošt called after her; "You, Miss Nana will become zee famous actress!" Curtis heard Nana laugh. Then Arnošt said, "I see an ally!" He waved and said, "Please, come in."

They shook hands. Curtis said, "Hello, Sir."

Arnošt said, "How is Mr. Trumbo? How is our friend? And how is Curtis Dark?" Curtis was absolutely thrilled that Arnošt remembered his name. The man wrote movies for crying out loud. Arnošt invited Curtis to have a seat.

It turned out Arnošt was the easiest guy in the world to talk to.

They talked about Trumbo and college and movies and the Marines.

Then Arnošt told stories about war and death and fathers and sons and Curtis listened and learned. "You see, I sink your father is a wonderful, wise man. Even this advice about wishing in one hand and shitting in the other. I have a nature like my father. I am able to take things from the sunnier side of life and it helps me. It is a slightly stupid way to look at life, but a beautiful stupidity, like being short sighted and taking off glasses. Everyone looks more handsome and nicer."

Curtis thought about D.L. Sherman.

About what he would and wouldn't see in the weeks and years ahead.

"The father gives the son a key gift," Arnošt said, "and sis gift is based on the father's own trauma. What made my father happy during the war were speeches of Hitler. I remember as a child that my father couldn't stop laughing and he called us to the radio and he said listen, and I didn't understand why I should listen to some strange man who was shouting, 'Rah. Rah. Rah.' And this was Hitler and my father loved it, because you know, sis Hitler was a fool, so he called the entire family to enjoy Hitler's speeches, too. We enjoyed our father's joy. The sad finish is that Hitler was laughing longer than my father, because I believe that in Auschwitz, my father did not laugh very much."

When Curtis told Arnošt about how nice Paulie had been and how he had died, just like that, Arnošt said that of course Ronald had to remain brave and tell his surviving son that, "'You live and you die, and so what?' but sis was in order to survive. He could not let your brother's death matter more than anything else or he would die, and you, too. Maybe you can see? A good father must try to manage trauma for his son."

Arnošt *knew* about fathers and sons and death.

"Thanks to my father," Arnošt said, "I claim optimism twenty-three hours and fifty-nine minutes of each day. One minute is truly dark each day from how they killed my father. But on balance, I am my father's son and I am a happy man."

Curtis stayed quiet.

He fished in his pocket and brought out a pack of gum.

He offered a stick to Arnošt. Arnošt took a piece.

"It's cinnamon," Curtis said. "Take two," so the professor took another stick. They chewed and then Curtis asked Arnošt if he thought of himself as a hero. Arnošt said, "Of course, I am not a hero. I am only a survivor." He paused, and then said, "I do know one hero. I have sis friend. He is hero. His name is Jan Wiener, a Czechoslovak Jew. He escaped Nazi camps and became a pilot in the Royal Air Force in the war."

"Do you like him?"

"I respect him. But I am cautious, too."

"Why would you be cautious if the man is a hero, Sir?"

"Because maybe heroes should be watched from some retreat. Maybe we shouldn't come too close. I sink fighters are important in time of war and maybe sis fighting nature is not so comfortable to be with in time of peace. Perhaps you know this as a Marine. Perhaps you are not so much a fighter, now?"

"Sir, I'd like to take your class if I get accepted."

"Your friend Trumbo and I will see that you do. Sank you for sis gum."

On the drive back, Curtis decided that Arnošt Lustig was the single most interesting person he had ever met. He gathered his gear and hauled his seabag down to Pat's kitchen. Pat and Larry were eating dinner. They asked him to join them, but Curtis was ready to get back to Quantico.

He'd already called for a cab.

Pat gave him a hug. She said she'd write Curtis a letter of recommendation for American University whenever he was ready, and Larry surprised Curtis again. He said, "I know a wonderful economist named Jim Weaver, who teaches at American. I'll introduce you." Goddamn Larry wasn't half bad after all.

At MSG Battalion, Ken Shipley checked Curtis in.

"You're back early, Corporal Dark."

"Took care of business. Sherman is squared away. No point in hanging around."

Sergeant Shipley said, "You still have four days on the books. Why not take a hop? Check out Buenos Aires? Or Machu Picchu? Peru is fun."

"Can I get a hop to Chile?" Curtis said. "I have a friend there."

The C-130 was fitted out just like the one he'd flown in with D.L. Sherman. *The Dirty Dozen* style aircraft had mesh seats that ran down the sides of the plane so you'd be looking across the aisle at other Marines if there were any on board, which there weren't. This was a cargo flight, so it was just the crew and Curtis and a planeload of crates. They stopped in Lima on the way to drop off supplies and refuel.

Curtis had to stay on the plane.

He read *Look Homeward, Angel* for nearly five hours.

Curtis put the book aside and stood up to stretch. It was cold on board and the plane jumped from time to time but other than that it was smooth. There was an awkward urinal in back with a curtain around it. He took a gander out of the paratrooper hatch. It was too dark to see anything, so he took a leak and sat back down.

He wanted to grab a little sleep but he couldn't.

The idea of finding Mercy kept him wide awake.

CHAPTER
Twenty Two

Curtis said, "*¡Hola Mercy! ¿Adivina qué? Estoy en Santiago!*"
That meant, "Hi Mercy! Guess what? I'm here in Santiago!"

Mercy said, *"Dios mio."* Then in English, she asked him to please wait.

It took quite a while for her to come back on the line and when she did, her tone was pleasant, but businesslike. Mercy told him to take the 10:00 o'clock bus to *La Parva*. The bus would be blue and white and have a big number seventy-seven on it. "Do be sure it is the 10:00 o'clock. The seventy-seven. Not the before or after." Curtis said OK.

Mercy said, "I will let Marcia know," and she hung up, just like that.

He wondered who Marcia was.

He also wondered why there'd been no trace of honey in Mercy's voice.

She'd talked to him as if she were issuing directions to a tourist. There was no hint of romance in the brief exchange. He pondered the wispy snow devils that danced outside the phone booth - checked his watch - then found his bus. Once he'd stowed his seabag and taken a seat, he gazed out at the endless snow in the Chilean mountains. He decided that if Mercy wasn't altogether thrilled about his being in town, he could go skiing. It amazed him that *June* was a winter month in Chile.

It took the catatonic bus driver nearly two hours to make it to *La Parva*. Curtis stepped off the bus. Colorful ski lodges were stacked up on both sides of the main street. Lifts fanned out in all directions. There was a stone church on a hill. The mountain range stretched forever. He put his hand to his forehead as a shield against the sun.

He hadn't walked three steps when he heard, "Curtis! Curtis, love!"

He turned toward a tall woman with a bushy crop of light brown hair.

She said, "Hey, babe!" in a British accent and threw her arms around him. She buried her face in his neck and Curtis instinctively gave her a big squeeze though he was ninety-nine percent certain he'd never seen the woman before. She put her lips to his ear and whispered, "Play along, right? Mercy's request. I'm Marcia Moyse. Act happy to see me." Marcia pulled back and said, "Look at you!" She cupped his face in her hands and gave him a kiss. Marcia stepped back and squeezed his hands through her mittens.

She smiled brightly.

Curtis said, "Marcia, Marcia, Marcia..."

He hoped that might get a laugh but it didn't land.

This particular Marcia behaved as if she'd never heard of *The Brady Bunch*.

"Let's go!" she said. It was obvious to Curtis that she wanted anybody who saw them to think they knew each other well and liked each other quite a bit. Marcia hung onto his left arm as if they were great friends or maybe sweethearts. As soon as they cleared the bus crowd, she leaned in to whisper, "We can talk by the church."

They strolled together and paused at the base of a huge sculpted Indian. The statue wore a headband plus a loincloth. He gripped a spear and stood barefoot in the snow. Marcia released Curtis's arm and pointed to the plaque at the base of the statue as if she were giving him a tour. It said, *"Lautaro. Nuestro héroe del pueblo."*

"Huh," Curtis said. "So, the big fuckin' Indian aside, what gives?"

Marcia laughed. She said, "You're a really good sport, mate."

"This is all very James Bond, sister. Are you some kind of British spy?"

Marica turned to Curtis and laughed. "My family is German." Curtis flinched. "We're German Jews, not Nazis in hiding. The thing is you're in one very, very, very small town. You're a surprise, Curtis.

Your job is to act like you've come to see *me* till Mercy can sort a few things out. Can you do that, mate?"

Marcia sniffed against the cold.

"I can do that," Curtis said. "Is she glad I'm here, at least?"

Marcia smiled. "Hold my hand. I'll take you to them."

He wondered who *them* was, but he let it pass.

Things were weird enough already.

They left the Indian on his pedestal. As they passed the church, a funeral service ended. Marcia threaded her arm in tight with Curtis. They ambled past the mourners and headed toward a hill which was jammed with kids on sleds and on toboggans.

Marcia continued to cling to his arm like a long-lost lover.

He asked her what she did.

"I'm a Shakespeare scholar."

"Any money in that?"

She laughed again. He squinted against the sun and scanned the mini mountain. The kiddie hill was crowded as hell. He pretended to know who he was looking for. "Ya! There!" Marcia pointed. "To the side of the tree." They waited for a toboggan to zoom past, then they started up hill. When they got to the tree, Curtis said, "I'll be damned."

The little girl who was maybe five, had to be Mercy's daughter.

She looked like a little tiny Liz Taylor. Mercy held her hand.

Mercy's skin was paler than he remembered. Her eyes were darker. The Chilean sun cast a different quality of light and he'd never seen her in snow. Her face was fuller now, more like the Liz Taylor in *Butterfield 8*, than the Liz Taylor in *Cat on a Hot Tin Roof*. Curtis was a fan of both looks.

Marcia said, "Curtis, this is my dear friend Mercy."

It was goddamn surreal. Mercy nodded. There was the tiny scar on her lip; her damaged mouth. Curtis took full measure of the woman. He felt himself exhale. Some of it was relief, some of it was disbelief, not all of it was joy. "How very nice to meet you, Mercy." Curtis cleared his throat. "How ya doin' there, kid?"

"*Mucho gusto, Señor. Soy Connie,*" she said.

She reached out and he shook her hand, all very proper.

So, Mercy was a mom. That was something she had failed to mention. Connie skipped off and they watched her pile onto a crowded toboggan.

"So here we are," Marcia said. "Welcome to Chile, my friend," and the three of them started down the slope after Mercy's daughter. Marcia continued to cling to Curtis.

Mercy walked alone.

At the base of the hill, Connie chirped, "¡Nos vamos a hacer galletas!"

Apparently, they were going to bake cookies.

Curtis wondered if Connie's dad was going to join them.

It was a short walk to the market. Connie asked in Spanish, "Who is this guy, again?" and Mercy answered, "He's Auntie Marcia's friend from Ecuador." Curtis waited outside the market with Auntie Marcia. They walked next to Marcia's place.

Curtis watched as the three of them unloaded flour and eggs and nuts and sprinkles in Marcia's kitchen. Marica pulled out a mixer and unwound the cord. Connie stood on a step stool and retrieved a big bowl. Mercy spoke to Marcia quietly and Marcia replied in English, saying, "You two go ahead. We're all good here." Mercy told Connie, "Yo quiero una galleta de vainilla con las nueces!"

That meant, "I want a vanilla cookie with nuts!"

He didn't know Mercy's story, so he listened to it sitting at Auntie Marcia's desk. Mercy had been married to a professional soccer player named Luis who played for Colo-Colo. She was pregnant with Connie when Luis died in a car accident.

Hans Hundekörper was her current husband.

Apparently, ol' Hans was a good father and a very jealous man.

Curtis asked her if she married him for money. He didn't ask it like an asshole. Mercy said his family was wealthy, but her family had even more money than his did. Curtis asked Mercy if she was rich and Mercy said, "Sí, sí en realidad, mi familia esta bien adinerada." That meant, "Yes, actually. My family is quite wealthy."

Mercy asked Curtis what he thought of that.

"It certainly doesn't make you any less attractive," he said.

They both laughed. They could smell cookies baking in the oven.

Curtis reached out and touched her face. "This has been quite a day," he said.

She was a skosh more beautiful than he remembered. He thought, "Fuck Hans," but he didn't say it out loud. They went into the kitchen.

Marcia and Connie lapped cookie batter off a wooden spoon.

"'*Tis an ill cook that cannot lick his own fingers,*'" Marica quoted.

She took the tray of cookies out of the oven. Mercy told her daughter that she could only have two because they were going to dinner. Connie asked if Auntie Marcia's friend was going to join them. Because he now knew the deal, Curtis slid his arm around Auntie Marcia's waist. He said, "Marcia, Marcia, Marcia," again, and he took a cookie for himself. Connie asked if he liked cookies. Curtis said "I do." In Spanish he said, "I would love to join my old friend and my new friends for dinner."

Curtis ate his cookie.

He kissed Auntie Marcia's hand.

"I get it," he said. "Mum's the word."

Then they all went out to dinner together.

Mercy acted like a stranger through the appetizers and the entrées.

Curtis figured she had to keep up appearances for her small-town neighbors.

After dessert was served, the restaurant crowd had thinned enough for him to make a few discreet inquiries as to where he stood with this married version of Mercy. She kept a neutral smile on her face. Her expression gave nothing away. Observing the two in conversation, people would assume they were in the midst of an amicable chat about la-dee-dah bullshit of very little significance.

Mercy quietly confessed that at the Ambassador's party she had admired his makeup and she could tell that he had a nice body under his baseball uniform. She said she had found him attractive. She lit a cigarette and explained that she enjoyed her private diversions whenever she was in Quito. Since she'd married Hans, Quito had become for her, "*Un lugar donde puedo olvidarme de la vida por un rato.*"

It was a place to forget about life for a while.

Curtis had fit quite nicely into that equation.

Mercy's explanation sounded *mannish* to Curtis.

He could imagine Mercy's explanation to hubby Hans, "*Yes, Honey, I fucked him, but it didn't mean a thing...*" He understood where Mercy was coming from. Pretty makeup and a nice body were attractive to Curtis, too. However, he had hoped there was more to it than that. This didn't make him stupid. Naïve maybe. But not stupid.

He wanted to say, "I wish I meant more to you."

But his father had taught him that wishing was futile.

So, Curtis stayed quiet. The meal was over. The waiter brought the check.

Mercy insisted on paying. She made a big show of how pleased she was to meet Curtis. They gathered up their things and for those few minutes, Curtis marveled at how well-coordinated their efforts were, all without speaking.

Mercy shifted Connie into Curtis's arms as she pulled on her scarf and then they headed to the door. Outside it was snowy and cold and the sky had become dark. Connie wasn't heavy at all. As they walked the few blocks to Mercy's house, Curtis pretended these were the natural steps of his everyday life. '*Yeah, great. We made cookies at Marcia's. Ate dinner in town. I had the schnitzel. Got in early. You?*'

Mercy worked the key in the lock. Connie slept. Curtis held the door. Marcia came in, too, of course. Hans wasn't home yet. No question, it was cozy inside. Jesus H. Christ, if things had been different, Curtis and Mercy could have been a family just like this. Mercy must have felt that vibe, too.

She took Connie from Curtis and went to put her to bed.

When Mercy came back, she told Marcia that Connie wanted to say goodnight. That left Curtis and Mercy alone. They kissed, but it didn't last very long. When Curtis asked, "Do you think we'll see each other again?" Mercy looked a little wistful.

"We let the life decide," she said.

Curtis slept on Auntie Marcia's couch and in the morning, he took the bus to Santiago and then caught a commercial flight to Quito. This approach was a helluva lot smoother than his original flight into the city. Curtis smiled. He was gonna go to college and really make something of himself. When he got there, he'd tell Arnošt Lustig about this great girl he'd fallen in love with. He'd tell him her name was Mercy.

He'd tell him how she was the girl who got away.

Curtis looked out the window at the mountains below.

He spotted the Angel of the Apocalypse. He thought of Paulie, of course, but for the first time Curtis didn't get clobbered by an overwhelming sense of grief. Paulie would have loved to know that. Goddamn Paulie wouldn't have wanted to be a perpetual source of sadness for anyone.

He wasn't that kind of a kid.

www.ingramcontent.com/pod-product-compliance
Lightning Source LLC
Chambersburg PA
CBHW021146060526
44107CB00146B/1340/J